MANCHESTER MESSIAH

Happy Birthday Dad!

lots of love

Sarah
x

MANCHESTER MESSIAH

How Kevin Keegan led
City to the Promised Land
... and where they
go next.

By Howard Johnson
with
Paul Lake

First published 2002 by Big Four Media
Copyright © Howard Johnson and Paul Lake

ISBN 0 9541006 2 X

Typeset by
Avon DataSet Ltd, Bidford-on-Avon, Warwickshire B50 4JH
www.avondataset.com

Printed and bound in Great Britain by
Cox & Wyman, Cardiff Road, Reading, Berkshire RG1 8EX

Big Four Media
Georgia House
6 Augusta Place
Royal Leamington Spa
Warwickshire
CV32 5EL

In the beginning

THERE was no sense of surprise when the end finally came.

It wasn't like the other recent times.

At home against Liverpool in 1996.

Away at Stoke in 1998.

On those two occasions there was a dull ache in the heart, a nagging, gnawing sickness that you couldn't ignore, could hardly contain . . . a slightly other-worldly feeling that said 'Yes . . . really'.

Despite the fact that you'd thought and believed all along that it simply couldn't happen, it actually did happen. City were relegated.

First from the Premiership, then from Division One.

Glorious Manchester City. Proud Manchester City. *Our* Manchester City.

But when the axe fell this time – following a 2-1 away defeat at Ipswich on May 7th 2001 – and City were again dumped out of the Premiership, there were no tears.

Maybe we had cried so much throughout that appalling season that there were no tears left. Maybe it was simply that the inevitability of our fate, during that horrible top flight escapade, had been so apparent for so long.

Whatever, there were no histrionics, no howling of anguish, no beating of breasts. There was only an air of quiet resignation when the end finally came.

Many of us expected another resignation. Some of us even hoped for one. Joe Royle, managerial stalwart of many a dogged performance in getting us back amongst the elite, had simply failed us in the Premiership. He had failed City not only because we were relegated. He had failed us because of a seeming inability to understand exactly what was required to maintain Premiership status.

The infamous 'Dogs of War' days were over. The times when a group of

1

well-organised, well-intentioned, ferociously-determined battlers could make a decent fist of it against the big boys, the artisans against the artistes, were consigned to history. It was no longer possible to scrape points through scrapping. All of the top sides had transformed themselves. They had now added swagger, panache and outrageous skill to their well-oiled defensive machines.

Arsenal, boring, boring Arsenal of all people, were playing open, inspiring, exciting football. They had put nine goals past us, without reply, in two league games. There was no greater evidence of the gulf in class and the need for change in order to survive. But change never came in that 2000-2001 season.

City were crying out for a creative midfielder to replace the magical Ian Bishop, whose legs were finally giving way. We were given Jeff Whitley and Tony Grant.

We clearly needed a rock solid defensive lynchpin. We had Spencer Prior.

We were desperate for a world class striker. Bloody hell, we even had one in George Weah! But Joe Royle thought it better to play Paul Dickov after a while instead.

City's performances were both horrible to watch and ineffective, a combination that made almost everyone who followed the club utterly, totally despondent.

When Joe Royle made it clear that he wasn't going to walk, City fans settled themselves for another dogged campaign the following season. Joe was too long in the tooth to change his style. After all, heed proved that it could succeed against lesser opponents and there was no doubt that we would be playing lesser opponents again. The chasm between the abilities of Premiership teams and outfits just one division down was getting wider by the hour. So maybe Joe *could* put in a good showing in the forthcoming season. But one sensed there wasn't much enthusiasm for it. Good as Joe had been to us, he had blotted his copybook in the Premiership and many fans felt the time was ripe for change.

Nobody expected such swift action from Chairman David Bernstein, though. Joe Royle was sacked on May 21st, just two weeks after relegation had been confirmed. Some criticised Bernstein for callousness. Others felt that the critical need of a club like Manchester City to retain Premiership status at all costs justified his decision and praised the speed with which he took it, not least to allow the new manager, whoever he might be, the time to build his own squad for the start of the forthcoming campaign.

But who on earth would that man be? David Platt? Steve McMahon? George Graham? Dave Bassett? The list seemed uninspiring and short. Mind you, who would want the poisoned chalice of managing Manchester City, the massive club that just didn't seem able to get its act together? Who was truly capable of making City great again. Was there even a Messiah out there? It would need a man of enormous character to stride into this hot seat. Who the hell was big enough for this job?

On May 24th, measuring just five feet seven and striding into a press conference, enter Kevin Keegan. Manchester Messiah?

The Manchester Messiah

It's a bright and breezy day as we swing into the car park at the side of Barca – the trendy bar part-owned by well known redhead and Reds fan Mick Hucknall – in Manchester's Castlefield area.

Sorry to disappoint all those cliché merchants who wish it was pouring down, so that we'd then be forced to go into another of those tired old monologues about the rain bouncing off the cobbled streets, rainbows in black and white and all the rest of it. But a sharp, crisp sunlight illustrates the mood of the place far better. The tired images of a once-proud northern industrial town lapsed into decay are a nonsense. Manchester has undergone an impressive urban regeneration these last 20 years. Gone are the empty, blackened warehouses and depositories down by the canals that snake their way into town from Liverpool. Gone, too, are the forbidding municipal buildings that clustered around the top end of Oxford Street, the serpentine sprawls of ugly old tower blocks like John Nash Crescent in Hulme. Now Manchester thrives with trendy canalside apartments for fashionable urban dwellers, with clean, imposing work buildings that throb with new purpose at Oxford Street, with community-oriented housing plans in Hulme.

As unrecognisable as all of this stuff may be to those like me, who went to school in the bleak and unfashionable Manchester of the 70s, so the image of a poor, rainy, downtrodden old city is merely the stuff of history books for everyone under the age of 25.

Manchester is vibrant and Manchester is happening and Manchester is a cool place to live and work and enjoy yourself. It has been since the explosion of the Madchester music scene at the fag-end of the eighties, when pig-headed pride in the place of our birth somehow gave impetus to new ideas, new ways of living, new purpose. For three or four years there, Manchester usurped London as *the* place to be if you were young, go-getting and, yes, mad fer it.

Manchester had the best music, the best fashion, the best club in the world in the Haçienda, the best bars, the best football teams. Well, not exactly the best football teams. Although Alex Ferguson was laying the foundations for – and this sticks in the craw – a decade of unparalleled success at Manchester United, Manchester City were about to enter one of the most turbulent periods in the history of a club long associated with instability, cock-up and the unerring ability to shoot itself in the foot.

Mind you, back in 1989 there was really no telling which way it was going to go. Both clubs were in the old First Division, both were struggling to find their feet and when the two sides met at Maine Road on September 23rd there was no guarantee that Ferguson would be in the job at Old Trafford any longer than City boss Mel Machin. It was all up for grabs. Of course, no City fan will ever forget the outcome of that game – whether they were there or not, or whether they were even alive then.

'The Five-One', as it is always referred to, is still the most precious derby memory that we have. Well OK, maybe not quite as spine-tinglingly sensational as the 1974 Old Trafford encounter, where the infamous Denis Law backheel helped to condemn United to relegation, but pretty bloody close to it. Each and every one of that young City side is a legend in the eyes of true Blues. Not only for the way they played in routing United, but for the sheer, unbridled pleasure that they took in cuffing their local rivals. There were a lot of local lads in that side – Andy Hinchcliffe, David White, Ian Brightwell, Steve Redmond, Paul Lake – and that made the victory all the more sweet. So what if we were beaten five-nil at Old Trafford a few years later? The Five-One is still the ultimate derby victory as far as we're concerned.

And there is Lakey, sitting alone in a quiet corner of Barca, waiting for our arrival. I'm with Kevin Cummins, City fan extraordinaire, NME photographer-in-chief during the heady days of Madchester. Though we've both known Lakey for some time now, it is always a bit of thrill to be in the presence of a 'Five-Oner', a legend. There is still a huge photo in the City Superstore of Lakey in the arms of, I think, Ian Bishop, arm aloft, face just beaming with pleasure as another City goal is celebrated in that game. I smile whenever I see it. But Lakey's not one for nostalgia. He is as much a fan as any of us and the first topic of conversation whenever we speak is inevitably of City's current fortunes. Many is the time when we have been on the phone and he has sadly had to report that City were 'diabolical', 'shocking' or 'minging'. It has almost made me glad to be exiled down in Watford. Almost: I still shell out for two season tickets every year, despite the fact that the M6 and two young boys under the age of five means that visits are heavily restricted.

Last season was different, though, very different. It's not just the fact that we ended up with a pot to show for it. In many ways that felt almost incidental to the plot. The real story was the way we played, the manner in which the victories were achieved and the astonishing turnaround in the mentality of the team that took to the pitch wearing Manchester City colours in comparison to what had been going on three or four months previously.

Watching Manchester City in the 2000-2001 season was one of the most dispiriting experiences I can remember in 30 years of following the club. Having brought the club back to the Premiership from the depths of Division Two (and let's face it, for that we should always be grateful), manager Joe Royle proved himself to be incapable of producing (or maybe pig-headedly unwilling to produce) a side that could hold its own in The Premiership. He seemed unable to identify the problem area of midfield creativity, when fans in the stands had, to a man, grasped the need for a player with vision in the middle of the park from the first few weeks of the season. Watching an inadequate and quickly demoralised City taking the field every week in the Premiership with the look of condemned men, wondering how many they were going to get tanked by that particular week, was utterly disheartening, utterly depressing.

Four nil at Charlton, Five nil at Arsenal, four one at West Ham, three one at Everton. The list felt never ending. And at home things were even worse. Four one against Charlton, four nil against Leeds, four nil against Arsenal. Painful stuff. We couldn't buy a win and ended up at the end of the season with exactly what we deserved: relegation.

The following season back in Division One, City's first with Kevin Keegan at the helm, couldn't have been more different. There was, admittedly, a jittery and unpredictable start, where they were as likely to lose and ship four goals as they were to run rampant and bag all the points in style. But from those uncomfortable beginnings, the side evolved into a consistent unit and a joy to watch, playing with a flair, swagger and confidence not seen since the halcyon days of Joe Mercer and Malcolm Allison in the late '60s and early '70s. Then, City had swept all before them to win a League

Championship, the FA Cup and the European Cup Winners' Cup. Now, fans fell over themselves to praise a manager about whom they had been unsure and lauded a side that played football with elan. The good times, it seemed, were ready to roll as City announced their arrival back in the big time with an emphatic First Division Championship win.

Of course City being City things were never going to work out as smoothly as that. The club's re-introduction to the Premiership has not been as silky as many would have liked and as many even predicted. With new signings of the quality of Peter Schmeichel, Marc-Vivien Foe and Nicolas Anelka on board, many were convinced that City would be right up there with the Premiership's elite at the first time of asking. Even Kevin Keegan was talking about a Top Six finish. So to reap just eight points from the first 10 games was hardly what the doctor ordered.

Paul Lake, though, is still convinced that City will be a force – and sooner rather than later. His enthusiasm for the new regime, and the manager in particular, knows no bounds. And for a man who has spent all of his adult life around Manchester City, witnessing the changes, triumphs and tragedy both from inside and outside, as player, media pundit and now as a chartered physio working for a medical company that supplies the Blues, he firmly believes that City are in the ascendancy. Ask him why and he'll give you a straightforward answer.

"Everything's changed at City. The whole atmosphere, the way of working, the approach to the game, the approach to the business. It's all moved on to another level. And there's no doubt in my mind that the catalyst for all that has been Kevin Keegan. I mean, how else can you look at it? How else can you analyse it? When City announced that Kevin Keegan was going to be the club's new manager there were a lot of doubting Thomas's out there, fans who had seen what had happened to Kevin with England and had bought into the idea that he was somehow a bottler, someone who turned on his heels and walked the minute the going got a bit sticky. But I spoke with a friend of mine, John Beresford, who was a trainee with me at City when we were both starting out. John went from City to Barnsley, but then ended up at Newcastle with Kevin. At the time of the appointment, I spoke to Bez on the phone. He was really excited for me, for City. He told me: 'Mark my words. Kevin Keegan will do the business for you, no doubt about it. You may have a blip sometime in the season because all sides go through something like that. But Kevin Keegan will get you into the Premiership at the first time of asking and you will be a top side within three years, never mind five,' which was what Keegan had been saying."

Despite the fact that these could have been seen as wildly optimistic claims, Lake is prepared to accept Beresford's viewpoint: "From what I've seen so far everything's come true and so I have no reason to disbelieve John. I am a City fan and I have seen enough false dawns to last me a lifetime. We are always capable of shooting ourselves in the foot by saying 'This is going to happen and that's going to happen' and maybe by the end of the Premiership season we'll have to admit that we've been talking out of our arses. But, slowly, I really believe it's taking shape."

Given the wretched performances that City have put in in the early part of the Premiership season – including defeats away at Aston Villa, at home to Liverpool and away at Southampton – Lake's get-out clause may well have to be invoked. But ask him quite seriously about City's prospects of a return to a place amongst the elite of English clubs and he is still confident that the Blues can achieve their goals despite this poor form at the time of writing, if for no other reason than that Keegan is an inspirational man with the ability to galvanise football clubs. When you ask Lake to explain what the appeal of Keegan is to football folk, he is unequivocal.

"John Beresford told me Kevin was the only manager he had known where all the players – every single one of them – was glued to every word that he said. Kevin's not an overly authoritarian man, so maybe it's something to do with what he's achieved in the game; European Player Of The Year twice, wasn't it? Bagful of England caps. Bagful of medals."

This would make sense. All players respond to bosses who do not just talk a good game, but who have a shared experience with players, a common bond, an understanding of life of a professional footballer. And if a manager has reached the absolute pinnacle as a player, then so much the better. Yet Lake once described one of former City manager Alan Ball's failings as having made *too much* of his achievements as a player, even going so far as to show the squad he had inherited from Brian Horton his 1966 World Cup Winner's Medal. It was, presumably, meant to inspire them to greater heights. It achieved the opposite effect.

"Kevin would never go around making a big deal of all his achievements. He just lets them speak for themselves. Ball set out his stall by saying 'Do you know who I am?', but Keegan took a different approach. He sat down and talked to the players when he first arrived. Nicky Weaver told me he said: 'This club is absolutely massive, I'm fully aware of that. You know my past, but that's by the by. We're in this together from day one. What I want you all to know is that I want to bring out the best in everybody.'

"That was really important and the players immediately responded to it. And his attitude to the game would have sounded so refreshing to the players after everything they went through in that awful Premiership season under Joe Royle. Keegan said 'I want to try things. I'm an attack-minded manager. We'll sort the back out, sure, but I'm positive, positive, positive. We're getting beat four nil, I'm still positive. I'm going to invest in all of you, from the youngest apprentice to the oldest player like Stuart Pearce.' And the players responded to that. Kevin has that happy knack of bringing the best out of everybody. You look at managers like Sir Alex Ferguson and Brian Clough. They're imposing figures and managers who will intimidate some players. Kevin's not like that. He's not scary, but he's able to command respect instantly and it's fantastic when you can get a squad of players together who respect and admire the manager and will do anything for him.

"You could see the results out on the pitch in that Championship season. He has the ability to keep people together, there were no cliques forming and he was able to keep players interested who were on the fringes and realistically weren't likely to get starring roles. He was able to take guys like Paulo Wanchope and Eyal Berkovic, players who had reputations for being enigmatic at their previous clubs, and keep them onside and on message. The players at the club have real respect for him."

And is that the single thing that matters most, to have a manager that the players respect?

Lake is unsure: "That depends. I wouldn't say that everything necessarily hinges on it, because a lot depends on the type of people that you have in your side. You get sides that have four or five players who are great guys and massive characters and they will drive everyone. When I was a young player at City there were people like Neil McNab, Gary Megson, Peter Reid, Adrian Heath, Mark Ward. All these guys weren't necessarily the greatest players in the world, but they knew how to bring the best out of the young guys around them. They made us feel like there was no pressure on us so that we could go out and play our natural game. They were just as important to that side as the manager was. If you look back at Manchester United when Eric Cantona was there, he could lift the team just by his mere presence on the pitch. Although City have some great players at the moment, there's no single guy like that. They look to the manager and it's really Keegan who brings it all together."

While Lake is clearly convinced as to Keegan's credentials, the manager's detractors have plenty of ammunition to fire in his direction. And the attitude towards Kevin Keegan before, during and after his ill-starred time as England manager provides a microcosm of the debate that surrounds him. When Keegan first announced that he would accept the F.A.'s offer to manage the national side (though initially for four games only) in February of 1999, the overwhelming belief was that Keegan would put the feelgood factor back into the England side following the rather sullen tenure of Glenn Hoddle. As striker Alan Shearer – who knew him well from Newcastle – said at the time: "It'll give everyone a lift. Kevin's enthusiasm is infectious. I'm sure everyone's excited, not only the fans, but players as well."

It was when Keegan decided to take the job full time, and lead England into the European Championships of 2000, that doubts were raised about his tactical abilities. Those doubts were magnified when the team only just managed to qualify, and after losing to a poor Scotland side at Wembley along the way.

Keegan's team then proceeded to throw away a 2-0 lead against Portugal in the first game of the Finals to lose 3-2. Some redemption came when they beat a poor German side 1-0 but their collapse in the final game against Romania sent them out of the tournament.

Former Republic of Ireland boss and passionate Englishman Jack Charlton gave voice to the thoughts of many when he told BBC Radio Five Live: "I would say Kevin is tactically naive, compared to other managers we've had. It all hinged on the first game against Portugal, when we were 2-0 up and getting run to death through the midfield. We had to do something about it, but nothing was done."

Football journalist Martin Lipton was even more damning of the manager. "It appears Kevin Keegan has learned precisely nothing about how to close up a game," he cried after the Portugal defeat.

Keegan stayed on but following a poor home defeat against Germany in a Wembley World Cup qualifier on October 7th, 2000 – the *Telegraph*'s Henry Winter memorably wrote of the match that 'Tactically, England were a mess and confidence drained away like rain from a broken gutter' – he resigned, leaving Sven Goran Eriksson to pick up the pieces. But the dramatic manner in which he walked out of the England job created new problems and new charges: that he was not only tactically naïve but that he was an emotionally fragile quitter who would fold at the first sign of trouble.

It seemed everyone believed that after the initial euphoria inspired by Keegan's legendary enthusiasm, the man would always be found wanting. Paul Lake, however, does not believe that this interpretation of Keegan the manager gives anything like the full picture.

"Some people say that Keegan was tactically naïve when it was a question of competing at the highest level. If you compare him with men like Arsene Wenger, Gerard Houllier and Alex Ferguson, it is true that Keegan didn't have the years and years of management experience that they have. But was that his fault? Another problem was the way he was built up too much by the press – remember the massive hype over Keegan when he first got the England job? He could never live up to it.

"But I believe that, ultimately, they main problem was the squad of players he had at his disposal. One or two, like Alan Shearer and Tony Adams, were coming to the end of their careers. Others, Gary Neville for instance, hadn't been performing well. And few, if any, of them had the flair required to play in the way Kevin wanted.

"Yes, there were one or two games where he made decisions that I couldn't understand. Against Portugal in that Euro 2000 game, for example, he took Michael Owen off and replaced him, almost like-for-like, with Emile Heskey, when it was clear that the midfield was getting over-run. But every football-watcher has seen a manager make what appears to be a weird decision which works out and which makes him a hero. Equally, he might do the obvious still get beaten by two or three goals. The hard fact for us all to acknowledge is that sometimes it is just pure luck. What if Emile had made it 3-0? Maybe Kevin would not be at City now!

"People should be more willing to accept that Kevin's still learning. I think he learnt a lot from that debacle with Sir Alex and the 'I would love it . . .' business on Sky TV when he was involved in the title race at Newcastle."

This outburst happened in the run-in to the 1995/96 Premiership season, as Keegan's Newcastle battled it out with Manchester United for the title. With the Magpies due to face Nottingham Forest (ironically then managed by Stuart Pearce) in a crucial encounter, Reds manager Alex Ferguson, schooled in the black arts of psychological warfare, suggested that Forest would put out a less-than-competitive team for the game. Keegan exploded live on TV, famously finishing: 'I would love it if we beat them (United) . . .!' But it was Ferguson's team which went on to win the title, with many commentators feeling Keegan's antics had revealed he was wilting under the pressure. Lake doesn't disagree.

"Yes, Kevin lost it there and yes, some people think he made a fool of himself over it. But he's always been a man who wears his heart on his sleeve. He's been volatile in the past, right back to the days when he was a player. He was sent off in the Charity Shield of all matches against Leeds in 1974 for fighting with Billy Bremner and threw his shirt off in disgust for good measure. There's a lot of passion in the man, though it was noticeable last season that he kept a much cooler relationship with the press than he ever has before. I think he's learnt from the England experience. Just before we lost to Germany, England drew with France, then World Champions, in Paris. Everyone was saying it was a great achievement by Kevin. After the next game, all of a sudden he was useless again. That sort of thing must have reinforced in Kevin the sense that much of what is written in the papers is nonsense, which is something we could all do to bear in mind.'

For a long time, Keegan kept his own counsel regarding his turbulent time as England manager. It was only after City won the First Division championship last season that he revealed his disappointment at what he saw as the lack of support he had been given by The F.A. Following the 5-1 home win over Barnsley which confirmed that the trophy was coming to Maine Road, Keegan praised Arthur Cox's work as Chief Scout. Speaking at the post-match press conference, he then added: "That's the same Arthur Cox The FA wouldn't employ because he was over 60, and then when Sven Goran Eriksson wanted someone of 64 – Tord Grip – they let him do it. But he is a foreigner so I suppose it's harder to knock. It's the most annoying thing the FA did. And it still rankles because I wasn't allowed to take the people I wanted and that was wrong."

Keegan clearly believes that he is not as effective a manager without his long-standing associate and this ham-strung his efforts to manage the national side.

Cox and Keegan had first crossed paths at Newcastle United some 20 years earlier, in 1982. It was during the twilight of the striker's career when then-manager Cox had brought Keegan to the Geordie club. A feeling of mutual appreciation was quickly fostered and Cox went on to work with

Keegan's management teams at Newcastle and Fulham. Immediately on being appointed Manchester City boss, Keegan once again sought out his old mentor, bringing Arthur in as Chief Scout (a position which would grow into Assistant Manager after promotion). Lake believes that the backroom team has settled down after a natural evolution when Keegan first arrived.

"I think it's looking good. On the coaching side he started off with Willie Donachie, who was obviously at the club with Joe Royle. Willie is a good coach. He may not have one of those shrieking voices that you can hear up the pitch but he knows his stuff and he was well liked and the players always knew he was there. He is also very inventive and different – he is very into the sports science side of things."

Indeed so. Rodney Marsh reveals how, during a recent meeting with Donachie, the Scot was constantly jotting down notes for a coaching book which he was putting together with the intention of explaining what it takes to be a good teacher. Donachie's talents have been praised by former City players Colin Hendry and Paul Dickov too, with both players expressing an opinion that Donachie fitted the bill to replace Scotland boss Craig Brown before the German Bertie Vogts was finally appointed. Despite this, Donachie did not last long at Maine Road after Keegan's arrival, handing in his notice on November 14th to move on and work with Terry Yorath at Sheffield Wednesday.

Was there a sinister element to this departure? On first taking the reins at City, Keegan had made such a big issue of his desire to hold on to Donachie that some people wondered whether the boss was protesting too much. Did Keegan already have an inkling that the Scotsman – a very close personal friend of Joe Royle – wasn't entirely committed to the new regime?

Lake is sceptical and believes the whole affair had more innocent motivations. "I just feel that Willie wanted more of a say than he was going to have Kevin; he wasn't involved enough for his own satisfaction. So I think Willie made up his own mind that he wanted out and he's moved to Sheffield Wednesday, where he's certainly got a challenge and a half. And I wish him all the best because he is a cracking guy."

Whatever, the speed with which Keegan appointed a replacement suggests that the manager already had a contingency plan in place. Rumours had immediately started to circulate that two men that Keegan had worked with previously, Derek Fazackerley and Paul Bracewell, were in the frame for Donachie's old post. Just six days after the Scotsman's departure, though, Bracewell, who had been Keegan's Number Two at Fulham, was out of the running, with Fazackerley announced as the man who had been appointed.

Keegan knows Fazackerley and his coaching credentials as well as anyone. The 51-year-old former Blackburn Rovers defender, who made a club record 596 appearances for the Lancashire side, had first hooked up with the current City boss at Newcastle United when Keegan became manager there in 1992. Fazackerley had arrived on Tyneside with Jim Smith in 1988, had also worked under Ossie Ardiles and at the time of Keegan's appointment was concentrating on developing the club's youngsters. Within four days the new manager appointed Fazackerley first team coach, "which tells you what I think of him," said Keegan. The pair masterminded Newcastle's revival, from languishing in Division Two to becoming a Premiership force again. When Keegan was handed the chance to become caretaker manager of the national side in February of 1999 he was quick to bring in Fazackerley as his coach.

Following Keegan's resignation, it was inevitable that his acolytes would find their positions vulnerable. So it proved. Fazackerley's contract with the FA was terminated by mutual consent a few weeks after his friend's departure.

Fazackerley was soon back in coaching work, this time under manager Nigel Spackman at First Division Barnsley, but the duo's poor record of just nine wins in 33 games led to both men being sacked on October 25th, 2001.

Keegan was unperturbed by this dismal performance, though, claiming "He is an excellent coach and I am delighted he is on board," when 'Faz' arrived at Maine Road.

Fazackerley's first thoughts on his new team were interesting. "Obviously they have a little bit of a reputation for leaking goals," he said, while still echoing his old-new boss's positive approach to what City could, potentially, achieve. "If you compared City to the clubs in the Premiership, then it would be among the top six or eight," he said.

Lake believes Fazackerly's was a key appointment. "If there's one single thing that Derek brought to the club it was the ability to get into the players' psyches and make them believe every single game was important. When he first arrived at City he talked about how important it was to keep clean sheets. At his first press conference he was emphasising the need to string results together, not to win one, lose one, win two, lose two. So maintaining focus was one of his key objectives. I remember when I was a player myself, if we lost one or two you'd start looking at the fixture list and thinking: 'Oh well, we've got so-and-so at home in a couple of weeks and we'll turn it around then.' It is human nature but it is not the right attitude and it was one Fazackerley clearly wanted to erase. He has succeeded in my view, because, from speaking to the players, that attitude doesn't exist at City now. It's all about the next game. If you lose you start again . . . right away. You try to turn it around."

Statistics seem to bear out this theory. Of the 20 games played while Donachie was coaching, City recorded a record of 11 wins, three draws and six defeats. After Fazackerley's arrival the record for the remaining 32 games of the season, including two meetings with Premiership sides in the FA Cup, yielded a record of 24 wins, three draws and just five defeats.

Lake says: "No disrespect to Willie, but I think Derek has added a bit more personality. He's a thinker and he has a real spark about him. When he arrived the side suddenly became settled. Perhaps Willie had known for a while that he wasn't happy and that he might be moving on, and maybe the players sensed that. When Derek came in the coaching team was in place and there were no changes in coaching personnel for the rest of the season. And it rubbed off on the players."

Lake, now training to become a physio himself, believes the medical element of Keegan's set-up has also made a quantum leap.

"Like all the top football clubs, and since Keegan's arrival, City seem to be taking the medical side of things more and more seriously. Rob Harris is currently the leading physio at the club. He's a Kiwi who came from the Wigan Warriors rugby league team with a reputation as one of the most clinically able men in the country."

Significantly for Lake, Harris was brought in by John Wardle, a City director. Significant, because this shows a forward-thinking manager backed by a forward-thinking board. Lake explains: "John is a very important guy at Maine Road and for him to be as aware as he is of the importance of the medical staff is a very good sign to my mind."

Wardle is, indeed, one of the most important figures at Manchester City. A self-made man and lifelong City fan, the one-time fireman has a personal wealth in excess of £30 million and sits on the City board together with his partner in JD Sports, David Makin (the 'J' and the 'D' of their business stand for John and David). Wardle first emerged as a significant figure at Manchester City as long ago as 1996, when Francis Lee was Chairman. A £10 million rights issue at the time was underwritten by John Wardle Associates, along with Stephen Boler, another wealthy businessman, in return for Wardle taking a seat on the City board. By 1997 Makin was being represented on the City board by former player and fans favourite Dennis Tueart (now the club's Director Of Football) and the JD axis was wielding considerable influence on the strategic direction of the club. It backed the appointment of David Bernstein as Chairman following Lee's departure in March of 1998. Indeed, this parting of the ways was partially instigated by Makin's passionate outburst where he demanded Lee's resignation on a local radio station phone-in. Both Makin and Wardle are hugely passionate about the club and have proved themselves more than willing to take tough decisions if they feel they are merited. The dismissal of Joe Royle after the club's disastrous Premiership relegation in 2001 is a case in point: Wardle is widely believed to have been the boardroom's strongest advocate of change.

Wardle is not alone in his burning ambition for his club; all of the current board members are bonded by a fierce ambition to restore City to the pinnacle of football's elite and move it out of the rank and file. But Wardle is a man who likes to make his moves behind the scenes. He never 'mouths off', he rarely goes on record and if he does it is usually in uncontroversial style. A typical example were his remarks to the *Manchester Evening News* at the start of the current campaign: "Our summer investments have been tremendous. It was something we had to do if we want to make an impact and do anything in the Premiership." Not much there to frighten the horses.

But Paul Lake is just one amongst many who feel that Wardle is heavily involved in all of the decision-making processes at City and the interest in developing a medical infrastructure is just one such example. Lake continues: "John Wardle started the ball rolling by bringing in a high calibre individual such as Rob and the effect then trickled down. Rob has brought in another physio called Jim Webb, who's worked at Chelsea and Spurs. At the Academy another Kiwi, Jeff Ross, was brought in in September of 2001 after coming up from New Zealand, where he'd worked with the national football team. We've been scouring the world to try and bring in what we consider is the very best talent available.

"We now have a medical team as good as Manchester United's or

Arsenal's – and that wasn't always the case. In the past we've had nice people who have done their best for City never a team this complete. The club even has a podiatrist – Steve Lyons – whose sole responsibility is for taking care of the players' feet."

Lake believes this investment is already paying off. "One of the things that pleased me most last season was the fact that when a player came back from injury you knew that he really was 100% fit. It was frustrating that Eyal Berkovic missed so many games last season but, ironically, this was a real indication that the backroom team was working well. They were not prepared to put players out on the pitch who were not in perfect condition. And you knew that everyone had worked really hard over the summer months to get to the root of the problem because Eyal didn't miss a single game for the opening ten matches of the Premiership campaign."

The treatment of players goes hand-in-hand with their overall conditioning and fitness. Throughout the First Division campaign, City rarely faded towards the end of a game and late goals actually became a feature of the side's play. Lake knows where much of the credit goes for the sheer physical power that the players have shown they possess.

"The fitness coach, Juan Carlos Osorio, has made a massive difference. He came with a big reputation from the States where he'd worked in football, but he's justified that reputation by really improving the players' conditioning. He's been a revelation." Osorio comes from Risaralda in Colombia, but already had an affinity with the North West of England long before arriving at City. The 40 year-old has a diploma in Science and Football from John Moores University in Liverpool. While studying on Merseyside, Osorio's obsession with analysing players led him to rent digs which overlooked Liverpool's Melwood Training Ground. From his bedroom he could spy on the players, watch their training routines and think about how he might use this valuable information in his own career. That career began as a midfield player in his native Colombia in the '80s and in The States in the 90s, where Osorio played for three sides in the New York area, The New York Fever, The New York Centaurs and, bizarrely, The Brooklyn Italians. But Osorio always had one eye on a career after playing, picking up a BA in Exercise Science from Southern Connecticut State University in 1990. He also has a UEFA 'B' coaching licence from the English FA and a coaching certificate from the Dutch FA. In January of 2000 Osorio was appointed to the coaching staff of MLS outfit The New

17

Jersey Metrostars, with special responsibility for conditioning, and quickly gained a good reputation working with highly-rated US stars such as Clint Mathis. The opportunity to join City proved too tempting, though, and he arrived at Maine Road in June of 2001 after pipping 30 other applicants for the position of Conditioning Coach, saying: "This was a very hard decision for me, because of the strong feelings I have for the Metrostars. But this is an opportunity I couldn't pass up." Eight candidates were interviewed initially before the final three were called back and asked to perform case studies on players from the City Academy. Director Of Football Dennis Tueart, who headed the team designated with the task of making the appointment, said: "We were very impressed by him." The players, too, were quick to warm to the new man, especially when he explained that his conditioning programme would be primarily based around working with the ball to allow the players to condition and train at one and the same time. This, of course, meant no long-distance running, the bane of all footballers' lives.

"The players have enjoyed working with him and have seen the results he can help you achieve," says Lake. "Guys like Darren Huckerby have said how much stronger they feel and how much more aware of their own bodies and their body's requirements they are. They're so much more aware of their ability not just to be able to finish 90 minutes, but to be able to *compete* for 90 minutes. People said early on last season that because we attacked so much we'd be dead on our feet for the last quarter of a game, but they soon found out that in the last two minutes of a game we were as strong as we were in the first two."

Huckerby agrees, saying "I think our fitness levels over the last season and a bit speak for themselves." Other players have also been quick to point out the inventiveness that Osorio has brought to the conditioning work, as evidenced in ideas like introducing swimming as part of the post-match warmdown routine. Even a seasoned campaigner like Peter Schmeichel believes Osorio is special. "Juan Carlos's fitness training is different from anything else I have encountered and for me that is tremendously exciting," he explained.

Lake continues: "The older players relished the new challenges because they could see and feel the benefit. Even an old stager like Stuart Pearce said he felt fitter and was able to give that extra yard when it was needed – and he was approaching 40. And with inner strength comes true belief."

Keegan has also demanded the best training facilities for his players – both first team and academy. "They've worked very hard to try to make the Academy an appealing place for youngsters to want to come to," says Lake. "They built the Carrington training complex, spending around £2 million on developing it in just 18 months. It's an exciting place, because it looks like somewhere that means business. It may not be as impressive as United's complex – which is also at Carrington – because that is really exceptional. But we're coming along very nicely, making steps in the right direction all the time."

Another example of the club's commitment to the training infrastructure is its recent investment in a new FieldTurf all-weather pitch at Carrington. Developed by an American company and approved by FIFA, the polyethylene and polypropylene blend looks like grass, feels like grass and plays like grass, but is light years ahead of the old-style all weather surfaces that would not allow the ball to roll as on a real surface and, perhaps more importantly, would cause burns injuries from tackling.

"You've got to give City respect because they've had the foresight to do these things properly, to spend the money," says Lake. "They're spending hundreds of thousands of pounds to get the right people and the right facilities but they're responsible for millions of pounds of talent and for trying to make sure that that talent will generate millions more in revenue, so it makes perfect sense."

Keegan is a players' manager par excellence. After City lost badly at Wimbledon in the Championship season, he spoke of his mystification at his side's poor level of performance. After all, he had done everything possible for the players, including flying them down to London to avoid a long, cramped, uncomfortable coach journey. The other side of that coin, however, is a requirement on his team to take responsibility for their own fitness and condition. The manager recognises that investing in the best possible environment in which to produce the highest levels of performance counts for nothing if players are not prepared to look after themselves.

Last season City players Nicky Weaver, Jeff Whitley, and Richard Dunne all found themselves in trouble with Keegan on this score. Dunne missed training without an explanation twice, Whitley was caught violating a curfew in a wine bar and Weaver was involved in a boozy nightclub 'incident' following the game against Crystal Palace in December. Finally, all three players were fined two weeks' wages after a 'drink-related incident' in a Liverpool nightclub the following February.

"It's very disappointing for me and what the long-term effects are on those players, only time will tell," said Keegan at the time. Given that one of the rumoured reasons behind Joe Royle's departure was that he had been unable to quash a supposed 'drinking culture' at the club, Keegan's treatment of these three players has been particularly interesting. He said little to the press about the breaches of discipline, insisting that the incidents, once discussed, are over with and forgotten. Behind this façade lurks steel. Whitley seems unlikely to feature in a Keegan first team again. Weaver first lost his place to Carlo Nash and would now find himself third choice keeper if he weren't out until mid-season anyway with a long-term injury. Dunne, perhaps the most talented of the three, has been given another chance after another incident *this season*, later described by the club as a 'serious breach of discipline'.

Lake believes this mirrors Alex Ferguson's actions in clamping down on a perceived 'drinking culture' at Old Trafford when he first arrived at Manchester United in the late '80s. "Bryan Robson was one player who liked a drink now and then but Ferguson knew that he couldn't afford to lose a player that pivotal to the team. He dealt harshly with a couple of other players – Norman Whiteside and Paul McGrath, who were shipped out. Dunne may not be as important to City as Robson was to United at that time but the managerial principal is the same. Discipline, yes, but carefully allied to pragmatism.

"Managers have to take a line on this issue these days because, more than ever, what you do off the pitch is as important as what you do on it. Whitley, Weaver and Dunne have let themselves down, no doubt about it. We've all had a few drinks when we shouldn't – I know I did – but, in today's game, with the very high levels of sophistication of preparation, it will find you out. There's a belief held by the public that if you're a top footballer and you're getting 10, 20 or even 30 grand a week then you shouldn't be out like the rest of us in pubs and clubs. And I think that's fair enough.

"Keegan knows there has to be discipline at a football club. He knows how to celebrate and enjoy himself – you just had to look at the way he lapped up the reaction from the fans when he did the lap of honour at Maine Road after winning the Championship last season – but he is not a big drinker like old-style managers such as Brian Clough and Malcolm Allison. Kevin comes from that slightly later era where players were starting to cotton on to the need to look after themselves if they were going to be a top class performer."

Keegan's managerial style, then, sees him set out clear – and not unreasonable – rules, provide support and encouragement to those players who abide by them and try to help those who fall by the wayside. Break the rules too often, however, and it is the iron fist, rather than the velvet glove, which you encounter. Lake agrees: "Kevin is very open and honest and is prepared to give players a chance. But if they keep screwing up then he'll deal with it. It's not Big Brother-like. He'll explain: 'This is how it's got to be. I'm there for you, I want to work with you and I can bring the best out of you. This can be an exciting place to work. This can be an enjoyable place to work. But there are certain rules that have to be followed.'"

In this age of the cosseted, millionaire player, presumably there has been a backlash against this? Lake says not: " Players who are worth their salt respond to that kind of attitude. I haven't heard a single player slag off anything about Keegan and that's no lie. He is egalitarian, straight, fair in the way he treats the players. Take Jeff Whitley: he is still at the club and they are still honouring their contract to him. If Nicky Weaver suddenly came back into the form of his life, and was abiding by the rules, then he would get his chance again. Above all his players are family and he will do anything for them in the hope of bringing out the best in them."

How does Keegan's era, so far, compare with that of another England superstar, Alan Ball? Lake is dismissive of the diminutive Ball's contribution to the club. "Alan was the kind of guy who wanted to show you his World Cup Winner's medal all the time but he did not earn the respect of the players. I couldn't relate to Alan Ball and I don't think many players could. He had his favourites, like Kinkladze, and that created disharmony in the dressing room. Kevin Keegan talks to players as players would talk, but he also knows when he has to put his manager's hat on. And that's resulted in a great atmosphere."

Stuart Pearce neatly summed up Keegan's ability to create a bond and inspire players in *Four Four Two* magazine in December of 2002 when he explained: "People really want to go and play for Kevin Keegan. He has great man-management skills. He brings that bubbly personality and that's a big strength, the sheer likeability of the man. I mean ... I wanted to leave my home in Wiltshire to come and work for him, so that shows you how I get on with him." Keegan thrives as a manager when he can create harmony and Manchester City has not always been a harmonious place in the recent past.

Lake says: "There used to be cliques in the past at City. There's nothing worse than turning up for training and not enjoying it because you don't like so and so or you've had a falling out with the manager and you're fighting for your place. The door is always open for you with Keegan. If a player isn't going to get a chance there then he will be the first to say: 'You don't fit in my plans, but I'll do my utmost to get you the best possible move I can.' He paid up Terry Cooke's contract and was very fair with Richard Edghill in the way he released him, giving him as much notice as possible and loaning him out to Birmingham City to give him a chance to impress there. John Beresford tells me that the peripheral players at Newcastle were always spoken to, Keegan's door was always open. You get it a lot in football where two or three players fall out with the manager and they're treated like dirt from then on. That won't happen at City. I haven't come across one player who's said: 'He's treated me badly. He hasn't given me a fair chance.' Maybe they exist, but I've yet to meet them. And you need that atmosphere to make things work. If you have problems on or off the pitch you really can go and see the manager and you don't often get it at clubs. Backbiting at football clubs is endemic and incredibly disruptive. But that's not happening at Maine Road right now."

The second coming

Manchester City's long-suffering fans understandably jumped on the team's performances of the 2001/02 season, when they ran away with the First Division Championship, and hailed this as the best side to play at Maine Road in more than 20 years. You have to go back to the League Cup-winning side of 1976 – featuring legends like Dennis Tueart, Joe Royle, Peter Barnes *et al* – to find a more naturally-gifted team, they say.

But is this really the case? The poor start to the Premiership campaign would suggest not, but Paul Lake is still confident that this team has what it takes to stamp its mark at the highest level.

"I went to my first City game about 1973 or 1974," he says. "So I can remember Francis Lee and Colin Bell, Kevin Bond and Tommy Hutchinson. I've seen some decent players over the years and, of course, I played in a fairly talented City side myself at the end of the '80s. But I have to tell you that we were never as inventive as this side is. This team can break so quickly and turn defence into attack in a split second. It's incredible. The side I played in that beat United five one in 1989 had pace, with lads like myself, Andy Hinchcliffe and David White. But I look at the set of players we've got now and not only can we turn defence into attack with three passes, but we can do it half a dozen times – in each half! It's awesome. That is not to say that the side is the finished article. It's not, especially when you think that we still concede too many goals. I was watching the video review of last season and that really brought the point home. After eight games we'd conceded 18 goals, which is a pretty poor showing. But you have to remember that we'd scored 23, which is almost an average of three goals a game. I think I speak for most City fans when I say that I'd much rather go out with that attacking philosophy, that desire to win games, and get the victories in that way than the old Joe Royle method of one-nil and two-one scraps and trying to nick stuff through set pieces. City fans in particular like to win in style.

"Think back to the Peter Reid era at Maine Road. We ended up finishing fifth in the old First Division in the 1991/92 season, but it was the dullest style of play you've ever seen. The fans didn't enjoy it. It wasn't down to the players, but the way they were asked to play. There will be lads in the current City side who'll know all about playing that more defensive style. Guys like Niclas Jensen will have been in teams where the manager will have gone: 'You're the full back. It's your job to defend. There's your man. You've got to win that battle.' Now it's like they have a new lease of life, a new perspective on the game, which a lot of these players have never had. Last season we even had Steve Howey scoring three or four goals, pushing up all the time on set pieces. The team is always looking for Shaun Wright-Phillips, always looking to get Eyal Berkovic and Ali Benarbia into the game. If you watch the matches all three of those players are always side on, looking for the ball and they're always three or four moves ahead. When I was playing under Peter Reid you'd get the ball facing your own goal and you'd look to play it to the full back and build that way. Now we're looking to go forward all the time. And yes, there's a risk in that. We lose the ball sometimes. But more often than not we're turning defence into attack in two or three passes."

It is certainly true that City were able to cut opposing teams to shreds almost at will in the First Division. This first season back in the Premiership has proved – and will continue to prove – a lot more difficult. Lake says that he wasn't surprised by the sharp learning curve the team has faced, but admits that there have been major disappointments.

"I expected City to acclimatise a lot quicker than they did in the early stages of the season but that hasn't dented my confidence in the system that Kevin Keegan has been playing or in the talents of the players. If you look at the man-for-man natural ability of the City squad in comparison to other teams in the Premiership, there's no doubt in my mind that City are superior to many of them.

"I thought it was interesting to see the differences between City and West Brom, who also came up last season. I paid quite a lot of attention to them because I worked with Gary Megson when he was at City and I have a lot of time for Mego. He's a really decent family man, but on the pitch when he was with me at City and now in his role as manager he has a real mental toughness and hardness that set him apart from a lot of other football people. As a player he was no Glenn Hoddle, but he knew how to make life very difficult for opponents with his constant harrying and his work ethic. He was also a very good talker, someone who could get their views on the game across to you in a very understandable way. He was a great communicator and you can tell that West Brom are extremely well drilled and every player really knows his job. It's no surprise that you see Mego's characteristics in the team he puts out now. West Brom were very solid at the back, scraped their wins in the First Division and were very consistent, much more so than we were. I have a lot of respect for what Mego's done, but I can't see them surviving in the top flight because being solid and well-drilled and well organised will not be enough. By nature Mego isn't as attack-minded as Kevin Keegan, but I think and hope that, ultimately, it will be to our advantage in the Premiership that we're capable of going out and unlocking defences. You saw it all the way through that First Division campaign. Sides came to Maine Road all through the season with a real agenda: 'We know what City are like, how they want to attack you all the time. So let's try and hold them and hit them on the break.' Yet in spite of that we managed to break those sides down and score two or three goals without too much of a problem. Take Birmingham City. We beat them six-nil and that was a side which had been defensively consistent, with a good manager who had a decent idea of how the game is played and how to combat the threats of their opponents. But it didn't do them any good, because with this City side the threat comes from everywhere. In the past City sides have been steady and you might have looked at one season where you'd get one particular player who posed a threat, a David White scoring 16 goals or a Paul Moulden, where the goals would come off his shin. But players like Neil McNab and Gary Megson have been just steady players, certainly not guys who could contribute at a creative level. With Shaun Wright-Phillips, Eyal Berkovic and Ali Benarbia there's creativity absolutely everywhere."

One area of concern for City fans on the return to the Premiership has been the midfield. Lake agrees that the collective performances in the Premiership have not been anywhere near as good in the early part of the season as they were in the last campaign.

"Extremely disappointing, there's no doubt about it. Ali was our star performer last season, but he's done nothing in the early part of the campaign. He's been poor, to be honest. It could be that the responsibility that rests on his shoulders has affected him, especially with being captain.

But the trouble is that it's not just been him. Foe hasn't delivered anything like the form we know he's capable of and has also been a passenger for much of the time. But nobody who knows about football can say they are lacking in talent. The trouble that City have faced in the early part of the season has been two-fold. Firstly, they have not matched the other teams for commitment and effort, which is the easy part of football and one for which there should be no excuses. The second part is that there have been far too many individual errors. You could point at Jihai for Owen's second goal against Liverpool or Steve Howey for Mark Viduka's goal for Leeds. We've put ourselves under needless pressure defensively by making unforced errors. You can be the best defensive coach in the world, but there's very little you can do about players switching off. They will obviously be doing a lot of role-playing work, going over the situations that have cost the side goals and trying to make the right decision an instinctive thing. But once the players go out on the pitch it's down to them. However, I think the players are good enough to eliminate those errors. We are still moving forward. If we work hard to eliminate mistakes I still believe we can be a threat in the Premiership. It only takes a few games to get confidence up, for one or two players to come back into form, and then we'll move forward.

"Once we do that teams will come to City with the agenda that they aren't going to get beaten and that they mustn't concede a goal. But the way that City play, pressing, pressing, pressing all the time, you'll find the sides that are pushing up will start edging back. And then the advantage will be with us. If you can get the sides that struggle to score goals, like Sunderland, on the back foot then we'll win. I don't think we'll be beating teams by the scores we did in the First Division, but we're going to win more than we lose because we're so positive."

Many pundits are less convinced that City do have the defensive quality. Both Ally McCoist and Ron Atkinson have lambasted the team's defensive naivety on ITV's 'The Premiership'.

Lake believes McCoist and Atkinson have been too harsh. But he concedes the defence is an area of concern. "I don't think they're right, but I agree that maybe Steve Howey and Richard Dunne lack that yard of speed to combat people like Thierry Henry and Ruud van Nistelrooy. Kevin Keegan must know that and it is obviously why he brought in Sylvain Distin."

The 25-year-old Frenchman spent the whole of last season on loan from Paris St. Germain at Bobby Robson's Newcastle and made 34 league and cup appearances for the Magpies in the middle of their defence. But a supposed dispute over terms led to City snatching the classy defender from under Bobby's nose for £4 million and he became a City player on 25 May. Director of football Dennis Tueart was in no doubt as to the player's abilities: "When it became clear that Newcastle were not going to take up their option on the player, Kevin moved very quickly and we a delighted to have Sylvain on board," he said. "He is a powerful, quick athlete who has already proved himself at the highest level." Tueart also earmarked Distin as a vital part of the team's structure for the new season, calling him a like-for-like swap for Stuart Pearce, though Distin's natural ability on the ball is clearly superior to Pearce's. He also revealed that City had tried to bring the player to Maine Road the previous season, but that Distin had been unwilling to drop out of the Premiership.

"Distin is a good player with a lot of ability," says Lake. "But you couldn't say that his partnership with Steve Howey has gelled quickly. You take a look at him, though, and you know he has all the attributes. He is not a bad buy. Would I make a change and bring Richard Dunne in? Players in the squad have told me that over the length of the pitch Richard Dunne is the fastest guy at the club, but my worry is his sharpness off the block and that's where you have to be really on it in the Premiership. If I were Keegan I'd be looking for one other central defender, just to give the side a few more options. Steve Howey's a good player, consistent and with a good football brain, but he can't go on forever. In general, as far as the defence is concerned I think the worst thing we could do is start dropping back straight away, because when a guy like Henry runs past you once you start thinking: 'What do I do? Do I try to stay with him? Do I drop off 10 yards so that I can try to defend facing him? How the hell am I going to work this?' And that could cause us a few problems.

"I believe that Keegan is right to play with the three central defenders and the two wing backs and in general I think the personnel is right. Niclas Jensen has to look at his performances and ask if he hasn't been hiding just a little bit. To my mind he's just been doing his job without having the commitment to express himself. But I believe he can make the grade. And there's no doubt that Peter Schmeichel has been inspirational from day one. He's been a man mountain and with the way he wants to dominate from the back, once things slot into place I think we'll be fine. Overall I'm convinced it's not a problem with the personnel."

But Keegan won't be afraid to make changes if he reckons the side isn't up to it – as he proved last season. Lake says: "When Kevin Keegan took over I think we were a club that knew what had to be done, but nobody there knew exactly how to change things. Everybody knew that the club was potentially massive. Everybody knew what the potential of the fan base was. Everybody knew that when we moved to the new stadium we would still be able to fill it. In Joe Royle we had a manager who you have to respect because he did do a hell of a lot for the club. He got us through the depths of despair. But he didn't have the level of managerial skill that would allow us to compete at the very top. I was talking to Glynn Pardoe – the City legend of the '60s and '70s – a while back. Glynn believes a manager needs 10 to 15 games to find his feet.

"We all knew after just five games in that season back in the Premiership under Joe that, with the squad he'd assembled, we just weren't up to it. We knew that there were certain players – Tony Grant, Danny Granville, Laurent Charvet, Paul Dickov – who couldn't raise their game to match the needs of being a top five side in the Premiership. Kevin knew straight away what needed to be done. He looked at the midfield, for instance, and knew we needed creativity. He said: 'All the endeavour of your Jim Whitleys and your Kevin Horlocks is there, but there isn't the spark to ignite it.' He brought Eyal Berkovic in straight away and when Berkovic got injured he brought in the ideal replacement in Ali Benarbia.

"He will do the same this season if he has to. He hinted as much during the opening 10 games, but of course the problem is who is available. I would like to see someone brought in to take a little bit of the weight off Anelka. I like Gudjohnsen. I also know that a lot of City fans would like to see Danny Murphy's battling qualities in the City midfield, but I think the chances of getting him from Liverpool are nil. I think Kevin might well be tempted to rest Ali more than he did in the early part of the season. He might be coming round to the view that while confidence is low he needs to shore up his midfield a little more and bring back the creative players once the confidence has returned. But people shouldn't forget that Ali is a quality player and he will come good."

Indeed, people shouldn't forget just how much of an influence the player was in the last campaign. "No doubt about it," concurs Lake. "And we all thought: 'Who the hell's he?' when we heard he'd been signed. Unless you're fully aware of European football you wouldn't have known who Ali Benarbia was."

Despite the ignorance of English football fans, Benarbia was certainly not a secret on the continent. Starting his career in the French Second Division with little-known Martigues, the Algerian has won a Championship at every club he has played for. Monaco, Bordeaux and Paris St Germain all picked up trophies with Benarbia in the side and the player was also voted French Footballer Of The Year in 1998. On being given a free transfer from the Parisian outfit in 2001, Benarbia arrived on Teesside for a trial with Sunderland, but again, City moved quickly to secure the player on a two-year deal. Benarbia shared an agent with the French striker Alioune Toure, who was on trial at Maine Road at the time and was himself also signed by the club. The deal to bring Benarbia to City was done over lunch at Carrington and Toure has since moved to Paris St Germain as the makeweight in the Nicolas Anelka deal. Astonishingly – and tellingly – Benarbia made his debut in the home game against Birmingham City on September 15th after flying in from Paris that very morning. An exemplary performance saw him leave the pitch to a standing ovation after 75 minutes.

Lake remembers: "Everybody was wondering what kind of player Ali would be, given that Kevin Keegan had immediately talked him up, so there was a lot of expectation before the home game against Birmingham. The fact that Ali had just got off the plane from Paris that morning didn't seem to bother him at all. He absolutely ran that game from the start until he went off. Truly great midfield players have everything to their game and Ali is not the best header of a ball. But he has speed, sleight of foot, he can use both feet, he can pass it short, he can pass it long, he can go by a man and he knows how to get the right side of a ball. He has the absolute awareness of what's going on around him to be able to get a yard ahead of somebody, yet it's all done with the coolest possible persona. You couldn't fluster that guy if you tried.

"When I saw Ali I was absolutely amazed at the kind of things he can do. I mean, we all know all about the idea of letting the ball do the work, but his astuteness to be able to pass a ball at speed, off balance and with either foot is sensational. Shaun Goater scored a tap-in during Ali's debut against Birmingham and it was entirely made by Ali's genius. He was at the corner of the box with four players around him. Even though he was off-balance he managed to pass it with his weaker foot for Paulo to get a shot in on goal and the ball popped out for Shaun. And it's all happened in a split second. Ali saw the possibilities in an instant. That wasn't a flukey pass in the hope that someone would get on the end of it. He passed it straight to feet and straight away I knew he was a very special talent. But that wasn't all he did in that game. If you watch the second goal, he played an incredible reverse pass to put Tiatto through. Wherever he is on the park he sees the potential. I was speaking to some of the fans and they were saying: 'You were a better midfield player than you were a defender', but I say no, because I didn't have the ability to control a ball with three players around me and see a pass.

"Once I had the ball at my feet and could get my head up I was OK, but with Ali he's already glanced up before the ball even reaches him and when the ball's at his feet and that ball's passed and it's on to his next one and you didn't even see him look up . . . that's phenomenal. He's got that low centre of gravity, which is ideal for a player in that position. I think Ian Bishop had it, but both Ali and Eyal are better at doing it than Ian was. You look at any quality player, any world class player, and the first touch is everything."

A horror story for Sunderland fans? "Peter Reid liked to consolidate every area of the park. He was a manager who looked for his sides to be drilled and disciplined, so I can see why he i might not have been too sure about Ali. You have to be prepared to adopt a more fluid style around Ali. He's not a player who will stick rigidly to a task. He needs to be given freedom to create and to invent. Peter Reid opted to sign a player like Kevin Kilbane rather than Ali, which has been great for City, of course. And who knows? Given the way things turned out at Sunderland Reidy might wish he'd made a different decision."

Signings like those of Berkovic and Bernarbia – later voted City's Player of the Year – show Keegan at his best: as with his style of play, he is adventurous, he takes risks and he has belief. Lake agrees: "He backed his judgement and brought this totally unknown player in. But not only that, he brought Ali in from the off with the specific intention of making him the kingpin of his side. He said: 'Mark my words, he's the best thing since sliced bread.' And he was proved absolutely right. And what's even more amazing is that he's done it on the cheap, really. So for no money he's got a guy who has made the difference in the side and who's been voted the Player Of The Year by fans and management alike. That whole episode was all about superb management."

There were other key players in the Championship side. Lake pinpoints Stuart Pearce and Shaun Wright-Phillips.

"I thought Stuart Pearce was a revelation and an interesting cog in the wheel. Keegan made statements about the way he wanted his teams to play – with style, flair and an attacking mentality – and then the first player he brought in was Stuart Pearce. In itself, that was a brave move: there were some very raised eyebrows, with fans wondering how we could play inventive, attacking football with an old warhorse like Psycho in the side. Hadn't his legs gone? Then we watched the first game at home to Watford, we saw how many chances we created and we even saw Stuart score his first goal for the club and they all started to believe.

"The point is that Keegan knew he had to have a leader out on the pitch and that's what Pearce provided. Every side needs someone like him, even the most creative and attacking teams. Roy Keane at United, Paul Ince and Bryan Robson before him, Souness at Liverpool, Peter Reid at Everton, Billy Bremner at Leeds . . . you always need that kind of a winner in a side. Stuart Pearce brought that driving force and steel. Keegan knows you need a blend; experience, flair, solidity, grit."

The criticism of Keegan that refuses to be quietened is that no matter how inspirational his man-management skills are, no matter how much the players like him, respect him and love to play for him, he simply doesn't have the technical ability to cope at the highest level. City's wretched start to the season has done nothing to hush these dissenting voices but the people who know him best and work with him are dismissive of this accusation. Stuart Pearce himself explained: "As I've found out with the media over the years, they like to put you in a little shoe box and label you with something. When I first got in the England squad I was labelled as being undisciplined and likely to let people down. Was I? I'm not so sure. You've only got to look at Kevin's club record as a manager to realise that he's not naïve. He had success at Fulham when he was there and if he hadn't left them when he did I think he would have taken them all the way to the Premiership and arguably to greater heights than where they are at the moment. Manchester City? In his first season here he's got us promoted. You can't argue with the club record he had at Newcastle either, so that's certainly not the club record of a tactically naïve manager. The facts speak for themselves.

"At international level he didn't have the best of times and people do look at his England record. But sometimes you take the helm at a time where there isn't an abundance of players. I think it was the same with Graham Taylor. He had a lot of players retiring and there weren't a great deal of top notch players coming through. Right now you've got Ferdinand, Gerrard, Beckham and Owen, so you could say we've got one or two who are world class. It's a good time to be involved as England manager.

"I wouldn't say Kevin's tactically naïve by a long chalk. He loves football to be played a certain way. He wants his teams to go out and try to win games, rather than settle for a draw. If you think that's tactically naïve, then that's down to you. But a lot of supporters would say it's a breath of fresh air to play that way. There's no doubt I'm more defensively minded, as is Derek Fazackerley, but that's down to the fact that I played as a defender for 20 years and so did Faz. Kevin's been a forward for 20 years, so common sense tells you that will be the case."

Keegan's ability to spot and develop players may well be his strongest suit. Many believe that he can take the lion's share of the credit for the development of Shaun Wright-Phillips, another outstanding success from last season and an import from the blossoming City academy. While the 21-year-old was introduced to the first team by previous manager Joe Royle and made 21 appearances in the 2000/01 season, he really flowered under Keegan, becoming a first team regular and contributing vital goals in the away wins at Millwall and Wolves. Paul Lake is full of praise for Keegan's work with the player.

"At the start of last season I was speaking at one of the supporters' club meetings and a lot of the fans were saying that Shaun was too small and that he wasn't strong enough. I said: 'I'm telling you, this lad is a star.' That's because I watched one of his very first games on trial at City, ironically it was against Stoke at Platt Lane when Danny Tiatto was playing for Stoke. Shaun didn't score four or five goals but he stood out purely and simply because of his first touch and his movement off the ball. He had intelligence beyond his years and he was only 16 then. I thought: 'We've got to sign this kid.' Let me make clear that I'm not taking any credit for Shaun Wright-Phillips. I wasn't involved at all. It was just my personal opinion that here was a player we should be making every effort to sign. But while the talent was always there it's obvious that Shaun has come on leaps and bounds under Kevin Keegan. Working with such quality experienced players as Ali and Eyal has helped, but Keegan has been very attentive to Shaun's needs. He's made sure that the two older midfield players have taken Shaun under their wing and I believe it's really important to have a mentor.

"I remember a certain player called Georghi Kinkladze arriving at Maine Road and he got in with the wrong crowd and became a liability. It was a shame really, because it didn't have to be that way, but Alan Ball put Kinkladze on a pedestal above the rest of the squad. He couldn't do any wrong and the other players responded badly to that. Clearly, Kevin Keegan has a real love of Ali Benarbia but the other players don't feel there's favouritism when they're all working together. Alan Ball wasn't like that. I can remember one day in training seeing Alan Kernaghan – of all people – score an absolute blinder, a world class goal. Alan Ball didn't even mention it. But if Kinkladze had scored that goal then it would have been praised to high heaven. Everyone knew Kinky was the golden boy and everyone had to work around him. Eventually, he decided he could do whatever he wanted: 'I can change a game so things must be done my way.' The guys at City now are allowed to be themselves, but they'll know they're part of a squad too. Look at Manchester United and Arsenal. There are some big, big names at those clubs and some real attitudes too. You only have to look at Patrick Vieira and Roy Keane to know that. But the management teams at those two clubs are skilled enough to be able to make it work."

Lake also believes that Keegan has not only introduced new and exciting talent to the City team, but has also significantly improved the abilities of squad stalwarts. Shaun Goater particularly springs to mind.

"Kevin has definitely done well with Shaun," says Lake. "The fans' opinions of Shaun Goater do frustrate me, because he has become a very, very intelligent footballer."

Goater's relationship with the City supporters has, indeed, been bizarre. When he was first signed by Joe Royle in March of 1998 for £400,000 from Bristol City, fans weren't sure what to make of 'The Goat'. His ratio of chances to conversions was poor and while his willingness to work and amiable personality gave him cult status ("Feed The Goat and he will score" is still a staple Maine Road singalong,) City fans have always been of the opinion that Goater really isn't a top drawer striker. Paul Lake doesn't agree.

"If you watch his positional play as a striker he's exceptional," he explains. "Alright, he's big and he's gangly, but look at the goals we've scored over the last few years. How many times has Shaun anticipated the knockdown? How many times has he been expecting the keeper to parry it in a certain place and been there for the tap-ins? He's so consistent and his runs are sublime. People say to me all the time: 'Yeah, fine. But put him in the Premiership and he hasn't got the ability.' But look at Gary Lineker. He couldn't beat an egg and he didn't have a stepover. But he was quick and he could finish. I'm not saying Shaun Goater's as good as Gary Lineker. But with the style that we have he will do well for us because, like Lineker, with Shaun it's all about anticipation."

The supporters' main gripe with Goater, though, is not the manner in which he scores goals but the number of chances he misses. Again, Lake feels this is harsh: "Darren Huckerby was probably more of a culprit on that score last season. And Shaun scored a hatful of goals – 32 in all competitions and 28 in the league. You'd much rather that players were getting 50 chances and scoring 25 of them, than not getting any chances at all. What I mean is that we have players throughout the team who can be the difference. And not just the star names either."

Kevin Horlock is a name he mentions. "Just think how many important goals Kevin Horlock scored for us last season. The only game in the home win against Wolves. The winner in that 2-1 midweek victory at Birmingham. A fantastic volley in the home win against Bradford. The list goes on. And we've got players throughout the side who can do that. I believe that Kevin's directly responsible for bringing the very best out of those lads. And he'll do it with the younger lads who he brings in as well. Look at Jon Macken. Things are evolving so quickly at the minute that he was our most expensive ever player when he signed, but now we've bought Nicolas Anelka, which means there's no extra pressure on Macken while he tries to step up to the Premiership. And that will help him. He scored a few towards the end of last season and he's settled in nicely. I like him, because I think he's a clever footballer, like a short Teddy Sheringham. He's got that footballing brain as well as the touch that will develop him into a very good player. But we're so strong at the moment that he knows he'll be a squad player. That's great for the club, though. I think there are other players who'll probably find themselves in that position this season too. I think Shaun Goater might well play a bit part. And maybe even Paulo Wanchope, though I don't know how that will sit with him. But it's so nice to see we have the numbers and the quality that will allow rotation."

In fact, Lake believes only one player will this season play every game for which he is available: Peter Schmeichel. He says: "Peter is such a big figure, and he's only here for a year, so he'll want to be playing every game he possibly can.

"But what a clever buy that was. He can develop Carlo and Nicky, who are both safe in the knowledge that Schmeichel's not going to stick around for ages. Added to which, he is the consummate professional who will raise standards all over the club. The staff tell me that even at his medical he was already setting his stall out as to what he expected. We've not even put our boots on, but it's got to be right. And I take my hat off to Keegan for that."

Some fans were concerned about Schmeichel's Manchester United connections but Lake believes that, while an element of City's support will never forget or forgive their keeper's Red history when the side has an off day, the Great Dane has the experience to handle any pressure. He also believes it is a signing which shows how Keegan is regarded by senior players. "No disrespect to Joe Royle, but when he was in charge you thought if he had five million quid to spend on a player, then who would want to come and play for him? The answers wouldn't be all that inspiring. But now you know there are loads of players out there who would jump at the chance to play for Kevin Keegan. Ali Benarbia said that one of the reasons he signed for City was that Kevin Keegan was a hero of his at Liverpool when he was growing up. Nicolas Anelka said that he'd been inspired to play for Keegan because of his amazing career as a striker.

This was another daring Keegan buy – and one surrounded by more than a little controversy. And it is a signing that, once again, underlines Keegan's attraction as a manager and his ability to see and execute daring possibilities. Despite the 23-year-old Frenchman's reputation for being surly and difficult, there has never been any doubting his abilities. His impact on the Premiership as a raw 17-year-old with Arsenal in 1996 was astonishing, his coolness in front of goal belying his tender years. And while his career failed to spark at either Real Madrid or during a second spell with Paris St. Germain, the esteem in which he is still held by his one-time mentor at Highbury, Arsene Wenger, speaks volumes for his ability. Liverpool chose not to pursue a transfer to Merseyside following a loan spell at the end of last season, with the reasons for this deal not being concluded shrouded in mystery. Gerard Houllier has since claimed that it was not for football reasons, though many believe the arrival of Senegalese striker El Hadj Diouf meant that Liverpool were happier to take a cheaper option.

Kevin Keegan had no doubts whatsoever about wanting to take the player and even conducted the £13 million negotiations for Anelka's signature during a family holiday in France. How likely is it that Anelka would have signed for a team which had just returned to the Premiership, which had experienced relegation or promotion for each of the previous seven seasons, without the lure of a manager with Keegan's stature and a man with Keegan's ambition? As Director Of Football Dennis Tueart explained at the time of Anelka's signing: "The signing of Nicolas Anelka reinforces the message that as a club we are moving forward. Kevin watched the situation unfold at Liverpool and once again his move for the striker is evidence of his ambitions for Manchester City. Kevin is a manager who doesn't stand still, he doesn't stand back and admire his last production – he is always moving forward." Tueart also revealed that showing Anelka highlights of City's Championship-winning campaign, the service he could expect from Benarbia and Berkovic and the style of play which Keegan insists on went a long way towards securing the player's signature on June 6th.

"Three seasons ago a player of Anelka's calibre signing for City would have been a pipe dream," Paul Lake rightly says. "A lot of City fans were pessimistic about Kevin when he got here as we all know, but I said to them from day one: 'Watch who he'll be able to attract. You'll see a different type of player coming to Maine Road now.' It's not only about the reputation he has a former player, but it's also about the reputation he has for the type of football he wants his sides to play as a manager. I had to laugh because I was talking to my son, who's four and a half, and we were talking about City and he said 'sexy football.' But if you look at the way we play that's the best description of it.

"Gary Megson was a team mate of mine. I called him 'Dad' when we played and I love Mego, but there's no way he could have brought the same calibre of players to City and changed City the way Kevin Keegan has. There were loads of managers who were linked with City who you thought might have been able to improve things, but there was no-one who could have brought the dimension that Kevin Keegan has. Over the next two or three seasons these top class players will come to City as well as Newcastle and United and Arsenal. There are very few managers who can have that effect.

"Then there is the support. How many fans have we attracted back to

Maine Road on the back of bringing Kevin Keegan in? It's so exciting and so pleasing to see young people who want to wear the City shirt again. Not just kids who are proud to wear it because their dad's a Blue, but also because it's exciting to be a City supporter again. It's something youngsters have never had before. We played quite exciting football in my time, but it doesn't even compare to what's happening out on the pitch right now. Even more fans will be attracted when we move to the new stadium. How fantastic does that look against Francis Lee's white elephant stall?"

Built during the 1994 close season to comply with new regulations insisting on all-seater stadia in the Premiership, the new Kippax Stand is indeed an eyesore, out of keeping with the rest of Maine Road, inelegant and universally unloved by the fans.

There are those who will say Lake – and the other Keegan enthusiasts – are crazy to be so positive about King Kev. He has never won a major trophy as a manager. Early Premiership results were not great. Inexperience is no longer an excuse. Is there a danger that, desperate for Keegan to be our Messiah, we are getting carried away?

Lake is unequivocal: "No. But I sense some football people and, particularly, some elements of the Press are hoping he will fail. Why is that? Because he quit the England job? At least he had the guts to do it and be honest. And he will have learned from that, as he will have gained from the Ferguson spat and from his time at Fulham dealing with Al Fayed. The moves he has made with City have proved he is a lot more astute than people give him credit for. Don't forget, too, that Keegan still has plenty to prove. He is a proven winner, he has massive ambition and I believe that will drive him and City forward."

Will City achieve the Top Six finish Keegan talked about at the start of the season? "That may not happen, especially after a shaky start. But we will not be relegated. We can hold our own in the Premiership, whether or not we add players who are worth £20 million pounds and more. We have a genuine squad, where everything isn't focused on building around a single player. If you invest in a player to be the difference that's dangerous. But if you add players to enhance *the squad* it takes the pressure off everyone. Our hopes are in several players, not just one signing. Even our biggest name player is Nicolas Anelka and, though he cost £13 million, that has not been a vast amount in recent times. Look at Chelsea. They've thrown so much money at building their team, but there's never been the feeling of a squad there, whereas there has been at Arsenal and Man United. If you compare City with United, Arsenal and Liverpool then it's obvious that we're not quite there yet. But we can beat any of them on our day and if you look at the other sides in the division . . . Sunderland, West Ham, Charlton, Birmingham, West Brom . . . I will always fancy us against those clubs.

"We performed so consistently in the last third of last season. I think that was a glimpse of what we're capable of at this higher level.

"Is Kevin Keegan our Messiah? Yes, I think he is."

Meeting the Messiah

It would be naïve to presume that a single meeting with Kevin Keegan could answer the question as to whether or not he really is tactically naïve. It wouldn't be beyond the realms of possibility, however, to attempt an eye-witness report on whether his oft-vaunted managerial strength, his motivational skills, are as impressive as many claim. After all, the function of the manager is almost as much to inspire the press that writes about both him and his team as it is to inspire his players. The power of the press is a legendary phrase, possibly invented by managers who are already lining up a ready-made scapegoat when the inevitable sacking occurs. But there is no doubt that the bigger football gets and the more voracious the public's appetite for tittle-tattle, gossip, hearsay and the occasional fact, the more the press does wield an influence on a manager's destiny. And that influence is undoubtedly on the increase. Sunderland boss Peter Reid learnt that lesson to his cost, when public pressure rather than real internal ructions led to his sacking as manager of the Wearsiders in October of 2002.

Meeting Kevin Keegan when he was England manager in May 1999 gave some insight into what preoccupies his managerial thoughts. The interview took place at Wembley Stadium a month before the key European Championships qualifying game with Sweden and two weeks after the 3-1 qualification win at Wembley over Poland. Keegan was launching a new England-centric initiative for kids. By the time he'd been wheeled out to kick a few balls about with some small boys and girls for the benefit of the cameras and then been interviewed by about three hundred different people, even Keegan's notoriously PR-friendly charm would surely have been stretched to the limit. Especially since we'd also been promised our own exclusive photo session for the cover of the particular magazine I was working for.

When Keegan was finally dragged into one of the banqueting halls to meet me he was looking a little bedraggled. He'd been out on the pitch kicking balls about and, of course, it had been raining. But he was still wearing his traditional smile and his mood was only temporarily darkened by the sight of a couple of lights and one of those photo umbrellas. 'Aw, fellas,' he protested. But he still sat down to have his picture taken while I chatted away with him.

I thought he looked tired. The skin underneath his eyes was darkened and wrinkled, but his enthusiasm for the game, for England, still shone through. Yet the answers to all of my questions focused on the emotional rather than the cerebral. His instinct was always talk about the attitude of the players rather than the systems he was asking them to play: "I was delighted with the performance against Poland because it was a very solid display from a team that really wanted to go out and both play for England and *win* for England," he explained. "That shone through in everything that my players did. It really put a smile on my face, because I knew that all the people who'd come to Wembley to support the team and the millions who'd tuned in to watch on television were happy with what they'd seen and could go out and have a great night of celebration. And I'm just the same as any England fan. We all feel good when England do well, don't we?"

Keegan was entirely concerned with the passion which he wanted his players to display and on what it meant to represent the country. Of course this may have been because Keegan is only too aware that this is, above all, what is expected of England managers prior to a crucial game. Flag-waving is all-important. But the more he spoke the more you could feel yourself getting dragged into this feel-good world where it's warm and cosy and where the players are all loved and cajoled into believing they're world-beaters. Of Paul Scholes, who had scored a hat-trick against a very mediocre Polish side, Keegan enthused. "He's a tremendous player; you've only got to watch him in training to realise that. We were seeing all week what you ended up seeing on the day, so it didn't come as too much of a shock to us. But scoring a hat-trick at Wembley. Well, it's a bit special, isn't it?". Talking about what we could expect from his side against Sweden he shot back with "100% commitment, because that's what the England fans always give and that's what I give too." Even when talking about potential Swedish threats, attitude and spirit was what he homed in on. "In many ways they're very similar to us, in that they have great commitment and they don't like getting beaten," he explained. And while it's easy to understand why all of these comments could send a player out feeling like his heart is ready to burst out of his jersey with pride, the professional game at the very top level is played with the head every bit as much as it is with the heart.

I am happy to admit that I too fell under Keegan's spell. When he talked he had this uncanny knack of making me feel as if he was engaged in the most interesting conversation he'd ever had. Keegan simply has that certain something that makes you feel you matter to him. And players – highly-strung, temperamental, egotistical – will clearly respond very favourably to that type of tender loving care. But whether Keegan adds the savvy to the soothing is the question that is hardest of all to answer.

Howard Johnson, October 2002.

Blow by blow

21 May
ROYLE OUT

Manchester City boss Joe Royle is sacked by the club after his side is relegated from the Premiership. Just a year after the euphoria of promotion from Division One, the manager's three year reign comes to an abrupt, but apparently amicable, end.

"I came in this morning with the idea of making plans for next season," says Royle. "But I sensed immediately that it wasn't to be. It all ended amicably. I spoke to the Chairman this morning. It was a three-minute meeting, I shook his hand and left."

The now-former manager makes a particular point of thanking the City fans for their support, saying that the club will always be a big part of his life. Then he leaves for Spain on holiday. His assistant Willie Donachie is asked to stay on but says he needs time to consider his future.

Immediately, the book opens on prospective candidates for the vacant position. Nottingham Forest manager David Platt emerges as the front runner, while odds are offered on Blackpool manager and former Blue Steve McMahon, George Graham, Dave Bassett (not for the first time) and Harry Redknapp.

22 May
WHO'S NEXT?

The papers begin to speculate on the reasons behind Royle's dismissal. *The Mirror* says it's because he couldn't put a stop to a 'drinking culture' is says exists within the club. *The Sun* gets hold of a player who won't be named, but who will say that it was "the best pub team I've ever played in". He obviously never laced up his boots with the Birmingham side of the early '80s, then . . . *The Daily Mail* appears to be the only paper to align itself with Royle, accusing City of being callous because both Royle's wife and father are recovering from serious illnesses.

Kevin Keegan is touted as a possible successor for the first time, alongside Republic Of Ireland manager Mick McCarthy. Other new names being bandied about include Preston boss David Moyes and Hibs manager Alex McLeish. Chairman David Bernstein admits there is a shortlist of potential targets and says he is prepared to look to Europe to get his man.

Fans are divided over Royle's departure. While some praise the Division Two Playoff Final win and successive subsequent promotions, others criticise his team selection during the Premiership campaign as naïve. City skipper Alfie Haaland talks on his own website of his sadness at losing his manager. "He's a very honest and open man and was always listening to the players," says the Norwegian.

Meanwhile, City's 22-year-old midfielder Jeff Whitley is named in the Northern Ireland squad for two World Cup Qualifiers against Bulgaria and the Czech Republic despite still being treated for a knee injury picked up in the home game against Chelsea. Kevin Horlock has already been ruled out.

23 May
WILL IT BE KEEGAN?
The Mirror and *The Telegraph* both claim that Kevin Keegan is the favourite for the City job, with the former claiming his 'special relationship' with City director Dennis Tueart gives credence to the rumour. Tueart is referred to as the 'Maine Road Axeman', pointing the finger at the former City player as an instrumental figure in Royle's departure.

Mark Kennedy rubbishes the stories of City having a drinking culture in *The Sun*. "They are entitled to their opinion," he says. "And I can only give you my opinion, which is that it was most definitely not the case." Kennedy then goes on to say that a manager can't be expected to keep his eye on players 24 hours a day.

24 May
CITY ANNOUNCE KEEGAN AS MANAGER
City Chairman David Bernstein announces that former Newcastle, Fulham and England boss Kevin Keegan will be the club's new manager. The 50-year-old Keegan has been out of the game since resigning as England manager in October of 2000 and drives down from his family home near

Middlesbrough to attend a euphoric 5pm press conference. He signs a five year deal worth £1.2 million a year. The Keegan magic takes no time at all to work, as City's women's side beat Manchester United 2-1 at Maine Road.

KEVIN KEEGAN'S FIRST MANCHESTER CITY PRESS CONFERENCE:
Chairman David Bernstein: Good afternoon and welcome to Maine Road. It's been a demanding week. Our club has a reputation for its frequent management changes. However, since my appointment as Chairman there has been only one change and it is an experience I'm desperately anxious not to repeat. Manchester City is now an extremely attractive proposition to manage. In three days we have had over 20 serious applications for this job. However, we had only one target. When we approached him on Monday his level of interest was obvious. He was fully aware of our club's great potential and described it as 'a unique opportunity.' I really am delighted that Kevin is joining us. As a player and manager he brings with him a tremendous record. Liverpool and Newcastle bear full testimony to that. He brings a whole range of talents and benefits to the club. I'd like to mention just three.

Outstanding achievements as a league manager. His record at Fulham was first class. And his performance at Newcastle was quite fantastic, taking them from the verge of relegation to the second division to virtually the Premier League Championship in just over three years. It's the stuff of legend and deservedly, Kevin is a legend on Tyneside.

Secondly, Kevin brings unique man-management and motivational qualities. History has shown that these are the first requirements of a really successful manager and Kevin has them in abundance.

Thirdly, he will bring something to this club that it has lacked for 20 or 30 years; real style and flair. We used to be renowned for this but over the years, as the club has struggled, it has been dissipated. This is something our fans really understand and will value.

Kevin has signed a five-year contract. This of course takes us into our new stadium. We look forward to playing successful, Premier League football in the City of Manchester Stadium and to Kevin inspiring our club to the success our supporters so richly deserve. Thank you. I think Kevin would like to say a few words himself.

Kevin Keegan: Yeah, obviously delighted to be here. It takes very little in the way of people trying to force you to join a club like this. It's a fantastic opportunity and I thank the Chairman and the Board of Directors for giving me that. It's a very similar situation, although not the same obviously, as Newcastle, in that there's a tremendous fan base, which of course Newcastle had. Maybe the club has underachieved over the years. People will have different reasons and opinions about why. That doesn't matter any more. Today's about what's going to happen from here on. I'll be judged on that. Obviously the Board of Directors at Man City will be judged on my appointment, on results. And I think this is truly a sleeping giant still and it's my job to turn it round with the help of an awful lot of people, not least the players. The supporters we know are there. It's a little bit different from Fulham, where the fan base isn't the same, and yet they've been very, very successful. And as I say, I'm really looking forward to it. I'm here today. I'm going to be to be here tomorrow in Manchester and what I don't know about Manchester City . . . I promise you, within three or four weeks I'll know everything about them; the youth academy, the training facilities. I'm going to look at the new stadium, which is very, very exciting. We can fill it, we know that, but we can win something, because that's what it's really about. That's all I want to say really, other than, as I said to you before, I'm delighted I've got the opportunity. And that's what it is, a tremendous opportunity. And it's up to myself, the staff, the players and the rest of the club to make sure that opportunity turns into something fantastic.

City's MC: What we're going to do is take a few questions. And please, this is about Man City today. Keep your questions to Man City.

Journalist: Why now? Why come back to management now?

KK: Because I'm ready for it. I really enjoy club management. I'm not saying I didn't enjoy the England job, because I enjoyed every minute of it. But I think my skills and what I'm about is more suited to club management, working with all the parts of the club, because football is a big, big business. Helping people who sometimes need help, that are not completely football-related, and building a club and hopefully building a successful outfit that people really want to be part of. I think that is my strength. I think I've already proved it twice at league level at Newcastle and Fulham; to a lesser degree at Fulham because I was only there a short period. And I'm pretty confident that, given that little bit of luck, which you always need in football – I don't care who you are, how talented you are, how much support you get, you need a bit of luck – I'm pretty sure we can do it here.

Journalist: It's been six or seven months since you were out of the game. Have you missed it?

KK: Yeah, I've missed it and that's why I'm back. I love football. I'm passionately in love with football in a real sense in that, you know, what you see is what you get with me. And I think the six months out have done me good. You look back and you can analyse things and you can see football for what it is. And when you're very, very much involved in the everyday, sometimes you can lose focus. I've got a nice clear picture, I know what I want to do here and I know where I want us to go and I'm sure my vision for Manchester City is the same as the board's and certainly it will be what the fans want, because that's what I try and deliver. I look at the fans, I look at what they want. They are our customers. What do they want? They want exciting football and they want to win football matches. And despite what people think it's possible to do both.

Journalist: How stressful a job is this? How do you feel about coping with the strain?

KK: Well, I can't go grey, can I? That's for sure, being almost white now, as we speak. And I suppose when you're a kid your mam always says "Don't go near a main road." So probably that's why a lot of people are scared about this place. But I do think it's got all the ingredients here. They've had some very good managers here. Joe Royle in particular did a fantastic job here. No doubt about that. I'm very close to Joe, so it's my job to take it on. And as I said to you when I made my opening statement, I'm really privileged to have the opportunity. It is a big, big club that, like the Chairman said, anybody in their right senses would want to manage.

Journalist: There were suggestions of a lack of discipline at Maine Road before. What's your stance on the behaviour of the playing staff?

KK: I'll be honest with you, I don't care what happened before. It's a new club for the players. I'll be seeing the players as soon as I can. It's a completely new club. What's gone is gone. I don't know anything about that. I know one thing. In the future we'll be looking to do everything we can to ensure success. And that's what my job is.

Journalist: Have you been told how much you've got to spend?

KK: No. We haven't really discussed that at the moment. We're going to have a meeting tomorrow. But if you just think that throwing a lot of money at it's going to solve problems at football clubs, it doesn't. I think Manchester City spent 17 million pounds last year trying to stay in the Premiership and we now find ourselves in Division One. So it's not just about money. But I'm pretty sure, having talked to the Chairman on Monday, that if the right player comes along and I want to sign him, then he'll do everything he can to make the money available.

Journalist: So what about your backroom staff? Can you say what you'll be doing on that front?

KK: To be honest with you we've got to get today out of the way. What I will try and do very much is be open as always. And as soon as we know what we're going to do . . . We can't let you know what we're going to do before *we* know, obviously, but we'll try. We'll let you know who the backroom staff are. But I want to say here and now. I haven't talked to Willie Donachie yet, but I do want him to stay. I told the Chairman that on Monday when he came to see me. I like Willie Donachie. He's a defender, which will balance well with myself. But if, when I talk to Willie, he decides he wants to go for whatever reason, then I fully respect that and I'm sure the board will.

Journalist: It's a five year contract to make the club great. Do you think that's realistic?

KK: Yes I do. I spent five years at Newcastle.

Journalist: What about the parallels with City and Newcastle? Similar clubs?

KK: Well the parallels are, they have the one thing you can't buy. They have a tremendous fan base. Passionate fans. Some clubs can never have . . . they have passionate fans, of course they do. It doesn't matter how small a club is, it has some passionate fans. But the number that they've got here, the way they've supported this team. I mean, 34,000 for the last game, already relegated. I don't think many clubs are like this one, I really don't, and that's what excites me and that's what would excite anybody in my position taking over a club like this. The rest is a lot of hard work and a lot of miles travelled looking at players and a lot of time spent looking at the youth set-up, all the things that are so important in the set-up today. You know, in five years' time hopefully we'll be looking back on a really successful period for the club. I mean, we proved at Newcastle what you can do in two and three years. It's fantastic. Once you get the momentum going. Once you get everybody rowing the boat the same way, once you get everybody believing in something, you can take it way beyond what even the most optimistic person – and I am an optimistic person – thinks. I mean, Newcastle surprised me. It would be nice if Man City does.

Journalist: Sitting next to you is an old friend of yours. How much was that important in deciding to come here?

KK: Well over the last two or three years Dennis (Tueart) and I have done a lot of business through his company and what he does and I know it's a well-run club. I know that for a fact. I know it's a club that has sorted out a lot of those problems from the past and is back now, geared to go on and be one of the big five, six clubs in the country because of the reasons I've said. You know, fan base, the fact that we're going into a 50-odd-thousand-seater stadium in two years that people think you have to have now to sustain the sort of finances you need to run a big club. So it's all there. The ingredients are all there. It's for us now to put them in a pan, for want of a better word, and to cook them. In the nicest way.

Journalist: Was there ever a time when you never saw yourself in this position of returning to football?

KK: No, there was never a point where I said 'Never go back'. I said that when I was allowed to come out of my house after the England departure.

It was strange because the press said 'You've been hiding', but they forgot to say that they were camped outside my house for three weeks, which made it difficult to come out. But I said then that I wouldn't rule it out. I'll be honest with you, I have had other opportunities but this is the only one that's appealed to me. And that's why it's been done very, very quickly. I'm not a fool. I know I've got a real chance of being successful. I've got a well-run club behind me, so there's a lot of pluses here.

Journalist: Is it fair to say that Manchester City is one of very few clubs that you would have said yes to?

KK: I think that's very fair to say and that's not me saying I'm choosy. I don't believe in people phoning you up and saying 'Here's a load of money. Come and make my small club into a big club.' You're looking at miracle workers there – and they don't exist. But this is a big club and what the board have told me they want to achieve at this club is achievable. They're not talking about silly things. It's achievable.

Journalist: Kevin, when were you asked to take over the job?

KK: I was approached on Monday. I had a phone call on Sunday to see if I would be in any way interested and I was approached on Monday and by Tuesday afternoon everything was sorted. It's been agreed since Tuesday really. And I'm here.

Journalist: You were in Spain, were you?

KK: No I wasn't. You don't always get it right, the Press. I was driving down from my home near Middlesborough and I heard I was coming in from Spain, so I went into a shop and bought some suntan lotion! I don't know who spun that one. But I've never been to Spain since I left eight years ago. But if you want to write that I came from Spain it sounds great.

Bernstein: If I can just add to that. When I first spoke to Kevin his initial reaction was 'Yours is the only club I'm interested in coming to', and it was fantastic to hear that. And I must say the way he's handled this thing over the last few days has really supported that. He's been fantastic to deal with and the negotiation, in a way, has been very easy. Kevin made it very easy indeed and his level of enthusiasm was really quite obvious and quite fantastic from our point of view to see that.

KK: I obviously sold myself a bit cheap, then. That's what the Chairman's saying.

Bernstein: Such a poor negotiator.

Journalist (to Bernstein): You said you wanted the new manager to have the summer to plan for the new campaign. How much did that mean to you?

Bernstein: A tremendous amount. I said we wanted the right person rather than do it too quickly. But to get the person we wanted in three or four days is quite incredible. And as you say it gives Kevin the chance to plan this thing properly. He's got the whole close season to work things out and that has to be a big advantage.

Journalist: There's a Fans Forum tonight Kevin. Are you going to be there?

Bernstein: We'll leave it out for the moment and see how Kevin's feeling afterwards.

KK: No I'm not going to be there. But I am going to be there, if you know what I mean. The Chairman doesn't want the fans to know I'm going to be there, but I'm going to be there. Have we given it away there?

Bernstein: I think we have somehow.

Journalist: Do you think you have a point to prove? To yourself if no-one else?

KK: I think you've always got a point to prove. In football, in management, in life. Every time you go somewhere what you've achieved doesn't count for anything. And yeah, I do think I've got something to prove. I always have felt that way ever since the day I can remember kicking a football around and people saying 'Oh, he's too small.' So yeah, that doesn't worry me. This game of football doesn't follow exact science, as you know. Just because someone's achieved something somewhere it doesn't mean to say necessarily that they'll achieve it somewhere else. And just because someone's failed somewhere doesn't mean to say they'll fail somewhere else. You know, it's been proved many, many times. Players get turned down at one club and they're successful at another. So yeah, I've got a lot to prove, always to myself because I demand that of myself to start off with. The book will be written and hopefully it will be a very successful one at Man City.

Journalist: Can you analyse the current squad? Are they equipped to get back to the Premiership?

KK: Well I'm not going to talk about the players in front of the press before I've even talked to the players. But if I look at the squad it's a very strong squad. It's got a nice balance of experience and youth. There are one or two youngsters come into the side towards the end of the season in particular and done quite well. I mean, it's all there. We're going down a division, so these players should be even more equipped for that division. It's a division I know, of course, having been there at Newcastle and having been at Fulham just recently.

Journalist: Dennis, perhaps finally you can talk about the characteristics of the man on your left, because you know him well and he was the man you wanted here . . .

(Director Of Football) Dennis Tueart: He has the desire. He has hunger and desire. As he said, he has things to prove. The bigger the challenge, the better the man he is and I think that's one of his best characteristics. It's the fact that he looks at a challenge, he looks it square in the face, and the bigger the challenge, then the better he performs.

Conference ends.

25 May
KEEGAN APPOINTS COX

Keegan immediately appoints Arthur Cox to run City's scouting network, explaining that the club must start looking everywhere for new talent.

However, he is careful to explain that the current squad will be given every chance to impress him. He again states – as in his press conference – that he wants Willie Donachie to stay at the club and will be talking to him when he gets back from his holidays the following Tuesday. He also says he would like to see City win the Premiership title within five years.

27 May
KASH FOR KEGGY

David Bernstein confirms that there will be multi-millions available to Keegan once City are back in the Premiership but that immediate funds will be more modest. Bernstein tells Radio Five Live: 'Kevin's quite satisfied with the funds available for the First Division. When we get back to the Premier League he will have substantial funds. We've promised him that and we will deliver on that.'

28 May
KEEGAN WANTS WILLIE

Keegan re-emphasises his desire to work with Willie Donachie, but again also accepts the possibility that the Scot may wish to move on. Displaying the first signs of his renowned management genius, Keegan explains: 'If Willie wants to go, then I'll look for someone else.'

29 May
THE KEEGAN BLUEPRINT

Keegan says he will spend the first six weeks in his new job putting the footballing side of the club under close scrutiny. Together with Arthur Cox, the manager says he will look at the City Academy, the training facilities, the assessment processes and the staff. And despite the smiling, joking Kevin Keegan that the press and public knows well, there is also the hint of a ruthless streak. Keegan says that anyone at the club who is not good enough at their job will go.

30 May
WHITLEY OUT OF BULGARIA CLASH, LEE BACKS KEEGAN, DUNNE PLEASED WITH APPOINTMENT

Jeff Whitley's knee injury forces him out of Northern Ireland's World Cup qualifier with Bulgaria and he doesn't travel with the party.

Former City chairman Francis Lee backs Keegan. Lee believes Keegan will get the club back into the Premiership at the first attempt. Given his turbulent time in charge, this doubtless puts the fear of God into most City supporters.

Defender Richard Dunne – away on World Cup duty with The Republic Of Ireland – is excited about his new club manager. 'You only get great reports from other players about him, so there's exciting times ahead,' he says.

31 May
DONACHIE TO STAY, MORRISON TO LEAVE

It's all smiles as coach Willie Donachie agrees to stay at the club and work alongside Keegan. Both men underline their commitment to getting City back into the top flight at the first time of asking. On the playing side, chunky defender Andy Morrison is handed a free transfer on the basis of his loyalty and 'the unique affection with which the club and supporters hold him.' Keegan says that Morrison deserves a chance to further his career, but it won't be with the Blues.

JUNE 2001
1 June
GINOLA TO CITY, MORRISON FOR BRISTOL?

City are linked with a move for Aston Villa midfielder and hair-washing expert David Ginola. City dismiss the stories as 'pure speculation'. Timotei are supposedly watching the situation closely. Andy Morrison could be on his way to Bristol City, while winger Mark Kennedy looks like he will get to start in the Republic of Ireland's World Cup qualifier against Portugal in just 24 hours' time.

2 June
TAYLOR TO LEAVE

City fans breathe a sigh of relief. 'Striker' Gareth Taylor is leaving. 'I definitely want to join Burnley,' he says. 'We definitely want you to join Burnley,' chorus the City faithful.

Keeper Carlo Nash, meanwhile, is delighted that Kevin Keegan has joined the club and predicts that it will be a speedy return to the Premiership under the new boss. 'With Kevin at the helm I'm confident we can do it,' he says.

LAKEY'S VIEW

"It's weird to see just how recently in City's history players like Gareth Taylor were at the club, but at the time they were important. Who remembers Robert Taylor coming in from Gillingham? Even when he scored goals people couldn't take him seriously. They were laughing, going "Fat Bob's done it!" People have said to me over the years that I was one of the better players who ever played for City and I think "No I'm not. There's Colin Bell, Frannie Lee, Mike Summerbee, Mike Doyle, Kinkladze . . ." But there again, there have been so many players at the other end of the spectrum. You know, you chant the name, you sing the song, you get the name on the shirt. And the next season they're gone and you've not thought twice about them. Under managers like Alan Ball, Brian Horton, Frank Clark and Joe Royle there were hundreds of them."

5 June
NEW FITNESS COACH CONFIRMED

City look set to appoint Juan Carlos Osorio, the assistant coach of American soccer side the New Jersey Metrostars as their new conditioning coach. The 39-year-old Colombian landed the job ahead of 29 other applicants following a rigorous interviewing process, which included putting together case studies on several City Academy players. Osorio has a degree in science and football from John Moores University in Liverpool and is so meticulous in his work that he once rented a house overlooking Liverpool's Melwood training ground so he could study the players at work. City are waiting on a work permit for Osorio, but Director Of Football Dennis Tueart says that Kevin Keegan has already met the coach. 'They spent a morning together talking through ideas and Kevin was very impressed with him,' says Tueart.

Richard Dunne looks likely to play for the Republic in Estonia in their World Cup qualifier. But Mark Kennedy now looks likely to miss out.

6 June
'KEEGAN WON'T WALK' SAYS SUMMERBEE.

City legend Mike Summerbee claims that Kevin Keegan has joined Manchester City for the long haul. Speaking at the launch of his book 'Fathers, Sons And Football', written together with Colin Shindler, Summerbee says: 'I know Kevin very well and I think you have seen the last of him walking out on clubs.'

8 June
PRIOR FOR CARDIFF?
City accept a £650,000 bid from Cardiff City for defender Spencer Prior, whose first team chances have been limited since the arrival from Everton of Richard Dunne. Prior was put on the transfer list by former manager Joe Royle.

9 June
CITY TO STAY AT CARRINGTON
The club's Chief Operating Officer Chris Bird says there is absolutely no truth in the rumours that Kevin Keegan wants to abandon the club's headquarters in Carrington and return to the training facilities at Platt Lane. City only moved out to Carrington at the start of the previous season and are in the middle of updating the facilities at the former University of Manchester-owned site. The total bill for the redevelopment could be in excess of £2 million.

11 June
'KEEGAN IS THE MAN' – HOWEY
Defender Steve Howey, who has already played under Kevin Keegan at Newcastle, explains why the new manager's arrival at Maine Road is great for City. 'He's a players' manager and I'm sure he will be able to get the best out of everyone here,' he says.

Defender Shaun Holmes leaves City for Wrexham.

12 June
BURNLEY NOT INTERESTED IN MORRISON
Burnley deny reports in the media that they are to move for City's Andy Morrison. 'We have enough defenders,' they say. Striker Gareth Taylor, however, looks set to sign a three year deal with the same club.

13 June
NEW KEEPING COACH RUMOURS
Rumours appear in the press that former City keeper Tommy Wright may be re-joining the club – as a goalkeeping coach. Wright is out of contract at Bolton and has worked with Kevin Keegan in the past.

Keegan, meanwhile, insists that City's pre-season friendlies against

Halifax, Tranmere, Scunthorpe and Huddersfield will all be honoured, despite the fixtures being pencilled in before he arrived at the club. 'It would be wrong of me to come in and change things,' he says. Keegan admits that he would have liked to have gone abroad for a game, but that is unlikely to happen now.

13 June
PRIOR MOVE OFF
It looks as if Spencer Prior's move to Cardiff is off after the player fails to agree personal terms with the Welsh club. Manager Alan Cork tells *The Western Mail*: "The deal is dead and buried. We just couldn't agree personal terms, which is a shame as it would have been a big signing for the club."

15 June
KENNEDY OUT?
Speculation mounts that winger Mark Kennedy could be the first high profile City player on his way out of Maine Road, with Wolves favourites to land the player as part of a £10 million spending spree.

Kevin Keegan talks of how important City's Academy is to the club and how he will be working hard on integrating senior and junior players within the club. He says that football is less "feudal" than when he was starting out and that the attitude at City must reflect that.

15 June
NEW TV DEAL ANNOUNCED
ONDigital announce that they have bought the rights to cover Nationwide League matches for their new ITV Sport channel, which launches on August 11. City may be asked to play on a very untraditional Thursday or a Sunday. The opinions of the fans seem to be of little importance.

16 June
PRE-SEASON GAMES CONFIRMED
City announce that they will play five glittering pre-season friendlies and confirm four of them. The games that are scheduled are:

Sat 21 July v Halifax Town 3pm
Tue 24 July v Scunthorpe United 7.45pm

Sat 28 July v Tranmere Rovers 3pm

Tue 31 July v Huddersfield Town away (Jon Dyson testimonial) 7.45pm

There will be another game scheduled for the first weekend in August, though the opposition has yet to be confirmed.

18 June
TIATTO GOES TO TOON?

The Sunday People claims that Newcastle are to launch a £6 million bid for City's Australian midfielder Danny Tiatto.

The Sunday Mirror claims that City are interested in Pierre Van Hooijdonk, who is leaving Benfica.

Keeper Nicky Weaver reckons he is slimmer and fitter than ever, having been working through the close season after injuring his ligaments during a reserve team game at the end of last season. "I feel so much better when I've been to the gym," he says, logically and unsurprisingly. City fans remain to be convinced.

A City Academy side returns from a tournament in Brescia, Italy where they lost on penalties in the semi-final to Scottish side Hearts.

19 June
NO BID FOR KENNEDY

Chief Operating Officer Chris Bird claims that talk of Mark Kennedy leaving City for Wolves is nonsense and says there is no offer on the table for the winger. Reports in *The Daily Mirror* suggest that Wolves have had a £1.8 million bid accepted by City for the 25-year-old Dubliner. Bird says that Kennedy and manager Kevin Keegan have met, but only for a cup of tea and a chat. Apparently no biscuits.

The Sun reports that Danny Tiatto is to become City's highest-paid player. Meanwhile, City are handed automatic entry into the second round of next season's Worthington Cup.

20 June
PSYCHO FOR CITY

Kevin Keegan makes his first signing for the club – and it's Stuart Pearce, who is out of contract at West Ham. "Having worked with Stuart before, I am confident that his strengths and leadership qualities will be a great addition to the team, not only on the pitch, but also in the dressing room and around the training complex," says Keegan.

Down in Australia midfielder Danny Tiatto is sent off in Australia's World Cup qualifier against New Zealand. The midfielder is red-carded for a challenge on Chris Killen, who just happens to play his football at Manchester City.

21 June
NEW SEASON FIXTURES
The new season's fixtures are announced and City will face Gianluca Vialli's Watford at Maine Road in Kevin Keegan's first game in charge. The season kicks off on Saturday August 11, though there is already concern that City's first game could be moved to accommodate television scheduling needs.

The bookies make City 9/2 favourites to win the league title. Notoriously sceptical City fans are not first down the betting shop.

22 June
KENNEDY FOR WOLVES
That cup of tea can't have been to his liking. Mark Kennedy *is* to join Wolves after all. The player has agreed terms and will move to Molineux, subject to a medical. He will cost the Midlands club £2 million. Speaking on the club's website, boss Dave Jones says: "He will be a big benefit to Wolves with his experience, pace and ability. He can not only provide goals, but score them as well." There appears to be little protest from City supporters over the departure of the undoubtedly talented but hugely inconsistent Irishman.

LAKEY'S VIEW
"I thought it was a bit of a surprise seeing Mark leaving before the season had even started, especially with him going to a perceived rival in the promotion race. But he was a bit of a loose cannon, a great player on his day, but very inconsistent. You really have to be the kind of player who wants to be the difference and with Mark I always felt that if he came up against a full back who was really up for it, then he might just disappear a bit. I think the truth of the matter is that in the cold light of day he wasn't really missed."

23 June

WEAVER WAS NOT MAN UNITED TARGET

City deny rumours that Manchester United made a bid for keeper Nicky Weaver shortly before the start of the Maine Road club's ill-fated 2000 Premiership campaign. "There was never an official approach by Manchester United," says a club spokesman. After some of Weaver's erratic performances in 2000/2001, United are not rushing to contradict him.

24 June

RULE CHANGES

Kevin Keegan admits there will be some new rules for the players when they return to the club after the summer break but refuses to announce exactly what these changes will be. "I believe they will be very important for them," Keegan explains cryptically.

25 June

HUCKERBY HOUNDED OUT?

The Mirror speculates that Darren Huckerby could follow Mark Kennedy out of Manchester City, with a return to former club Coventry on the cards. This, despite the fact that Kevin Keegan insists that all City players will be given a fair chance to make an impression on him. "It is clean slate for all the players, and it always is with me," he maintains.

26 June 2001

KENNEDY MOVE STILL ON

City deny that there are any last minute hitches in the proposed transfer of Mark Kennedy to Wolves and that the player will sign, subject to a medical, when he returns from his holidays. The player has not demanded a pay-off from City, despite rumours to the contrary. Nor is there any truth in the rumours that missing-in-action winger Terry Cooke is set to join Wigan.

27 June

WILCOX WANTED?

The Sun, The Mirror and *The Daily Mail* are all convinced that Leeds winger Jason Wilcox is on his way to City for a fee which varies between two and three million pounds. Both clubs deny the story. Dundee United also rubbish talk that midfielder Charlie Miller is a City target. One move that *is* seemingly on, though, is Spencer Prior's stuttering transfer to Cardiff. The fee is set at £700,000.

28 June
SEASON TICKET SALES SOAR

City announce that they have sold more than 22,000 season tickets for the forthcoming First Division campaign and believe they will easily surpass that figure. Chairman David Bernstein says: "The support of our fans continues to be outstanding. In spite of our relegation, season ticket sales are well ahead of last year and will reach a record level."

LAKEY'S VIEW

"Though we all know the unbelievable loyalty of the City fans, to my mind such a huge number of season tickets being sold despite dropping down a division was a definite example of 'The Keegan Factor' at work. But that's no surprise to me coming from City fans. I'll never forget that I had 22,000 people come to my testimonial – on a Sunday. If that doesn't show the depth of feeling the supporters have for the club, then I don't know what does. When you've had a club like Manchester United as your rivals, a club that has had so much success, it really has bred that type of dogged, determined and loyal character in City fans."

28 June
YOUNGSTERS GET THE CALL-UP

Academy players Lee Croft and Dorryl Profitt are selected by England for July's Nationwide international Under-17 tournament, while Shaun Cartwright is put on standby.

29 June
CITY ON TV

As expected, City's first Nationwide game against Watford ("It's Keegan v Vialli!") will be the first televised game on ITV Sport. It looks like a 6.15 kick-off on Saturday August 11. The game away at Nottingham Forest, scheduled for Saturday October 27, looks like it will be switched to a 6.15 Sunday kick-off.

30 June
COLOSIMO BAGGED?
City admit an interest in Australian defender Simon Colosimo, the man who hit the headlines back in 1999 after a high challenge from Manchester United's Andy Cole put him out of the game for six months.

JULY 2001
1 July
GAME CHANGES
Three more games are subject to the vagaries of ITV Digital's scheduling. Games against Bradford, Burnley and Birmingham are all moved to new kick off times.

2 July
PAULO POUNCES
Paulo Wanchope scores the first Costa Rican goal in a 3-2 World Cup qualifier win over Honduras. But it makes bittersweet viewing for City fans. The lanky striker may miss as many as five club matches because of international commitments in August, September and October.

An academy Under-15 side will compete in a tournament in Switzerland in August against Borussia Dortmund, Red Star Belgrade, Feyenoord, FC Grasshoppers and the Switzerland and Liechtenstein national teams, amongst others. In the same month an Under-14 team will be in Cologne to take on sides including Schalke and Bremen, while an Under 21 Academy side will compete against Aston Villa and Juventus in Wrexham.

Academy head Jim Cassell says: "If we get one youngster through every year who is capable of sustaining his performance at first team level, then we are doing a fantastic job."

3 July
THE CAT CREEPS IN
Keegan appoints Peter Bonetti, 59, as City's goalkeeping coach on a one-year deal. The former Chelsea and England man worked alongside Keegan in the England set-up, as well as at Newcastle and Fulham.

The club denies having signed Australian defender Simon Colosimo on a two year deal.

LAKEY'S VIEW

"Ah, The Cat! When I was with the England Under 21s he was the keeping coach under Dave Sexton and Ian Brightwell and I used to laugh about his nickname all the time. "Here comes The Cat!" But he was good at his job and he's still at Maine Road now, which says a lot about how he's regarded. He's not quite as mad as John Burridge who used to play in goal for us, who actually cried when he wasn't selected against Spurs one time!"

4 July
COLOSIMO TALKS TO BEGIN

City admit that they are preparing to open negotiations with Australian club South Melbourne for Simon Colosimo. However, the club is irritated by the amount of speculation surrounding Manchester City transfers. A spokesman claims that in the previous pre-season City were linked with no fewer than 146 players!

New goalkeeping coach Peter Bonetti says: "If anyone is going to get City back into the big time then it is Kevin." He then goes on to suggest that City have two great goalkeepers, suggesting he didn't watch too much of Nicky Weaver in the Premiership.

5 July
KENNEDY SAD TO LEAVE

Mark Kennedy says that the two years he spent at Maine Road were the most enjoyable of his career and that he didn't want to leave. "I had no intention of leaving Maine Road and it was no exaggeration to say that I was stunned."

6 July
PLAYERS REPORT BACK

The senior players report back for training at Carrington. There will be three days of fitness tests before Keegan takes charge. Danny Tiatto, Paulo Wanchope and Terry Dunfield are all missing due to international commitments.

Another fixture change is announced to suit the telly. The away game at Preston is moved to a Sunday, October 21 kick off at 2.15pm.

Ah well. At least the clubs can rely on their money. Can't they?

7 July
HAALAND PREPARED TO LOSE CAPTAINCY
Club captain Alfie Haaland says he will have no problem if Kevin Keegan decides to appoint his new signing Stuart Pearce as captain in his place, calling his one-time Nottingham Forest team mate "inspirational."

Simon Colosimo has returned to Australia and City expect to tie a deal up in the next 10 days.

LAKEY'S VIEW
"Of course Stuart Pearce did become captain and I do think it was the right decision to take it off Alfie. Stuart has such respect amongst professional players and was a driving force on the pitch for the full 90 minutes. Ultimately, if Stuart Pearce shouts jump, you'll say 'How high?'"

9 July
PSYCHO BABBLES
Stuart Pearce admits that he was ready to sign another one-year contract at West Ham before manager Harry Redknapp was sacked. Once the manager had gone, however, he was open to offers and quickly accepted the challenge of trying to get City back in the Premiership from Kevin Keegan.

10 July
WANCHOPE OFF?
City dismiss as "utter nonsense" stories linking striker Paulo Wanchope with a move to Malaga in Spain.

LAKEY'S VIEW
"I thought Paulo would go to be honest, knowing the past he'd had with Joe Royle. You knew Joe wouldn't stand for any nonsense and while Paulo would have known that City is a bigger club than Derby, he would also have known that he would have been able to get a decent move. Unless there was an arrogance about this particular player, then Joe's method of treating footballers might have been questionable. Of course that depends on the overall team ethic, too. We just don't know what happened between the two of them on a personal level."

11 July
NO-GO GOATER
Now it's striker Shaun Goater himself who's dismissing any talk of a move away from Maine Road to Wolves. "The only time I would consider leaving this club is if they accepted a bid for me," says the popular and loyal striker, who still has three years to run on his contract.

The Mirror suggests that Simon Colosimo has returned to Australia after City discovered that the player doesn't have an EC passport. His Italian parents apparently gave up their Italian citizenship when they emigrated to Australia. City vigorously deny the story.

13 July
COOKE DESPERATE TO IMPRESS
City's forgotten man Terry Cooke meets the new manager face to face and wants to stay and fight for his place. "I am hoping this is a new start for me," he says. *Any* kind of start would suit the forgotten former Manchester United man.

14 July
STEVE HOWEY LARGES IT
Steve Howey has a rush of blood when he says he wants to clinch promotion by Christmas! "I think we are going to bounce straight back," he says, slightly more realistically. "I think we will only do ourselves justice if we win the Championship."

16 July
AUSSIE SOAP TO END
City claim the on-off transfer saga of Simon Colosimo is due to end, with the player due to sign for the club at the end of the day. One player who definitely won't be joining the Blues, however, is defender Des Walker, who has been released by Sheffield Wednesday.

New fitness coach Juan Carlos Osorio reveals that he wants the players to eat six to eight meals a day. Richard Dunne seems already to have taken the advice to heart. Unfortunately, he also seems not to have grasped that these are small, grazing-type meals.

17 July

WANTAWAY WANCHOPE?

Plenty of national newspapers are carrying the story that Paulo Wanchope has told Kevin Keegan that he wants to leave the club. The player is away on international duty with Costa Rica but City deny the stories, which insist Wanchope is heading for Spain or Italy. Wanchope scores his country's goal in the one-all Copa America draw against Uruguay.

Simon Colosimo finally signs a two-year deal at City and starts his first full day's training. It's unlikely he'll be ready for the pre-season friendlies. "The desire which the player has shown to make this happen has been terrific," says Dennis Tueart. Surprising, that, given that Colosimo's lately been playing for giants of the game South Melbourne.

20 July

LAST HURRAH FOR PEARCE

Stuart Pearce confirms that this will be his last season as a player. "I'm taking liberties now with my fitness and maybe that tell later on in the season," he says. "But that will be that. If I get Man City back in the Premiership it will be a fantastic way to finish my career as a player."

21 July

EYAL BE SEEING YA

Eyal Berkovic agrees to join City in a £1.5 million deal from Celtic, subject to a medical and the granting of a work permit. The 29-year-old former West Ham, Southampton and Blackburn man has agreed a four-year deal and Kevin Keegan says: "Eyal will bring additional experience and creativity to the squad."

City play their first game under Kevin Keegan in a friendly at Halifax – and run out 2-1 winners. There are debuts for Stuart Pearce and Simon Colosimo and goals for Darren Huckerby and Kevin Horlock.

24 July

CITY SALVAGE A DRAW

A late header from Shaun Goater spares City's blushes as they draw 2-2 at Scunthorpe. The 19-year-old Dickson Etuhu scores the first. Despite the draw Darren Huckerby is unequivocal in his target for the season. "Every season has an aim and this season it's to win the First Division," he says.

25 Jul
BERKO SIGNS ON
Eyal Berkovic completes his move to City and the Israeli international seems more than happy with his decision to play under Kevin Keegan. "He was a very big reason why I decided to come here and I think everybody respects him," says the midfielder. He denies any rift with his former boss Martin O'Neil at Celtic: "It was his decision not to play me," he says. "But with the success they had you can't argue and I think he did a very good job. I had to move because I wanted to play."

27 July
"CITY MY LAST ENGLISH CLUB" – BERKOVIC
Eyal Berkovic wants to end his career in this country in Manchester. He says he will fulfil his four-year contract with the Blues, then return home to Israel with his family. He also insists he will be fully fit for the start of the season, despite some rumours to the contrary.

30 July
KNOCKOUT BLOW
City are beaten 1-0 by Tranmere in the friendly at Prenton Park, but the game is most memorable for a bizarre incident where defender Steve Howey catches referee Mike Jones and knocks him out. It's that kind of fight that will see City back to the big time!

The FA Premier Reserve League fixtures are announced. City's first match is against Blackburn on August 14.

30 July
OFFERS TO FEED GOAT
Chairman David Bernstein admits to having received two offers for striker Shaun Goater, but insists the fans' favourite is going nowhere. "We are looking for him to do what he did in the First Division last time when he scored 29 goals," says Bernstein.

31 July
CITY BACK TO WINNING WAYS
Eyal Berkovic and Paulo Wanchope both feature as City record a 2-0 victory in the friendly against Huddersfield.

AUGUST 2001

1 August
WANCHOPE HAPPY AT MAINE ROAD
Paulo Wanchope dismisses speculation of a move away from Maine Road. "I'm very happy here," he insists.

2 August
GOATER STAYING PUT
Now Shaun Goater gets in on the act by again saying that he doesn't want to leave the Blues.

Meanwhile coach Willie Donachie declares that City can do much better than the form of their pre-season games has shown. "We all know there's room for improvement and we're still a bit rusty," he says.

3 August
MORE SIGNINGS TO COME
Kevin Keegan explains that his three new signings for the club do not mean the end of his spending spree and says that a good manager must always be looking to strengthen his hand. He promises to keep going to the board for money when a decent opportunity comes along.

4 August
ETUHU SINGLED OUT
Both Shaun Goater and Eyal Berkovic single out 19-year-old Dickson Etuhu as one of the pre-season's star performers and suggest he has a big future in the game.

6 August
KEGGY CONFIDENT
Kevin Keegan again states that he is confident his side can get out of the First Division – and he insists they can do it by playing attractive football. "I think we have a great chance of promotion, and I've told the players that," he says. He also states his aim to make City a top six Premiership club within five years (wasn't it a Premiership title within five years not so long ago?), but warns that the club will have to be able to sustain £25 million investments in a single player to make the dream a reality.

LAKEY'S VIEW

"I must admit I was confident that we'd get out of the division too. Even when Kevin Keegan first arrived I was confident. I was having to fight his corner with City fans who were very unsure about Kevin's staying power and who were a bit hurt, because they loved Joe Royle and were sorry to see him go in the way that he did. They didn't like the way he was treated. But ask any fan what they want and they will tell you they're after exciting, attacking football and everyone knows that's what Kevin Keegan is about. But let's be clear about one thing. Kevin Keegan didn't think for a minute the players he had at the club at this point were good enough to get them up. He knew he'd have to keep adding to his squad and then adding to it again."

8 August
INJURIES MOUNT

City's plans for the opening day of the season meeting with Watford are thrown into chaos by a large number of injuries. Alfie Haaland and Darren Huckerby are almost certain to miss out, Shaun Wright-Phillips has only just returned to training and won't make the game, Paul Ritchie and Jeff Whitley have knocks and Nicky Weaver has picked up a thigh strain.

City's November 17 fixture away at Portsmouth is switched from a 3pm kick off to 12.30 to – why else? – fit in with TV demands.

9 August
KEEGAN LOOKS TO WATFORD GAME/ HAALAND OUT FOR SIX WEEKS

Kevin Keegan explains that he has opted to play with wing backs for his first competitive game in charge of Manchester City. City skipper Alfie Haaland looks likely to be out of action for six weeks after having a second operation on his cartilage. The unlucky Norwegian missed the last two games of last season.

It looks as if Nicky Weaver's thigh strain will keep him out of the England Under-21 squad for the game against Holland next week, though both Eyal Berkovic and Richard Dunne have been called up for the full Israeli and Republic Of Ireland squads. Danny Tiatto and Simon Colosimo haven't been called on for Australia's match against Japan.

10 August
KEEGAN LOOKS TO HIS OWN SQUAD FOR ANSWERS

Kevin Keegan again insists that his Manchester City players will get a chance to impress him at the start of the season.

"I did promise the players that I would look at what they are about and would give them the first opportunity to put right what went wrong last season. They have responded really well to that."

City are linked with the Burnley winger Glen Little, with *The Sunday People* suggesting that Kevin Keegan is preparing to make a £4.5 million bid to sign the player.

The manager watches a City Under-21 side beat the Juventus equivalent 4-0 in a pre-season tournament. can't be bad.

12 August
CITY 3 WATFORD 0
DREAM START FOR KEEGAN'S NEW BOYS

A convincing start to the new season as goals by Goater, Berkovic and Pearce seal a memorable victory.

"We scored one great goal and were unlucky not to win by more." says Kevin Keegan on the City website *www.mcfc.co.uk*. "We laid siege to them in the second period of the first half, but they held out. We kept believing, kept passing the ball and I knew that we were always going to create chances."

WHAT THE PAPERS SAY
THE SUNDAY MIRROR

'Kevin Keegan brought the good times back to Manchester City last night – then revealed how he had talked Stuart Pearce out of quitting football. Pearce scored City's third goal on his debut in the 3-0 demolition of Gianluca Vialli's Watford at Maine Road. And Keegan later explained how close the former England defender had been to turning his back on the game.'

THE SUNDAY PEOPLE

'Keegan and Berkovic – a marriage made under a blue moon. Last night they fairly danced up the Eyal. Israeli midfielder Eyal Berkovic made more impact than John Hartson's boot on his Manchester City debut. "When you sign someone like Eyal Berkovic, you get a kaleidoscope – he will give you a different pattern of play in every game," said Keegan.'

THE SUNDAY TIMES

'They called him a mug with England, but Kevin Keegan was back in his old Messiah's role at Maine Road last night, when second-half goals from Shaun Goater and the two debutants, Eyal Berkovic and Stuart Pearce, saw him off to a triumphant start as manager of a club that has spent the past six seasons in different divisions, and not too long ago had five men in charge in the space of six months.'

THE MAIL ON SUNDAY

'It will be some considerable time before two teams boasting such celebrity managers can expect to be judged simply on their own merits. Kevin Keegan, the self-confessed inadequate with England, suggests that, operating at a more mundane level, he is capable of establishing City as a Premiership top-six outfit by the time his five-year contract has been honoured.'

LAKEY'S VIEW

"I remember the match well; Berkovic and Pearce's first game and a match that was billed as Keegan versus Vialli, the football enthusiast against the football artist. It turned out to be the perfect start. Eyal showed all the touches straight away. His use of the ball, pinching it and getting forward, told me that he was still as good a player as I remembered. He had it all. And then he scored a goal on his debut! Marry that with the defensive abilities of Pearce – The Rock – and I was starting to think that maybe we were onto something. And then the Old Warhorse goes and scores the third goal! It was incredible. What better start could Keegan have asked for?"

13 August
KEEGAN HAPPY TO SET STANDARDS

Kevin Keegan is happy with the win against Watford. "We set a high standard with the win and there is nothing wrong with that," he says. Eyal Berkovic says he is delighted with his debut goal but warns that he doesn't want to be compared to City hero Georghi Kinkladze, before jetting off to join up with the Israeli national squad for a friendly against Lithuania.

The City Under-21 side wins the round robin tournament in Wales with a 2-1 victory over Aston Villa.

Meanwhile City's women's team take part in the Reebok Women's Soccer festival.

14 August
CITY FANS BANNED FROM VISITING NEW DEN
City Chairman David Bernstein and Millwall's Theo Paphitis issue a joint statement where they announce that away supporters will be banned for the club's two fixtures this season. The statement reads: "After careful consideration and full consultation with the football authorities, both Manchester City FC and Millwall FC have decided to limit this season's fixtures between the two clubs to home supporters only (ie no away supporters will be allowed). This decision has been taken on intelligence and information that the fixtures may be used as a catalyst for football troublemakers from a number of clubs to cause problems. This behaviour impacts on local communities and presents opportunities which may be used by others as a cover to commit crimes and engage in anti-social behaviour. Manchester City and Millwall are both aware of their excellent relationships with their local communities, exemplified by the clubs' community schemes. Both clubs do not want to subject their localities to the difficulties experienced two seasons ago and hope their supporters will understand and endorse this action. The clubs are hoping that both matches at Maine Road and The Den will be beamed back live so that away supporters will be able to see the matches as they happen." Nicky Weaver is due to join up with the City squad for the visit to Norwich after recovering from his thigh strain. The reserves record an emphatic 4-1 win in their first game against Blackburn with goals from Colosimo, Cooke, Horlock and Wright-Phillips.

15 August
KEEGAN – I WANT FOWLER
Kevin Keegan now says he needs to improve the City squad, with a goalkeeper and a striker his two top priorities. He makes no secret of the fact that he would love to bring Robbie Fowler to the club, given that the player is unsettled at Liverpool, but accepts he has no realistic chance of doing so.

16 August
LOSS LEADER
Skipper Stuart Pearce says that the club can't afford to lose more than eight games during the season.

Eyal Berkovic is injured playing for Israel.

17 August
UNLUCKY LADS
Keegan admits that two City youngsters, Dickson Etuhu and Shaun Wright-Phillips, were very unlucky not to make the squad for last Saturday's game with Watford. In the end the boss decided that it was a day for experience and the result proved him right.

19 August
NORWICH 2 CITY 0
LACKLUSTRE BLUES GO DOWN
City turn in a poor performance and are deservedly beaten 2-0.

Jeff Whitley breaks his ankle and Paulo Wanchope is involved with a scuffle with a ball boy.

"We were out-fought by Norwich and failed to think our way round the park," says a disappointed Kevin Keegan on the City website. "It was just one of those days and we have to get on with things when we play Crewe next week."

City will wait on news of keeper Carlo Nash, who had to go off after half an hour following a clash with Norwich striker Iwan Roberts. It could be broken ribs. Keegan will look to bring a keeper in on loan as cover. Jeff Whitley will be out until the New Year at least with a broken ankle. In addition, there could be trouble over the incident where strapping Paulo Wanchope tangles with a (presumably mad!) ball boy.

WHAT THE PAPERS SAY
THE SUNDAY TIMES
'Kevin Keegan has had better days. Not only did his team surprisingly lose at Norwich, but three serious injuries have thrown a considerable spanner into the works of Manchester City's promotion bandwagon. On top of all that, his striker Paulo Wanchope will this week find himself the subject of interest from Norfolk police after an unfortunate clash with a teenage ball boy.'

THE MAIL ON SUNDAY
'Kevin Keegan was brought crashing back to earth as Norwich scored two goals in the last 15 minutes to sink Manchester City at Carrow Road. Keegan's side started the season in rampant form with a 3-0 victory against

Watford at Maine Road, but Norwich were in no mood to succumb in similar style. Goals from substitutes Marc Libbra and Paul McVeigh were enough to make sure of the points.'

THE SUNDAY MIRROR
'Manchester City striker Paulo Wanchope is facing a police investigation into an alleged incident with a ball-boy towards the end of yesterday's 2-0 defeat at Norwich. Witnesses in the crowd said Wanchope appeared to knock into 15-year-old Stuart Frohawk in the 85th minute as the Costa Rican striker tried to bring a dead ball back into play.'

THE SUNDAY PEOPLE
'Manchester City striker Paulo Wanchope is the subject of a police investigation after he was accused yesterday of striking a 15-year-old ball boy. He could face charges after schoolboy ball-boy Stuart Frohawk insisted: "Wanchope struck me in the neck."'

LAKEY'S VIEW
"A very disappointing game and one that highlighted the fact that we were a bit thin on the ground for quality at this stage of the season. Nothing to get too worried about, seeing as it was only the second game of the campaign, but I was interested to see how the lads would react to a defeat after the euphoria of the opening game's victory."

20 August
WANCHOPE IN TROUBLE?
The rumpus rumbles on over Paulo Wanchope and the Norwich ball boy but City are not prepared to comment just yet.

Carlo Nash hasn't broken his ribs, but has badly bruised them. It's not known how long he'll be out for and the search for a loan keeper will be stepped up.

City striker Paul Dickov is surprisingly called up for Scotland's World Cup qualifying tie against Croatia in Glasgow. This despite not making the City squad for the Norwich game.

21 August

CHANGE OF HEART ON KEEPER

Kevin Keegan now says he will not be looking to bring in a loan keeper but will have young Brian Murphy on the bench for the weekend visit of Crewe.

22 August

WHITLEY OUT FOR SEASON?

Jeff Whitley has an operation on his broken ankle, but there are fears that the player could be out for the rest of the season.

The reserve team start their defence of the Manchester Senior Cup with a 3-0 win away at Bury.

City legend Bobby Johnstone, who scored for the Blues in two successive Cup Finals in the 50s, dies at the age of 71.

24 August

DON'T LOOK AT THE TABLE – KEEGAN

Kevin Keegan insists that his side needs to be judged on half-a-dozen performances rather than just two. "I won't be looking at the table for six to eight weeks," he insists.

Kevin Horlock insists that he won't be leaving City of his own free will. "I've been going to Birmingham for the last four years," says the midfielder on the latest rumours.

25 August

CITY 5 CREWE 2

BLUES BAG FIVE IN STRANGE HOME VICTORY

City banish the memory of defeat at Norwich with a bizarre 5-2 home victory against Crewe. There are two goals from Wanchope, two from Goater and a penalty for Stuart Pearce, but the scoreline is hugely flattering to a none-too-convincing City.

"We have scored eight goals in two home games and it could have been a lot more," says Kevin Keegan on the City website. "We can do better and I am sure we will get better."

Keegan also announces that new fitness coach Juan Carlos Osorio has got the team swimming as part of their post-match warmdown.

26 August
KEEGAN BACKS HORLOCK AND WRIGHT-PHILLIPS

Kevin Keegan praises Kevin Horlock after the midfielder came off the bench against Crewe at the weekend and also singles out Shaun Wright-Phillips. "I think he has a tremendous future in the game," says the manager."

27th August
BURNLEY 2 CITY 4
GOATER HAT TRICK AS CITY ROMP HOME

Shaun Goater hits a hat-trick on one of his luckiest grounds as City record their first away win of the season, 4-2 at Burnley. City's other strike is from Paulo Wanchope.

"This is a good ground for me," says The Goat. Boss Keegan is also happy as he tells the City website. "I was very pleased with the performance. The fitness looked good, we were controlled and when we had to battle we certainly knew how to do it."

LAKEY'S VIEW

"Burnley were a side that everyone was surprised to see right up at the top of the table. But this game was a big test for us, make no mistake, and we came through it with flying colours. You couldn't help but be impressed by Shaun Goater's hat-trick. He was so sharp, so alive, despite that famous spidery appearance of his. Granted, there are times when Shaun will hit the corner flag instead of the back of the net, but to my mind he's still quality."

30 August
RESERVES WIN

City's second string side record a 1-0 win away at Bolton thanks to a Chris Killen strike. The team remains unbeaten in the FA Premier Reserve League.

31 August
ON TRIAL

Keegan admits he has a French and an Italian striker on trial at Carrington this week but refuses to name them. He also admits that he fully expects to have more players over on a trial basis in the future.

SEPTEMBER 2001

3 September
CITY LOSE TOP SPOT

With City players away on international duty there is no weekend game for the Blues, who lose top spot and drop down to third as both Burnley and Grimsby overtake them.

Richard Dunne plays for The Republic, who beat Holland 1-0 in a World Cup qualifier. Kevin Horlock plays his part in a 1-1 draw for Northern Ireland against Denmark and Paulo Wanchope appears for Costa Rica in a 2-0 victory against the United States.

4 September
BUZZER'S BACK

Nicky Summerbee, former City player and son of legend Mike, is back at Maine Road. Fans are underwhelmed by the return of a player many were glad to see the back of due to feelings he is lazy on a football field. Having been released by Bolton it looks like 'Buzzer' will sign a three month contract and is included in the squad for the night's friendly game, a testimonial for Earl Barrett away at Oldham.

French striker Alioune Touré, on trial from Nantes, scores the winner in a 2-1 victory. City's first strike is an own goal from Oldham's Shaun Garnett.

City's reserves extend their lead at the top of the Premier Reserve League with a 2-1 victory against a much more experienced Leeds side.

5 September
IT'S UP TO YOU, NICKY

Kevin Keegan tells Nicky Summerbee he can win over the City fans with good performances. Keegan, however, may not have seen too many of Summerbee's performances during his first spell at Maine Road.

LAKEY'S VIEW

"I think Nicky only lasted about two weeks. There was talk of the strikers needing good service, which we all know Nicky can provide, but the next thing I knew I had a call from a mate at Forest saying he was in their reserves. Something odd happened there, but I don't know what."

6 September
LATICS WANT DICKY
Oldham make a bid for Paul Dickov but City have no interest in selling. Eyal Berkovic has an outside chance of making a speedier return to first team duty than anticipated. The Israeli international may make the trip to West Brom at the weekend.

Keegan is also close to signing French striker Alioune Touré for £500,000. "He is quite a clever player and will be a really useful addition to the squad," says the manager.

7 September
OPTIONS FOR BAGGIES
Kevin Keegan looks like he will play Darren Huckerby upfront alongside Shaun Goater when the Blues visit West Brom, as Paulo Wanchope is suspended. He will have young keeper Brian Murphy on the bench again as Carlo Nash struggles to recover from injury.

The manager has also blocked any loan moves out of the club, saying he wants to see exactly what he's got at the club first.

8 September
WEST BROM 4 CITY 0
ABJECT CITY CRASH TO DEFEAT
An appalling display from the Blues sees them soundly thrashed at West Brom. There is nothing positive to take from the game.

"My players know how I feel about this performance," says Kevin Keegan on the City website. "It is not good enough for Manchester City, it is not good enough for our supporters and it is certainly not good enough for me." Keegan keeps the players locked in the dressing room for 30 minutes after the game finishes to vent his frustrations.

WHAT THE PAPERS SAY
THE SUNDAY TIMES
'One week brilliant, the next utterly dreadful. Just where do Manchester City go after this? Well, evidently not straight back to the Premiership according to manager Kevin Keegan, who once again witnessed the Jekyll and Hyde nature of his side.'

THE SUNDAY MIRROR

'Any hopes City had of taking anything from this game were thwarted by a penalty which infuriated Kevin Keegan and led to a West Brom goal-fest. Keegan was seething as Neil Clement blasted home the spot-kick that put his side 2-0 ahead, following Derek McInnes' opener. Certainly, the decision to give West Brom a penalty after Richard Edghill was adjudged to have bundled over Scott Dobie, looked harsh.'

THE SUNDAY PEOPLE

'Neil Clement's educated left foot destroyed promotion favourites Manchester City at The Hawthorns. Clement, one of the outstanding young players outside the Premiership, drilled in a controversial penalty and then a delightful 28-yard free kick to leave visiting boss Kevin Keegan seething. And it got even worse when substitute Scott Dobie danced through City's ravaged defence to make it 4-0 late on.'

THE MAIL ON SUNDAY

'West Brom finally rediscovered the form that earned them a flirt with promotion in last season's play-offs as they staged a dramatic destruction of Kevin Keegan's men at the Hawthorns.

Captain Derek McInnes fired the Baggies ahead with a spectacular ninth-minute opener. And although City disputed the 66th minute penalty that provided Neil Clement with Albion's second, they were comprehensively out-gunned as further goals from Clement and Scott Dobie secured Albion's second win of the season.'

LAKEY'S VIEW

"This game was a real surprise. We didn't play well generally and didn't defend at set pieces at all. If nothing else the game proved to me that there was still a lot of work to be done defensively and this seems to be the match when Kevin Keegan finally decided that the players had had enough of a chance and that changes would have to be made. But it was a weird game. I spoke to West Brom manager Gary Megson and he said he'd felt that City were capable of going up a gear at any time, but they simply didn't do it, they never pressed the lever. I think the game made me realise that if we were going to do well in the First Division, then we would have to be able to compete with the battling sides as well as outperform them for creativity."

10 September
KEEGAN STILL SMILING

The boss proves he hasn't lost his sense of humour, despite the awful showing from City at The Hawthorns. Explaining that the young players do deserve a chance, Keegan quips: "Chris Killen will have looked at the performance against West Brom and wonder why he wasn't in the side. I looked at it and wondered why I wasn't!"

He does, however, admit that his current squad is not yet good enough to claim automatic promotion. There is a rumour in *The Daily Mail* that he will move for Tranmere midfielder Jason Koumas, using Tony Grant as bait.

11 September
NOTTS COUNTY 2 CITY 4
BLUSHES SPARED AT COUNTY

The day is dominated by the tragic events in New York, but City's game still goes ahead. Shaun Goater grabs a goal five minutes from time to save City from an embarrassing Worthington Cup defeat at the hands of Notts County after Chris Shuker had given the Blues the lead. It's two all at the end of 90 minutes and City power on to win with goals from Paul Dickov and Darren Huckerby.

"This was not a day for football," says a grave Kevin Keegan on the City website. "We are in the hat by the skin of our teeth," he adds, turning reluctantly to matters sporting and mangling metaphors left, right and centre.

Eyal Berkovic pulls up with a recurrence of the hamstring injury he suffered in only his second game against Norwich. The midfielder could be out of action for as long as six weeks.

13 September
CITY TO SIGN BENARBIA?

The Mirror claims that Keegan is to strengthen his midfield with the free transfer addition of Paris St. Germain's Algerian midfielder Ali Benarbia. City confirm that talks for the 32-year-old, who almost moved to Sunderland earlier in the month, will open on Friday. He could be in the City squad for Saturday's game against Birmingham.

Jeff Whitley says no-one is to blame for the tackle with Norwich's

Darryll Russell which has put him out of the game for the season.

Eyal Berkovic's hamstring injury isn't as bad as first thought and the player could be back in action in as little as 10 days. Keeper Carlo Nash is back in training.

14 September
KK IS A FOOTBALL GENIUS

Kevin Keegan is happy that his side is scoring so freely but is clearly concerned about the amount of goals being leaked by a somewhat porous defence.

He thinks he knows the solution, though. "If you keep a clean sheet you don't lose many games," he states with some degree of certainty.

Ali Benarbia signs a two-year deal with City and may be pitched straight into the first team to act as playmaker against Birmingham in the absence of Eyal Berkovic. He is Keegan's sixth City signing.

15 September
CITY 3 BIRMINGHAM CITY 0
ALI THE MAGICIAN ARRIVES

City brush aside Birmingham in a display that is wholly inspired by the performance of new signing Ali Benarbia. Shaun Goater bags a brace and Richard Dunne pitches in with one, but it is the Algerian midfielder's dynamic performance that catches the eye.

"He is a top class player and what you saw today was the tip of the iceberg," says the manager on the City website. "If we can get it right and support players like Benarbia and Berkovic, we will be able to play football against anyone."

WHAT THE PAPERS SAY
THE SUNDAY MIRROR

'Kevin Keegan compared new boy Ali Benarbia to City legend Colin Bell after watching the French star dazzle Maine Road on his full debut. The 32-year-old enjoyed an outstanding game as City trounced Birmingham. The scoreline flattered the visitors, and Keegan's men could have had even more. And that was mainly down to Benarbia and fellow debutant Dickson Etuhu, a rangy midfielder plucked from the club's academy.'

THE SUNDAY TIMES

'"One of those players who takes pictures in his mind," said Manchester City manager Kevin Keegan, his eyes shining with wonder. He was talking about Ali Benarbia. Remember the name, because if he stays fit, this man will take City back into the Premiership.'

THE MAIL ON SUNDAY

'Kevin Keegan elevated Ali Benarbia, snapped up 24 hours earlier on a free transfer from Paris St Germain, to the ranks of Manchester City greats after drooling with the fans over the midfielder's performance in the defeat of Birmingham. The 32-year-old Algerian transformed a side thrashed 4-0 at West Bromwich a week earlier and was given a standing ovation as he walked off after 74 minutes. Keegan said: "I don't think the City fans in the last 20 or 30 years will have seen many players like him. They will come up with names like Colin Bell – and he's in that category."'

17 September
INCONSISTENT PLAYERS NOT NEEDED

Kevin Keegan has pointed out to his senior players that he will not accept inconsistency.

Meanwhile defender Richard Dunne talks about Ali Benarbia's debut against Birmingham. "His performance was unbelievable," he says. City are now being linked with another midfield talent; this time it's Blackburn's Jason McAteer. One player who is definitely interesting the club is Cameroon defender Lucien Mettomo of St. Etienne. The 24 year-old flies in for a three day trial.

18 September
GOATER DISAPPOINTMENT

Despite scoring twice in the weekend victory over Birmingham top scorer Shaun Goater is disappointed not to have notched more goals. "As a striker I am always greedy," he says.

Alfie Haaland returns to training with the squad for the first time in three months. There's still no date set for a prospective return to competitive action.

19 September
COVENTRY CITY 4 CITY 3
CITY LOSE OUT IN SEVEN GOAL THRILLER

Another crazy goalfest sees City go down 4-3 at Highfield Road after having equalised three times. Ali Benarbia, Kevin Horlock and a Marcus Hall own goal account for City's strikes, but it's another worrying defeat with goals leaked.

"It was a game with a lot of chances but I was not happy with some of our defending," says the manager on the club website, rather stating the obvious.

Keegan also reveals that defender Richard Dunne was left out over a disciplinary matter. "He didn't turn in for training on Sunday, so I told him he would have no part in the game tonight. I don't want to say any more about it."

20 September
DUNNE IN DANGER

Kevin Keegan admits that he will leave wayward defender Richard Dunne out of the City squad for the weekend's game against Sheffield Wednesday but denies that this signals the end for the player at Maine Road and insists he hasn't transfer-listed Dunne.

21 September
A GOOD PERFORMANCE OFF THE PITCH

City's reporting of the club's annual figures shows a £5m operating profit and an 85 per cent rise in turnover, which soared from £17.5m to £32.4m in the year to May 31st. Operating profits, before the costs of player transfers, jumped from £832,000 to £5.1m and pre-tax losses fell from £1.9m to £0.6m.

"We are a Premiership club in all but name and we have made immense progress over the last three years," says Chairman David Bernstein.

City spent a net £13m on strengthening the squad for the Premiership, as players including Steve Howey, Paulo Wanchope, Richard Dunne and Darren Huckerby were brought in.

The club's total wage bill, including all staff, rose from £9.5m to £18m and is likely to remain the same in the next financial year. "It is not our intention to weaken our squad, unlike other relegated teams who have sold their best players," says the Chairman.

Kevin Keegan says that Terry Cooke can leave Manchester City if the right offer comes along, though there will be no loan deals for the player. It's believed that Oldham wanted to take the player but were not interested in making a firm offer. The trip to Millwall (for players, not fans) has been rescheduled and will now take place on November 20.

22 September
SHEFFIELD WEDNESDAY 2 CITY 6
RAMPANT CITY SHOW THEIR CLASS

It's yet another goalfest but this time City take all three points after firing six past a hapless Sheffield Wednesday. Goater and Wanchope plunder two each, while Benarbia and Danny Granville weigh in with one apiece.

"There is still a lot of work to do despite winning 6-2 here today," says Kevin Keegan on *mcfc.co.uk*. "The goals are flying in . . . at both ends."

Richard Dunne makes the bench after all. "I changed my mind. He will not miss training again," says the boss.

WHAT THE PAPERS SAY
THE SUNDAY MIRROR

'Poor Wednesday are the latest victims left wondering how Kevin Keegan managed to get Ali Benarbia on a free. The one-time French Footballer of the Year turned in another master show to crush Peter Shreeves' gallant triers. The 32-year-old magician scored once and inspired three others – and there could have been more.'

THE SUNDAY PEOPLE

'Sheffield Wednesday were hit for six as they crashed to their heaviest defeat of the season. It ended a dismal week for the club who announced debts of £16 million in their failed attempt to compete with the elite.'

THE SUNDAY TIMES

'Although Wednesday were booed off by their fans at the end of this eight-goal epic, in truth they did not play that badly. Had they been the team fielding Ali Benarbia yesterday this could have been a different result. At last Manchester City fans have a new idol to replace Georghi Kinkladze.'

THE MAIL ON SUNDAY

'Over the past few weeks Kevin Pressman has been in the form of his life but he could have had another two goalkeepers alongside him and it would not have made any difference. There were more holes in the Sheffield Wednesday defence than you would find in a packet of Polo mints and Manchester City exposed them ruthlessly on a day when they might have run up double figures. When Tommy Johnson's eve-of-match illness ruled him out, Peter Shreeves must have thought there was a curse over the club.'

Nice report, but surely *three* keepers would have made a difference?

24 September
NO DANNY DING-DONG

Danny Tiatto and Kevin Keegan insist that there is no chance of the Australian midfielder leaving the club despite there being a row between the two men after the player was substituted in the defeat at Coventry.

Richard Edghill could be out for up to two months after damaging medial ligaments in the win at Hillsborough.

25 September 2001
CITY 3 WALSALL 0
BENARBIA CATCHES THE EYE – AGAIN

The start of a run of four home games sees City overcome Walsall at Maine Road courtesy of goals by Benarbia, Goater and a Wanchope penalty. "We never hit the heights of the Birmingham game," says Keegan on the club website. "I don't think 3-0 flattered us at all, but it was a good night's work by the boys."

There is another excellent performance from Ali Benarbia, who is taken off after 70 minutes. Keegan describes his skills as breathtaking and immediately plays down claims that he is the new Kinkladze, saying Benarbia is more of a team player than the Georgian.

Danny Tiatto picks up another yellow, which means he'll be banned for one match if he receives another one.

It looks as if defender Lucien Mettomo has done enough during his trial with City to secure a move to Manchester. The 24 year-old almost joined both Middlesbrough and Blackburn, but neither club committed and now City look set to step in.

The reserves draw 1-1 with Everton to maintain their unbeaten record.

Carlo Nash makes his first start since the Norwich game and the goal comes from Joey Barton.

27 September
METTOMO SIGNED?
The Mirror claims the Lucien Mettomo deal is done and dusted, with City paying £1.5 million down with the promise of a further million dependant on certain performance targets. The paper says the Cameroon ace is due to fly in for a medical today. Paulo Wanchope makes his soon-to-be-famous comment about Ali Benarbia. "He sees you before you see yourself," he claims. What *does* that mean?

28 September
TWO POINT AVERAGE
City are averaging two points a game and although they lie in fourth place in the First Division, Kevin Keegan is convinced that this average will be enough to win City promotion. He wants to see the 100% home record maintained with Saturday's game against Wimbledon. The manager says that the Lucien Mettomo signing is completed but that the player will not be available for City until the Birmingham game on October 10 due to international commitments with Cameroon. He explains that the player's versatility was a factor in deciding to sign him.

Eyal Berkovic will not be risked against Wimbledon, despite having trained well all week.

29 September
CITY 0 WIMBLEDON 4
BLUES THRASHED IN AWFUL DISPLAY
City's unbeaten home record crashes around their ears as Wimbledon make a mockery of City's supposed class.

"We looked like a team that thought, 'Here we go. We're at home, it's Wimbledon and they won't expect to get anything,' says Kevin Keegan on the City website.

Paulo Wanchope doesn't make the starting line-up due to a knee injury. Keegan says the striker will be out for six weeks.

WHAT THE PAPERS SAY
THE SUNDAY MIRROR

'Kevin Keegan hit out at his Manchester City flops after seeing Wimbledon storm the so-called Maine Road fortress. Terry Burton's men tore City apart to consign their 100 per cent home record to the dustbin – and Keegan admitted that he had seen the writing on the wall before the start of the game. Keegan said: "I'm obviously very disappointed about the result, but I told the players before the game that they had to make things happen themselves."'

THE SUNDAY PEOPLE

'Confused Kevin Keegan must address Manchester City's chronic problems at the back or kiss goodbye to his dreams of inspiring an instant return to the Premiership. Two first-half strikes from Irish ace David Connolly put the skids under the erratic Maine Road side, before sub Neil Shipperley finished them off. Only in an early 10-minute first-half spell did City threaten a superbly-organised Wimbledon side that went on to dish out a harsh football lesson.'

THE SUNDAY TIMES

'Terry Burton's side may have long since shaken off their Crazy Gang tag, but party-pooping is a hard habit to break. So, faced by a Manchester City side that has swept all before them at Maine Road this season, the Dons revelled in romping to an emphatic victory that Burton ranked as arguably the best he has enjoyed since taking charge at the start of last season. "We have had some good results away from home, but put in order this would be close; they are such a big club with good players," he said.'

THE MAIL ON SUNDAY

'Wimbledon stunned Manchester City with a scintillating 4-0 victory at Maine Road. City were as woeful at the back as they had been wonderful in attack when they scored six at Sheffield Wednesday last Saturday. They were caught on the break for the first goal when David Connolly scored from the penalty spot and the Blues backline then went AWOL for Connolly to head home the second. Substitute Neil Shipperley added to Keegan's misery and condemned his side to their first home defeat of an already topsy-turvy season when he scored twice in the last seven minutes.'

LAKEY'S VIEW

"What a mad month September was, totally up and down. I don't think the manager changed the formation or the side that much during the month, but the results just showed that what really needed working on was consistency. And the effort paid off as it was something we definitely had later in the season."

OCTOBER 2001
1 October
SKIPPER TAKES STICK

Stuart Pearce knows that Saturday's four-nil home defeat to Wimbledon is not acceptable. "It hurts me to say it, but they turned us over," he acknowledges. "We were slap-dash all over and there can be no excuses for anyone."

City now lie sixth, six points behind leaders Wolves and, with international matches coming up, there is no game to help banish the Wimbledon memory for two weeks.

City have denied that Eyal Berkovic pulled up in training and insist he has travelled to join up with the Israeli national squad.

Richard Dunne's calf injury forces him out of the Ireland squad.

The boss also says he is ready to listen to offers for out-of-favour striker Paul Dickov, though he insists that this is not merely a polite way of forcing him out of the club.

2 October
ROYLE TO SUE CITY

City's former manager Joe Royle is to sue the club for unfair dismissal. Joe Royle, who was sacked one year into a four-year contract tells the Manchester Evening News "The matter is in the hands of my solicitors and that is all I can say. The issues at stake are the level of settlement and unfair dismissal." The case apparently and incredibly sits on an abstract legal point: whether Royle was technically in charge of a Premiership or First Division side when he went in May.

"This is not a matter I wish to comment on," says City Chairman David Bernstein. "But clearly the club will strongly defend this unnecessary action."

LAKEY'S VIEW

"I really wasn't surprised by Joe's actions at all. In the previous year before the Premiership campaign Joe did the business for the club; he was committed. In my view he's not quite the Premiership manager but as far as Joe was concerned he was coming back from his holidays after relegation and he was coming back to his job. We all know that's not what happened and Joe felt it was all done behind his back. It wasn't handled very well. Joe's not taking legal action to take a chunk out of City. He's doing it because he feels people let him down and took his livelihood from him. There's a hell of a lot of pride that was dented there and I feel for the guy. He will now be perceived as a failure, but for what he managed to achieve at a difficult time for City I think he was a success."

3 October
ALFIE BACK

Alfie Haaland returns to competitive action as City's reserves thump
   Manchester United 5-0. Goals come from Leon Mike, Shaun Wright-Phillips (2), Joey Barton and Tony Grant.

4 October
SECOND OPINION FOR PAULO

Paulo Wanchope is to fly to Spain for a second opinion on his injured knee before a final decision is taken on whether the Costa Rican striker needs surgery.

5 October
BERKO FLIES BACK

Eyal Berkovic returns to City as Israel's World Cup qualifier against Austria is cancelled in the wake of a plane's crashing after leaving Tel Aviv.

6 October
ETUHU CONTRACT TALKS

Youngster Dickson Etuhu, who only has a one year contract at City, will be free to talk to other clubs in January, though Kevin Keegan hopes to have the player under a longer-term contract shortly. Kevin Horlock plays in Northern Ireland's 1-0 World Cup qualifying win over Malta.

9 October
THE NEXT GREAT DANE?
The 18 year-old Danish keeper Kevin Stuhr-Ellegaard arrives on trial at City and will be thrown into a specially-arranged reserve game against Blackburn Rovers. The keeper, who plays for Danish second division side Farum, has already spent time with Manchester United, Charlton and Spurs.

Both injured first teamers Eyal Berkovic and Richard Dunne will play some part in the Worthington Cup tie against Birmingham City on Wednesday. "I want a Cup run and will play my strongest side," says Keegan.

10 October
CITY 6 BIRMINGHAM CITY 0
CITY ANNIHILATE BIRMINGHAM
The Blues trounce Birmingham City at Maine Road with four goals from Darren Huckerby, one from Shaun Goater and a Birmingham own goal.

"I thought Darren Huckerby was outstanding," says Kevin Keegan on the City website. "Darren is hungry and what he did continually was to use that pace to cause Birmingham problems."

WHAT THE PAPERS SAY
THE DAILY MAIL
'Darren Huckerby led Manchester City on the charge that quickly made sure the interest of Birmingham, beaten Worthington Cup finalists last February, would last no longer than the third round of this season's competition. This third-round tie at Maine Road was really over as a contest after 25 minutes. In that time Huckerby, only starting in the absence of the injured Paulo Wanchope, struck twice, while Tresor Luntala conceded an own goal. Huckerby completed his hat-trick in the 81st minute and Birmingham were rocking when he smashed home his fourth with two minutes remaining.'

THE SUN
'Darren Huckerby grabbed an awesome foursome as City hit Birmingham for six. Kevin Keegan's reserve striker was simply sensational and could easily have had a hatful of other goals. He also played a part in the two

other strikes as City hammered last season's beaten finalists. But boss Kevin Keegan did not even think it was City's best performance of the season. He said: "People will look at 6-0 and think 'Wow', but we have played better than that. I was pleased there was a lot of hunger in the side.""

THE DAILY TELEGRAPH

'Trevor Francis' Birmingham career played out its death throes at Maine Road last night as his team were torn to pieces by Manchester City. Kevin Keegan's men were made to look one of the best teams in the country by a Birmingham defence that can surely never have performed so poorly. Unfortunately for their manager, it was just when he needed them.'

11 October
"I HAVE NOTHING TO PROVE" – GRANT

Tony Grant leaves City for Burnley in a deal which could be worth up to £400,000. He then predicts that City will be promoted.

"I never really did too much at City," he admits, though the City fans won't need telling twice. "But I don't think I have anything to prove."

Paulo Wanchope has an operation on his troublesome right knee in the States. He most likely won't be available for City until December.

The infamous away game against Millwall will now be played on December 4.

LAKEY'S VIEW

"I don't think Tony Grant was ever a City player. I just don't think he was good enough. People said that the experience he'd gained at Everton would bode well and blah blah blah. But he was never up to speed. I think he was out of his depth from day one."

12 October
THE WRIGHT STUFF FOR ENGLAND

Kevin Keegan says Shaun Wright-Phillips is good enough to be playing for his country's Under-21s side. City are linked with Newcastle midfielder Robert Lee after the player hands in a transfer request at Newcastle. Keegan denies making an enquiry about him.

There will be no changes from the side that beat Birmingham 6-0 in midweek for the derby game against Stockport County.

13 October

CITY 2 STOCKPORT COUNTY 2

HOODOO STRIKES AGAIN

City's bogey team again thwart the Blues as neighbours Stockport take a point at Maine Road. City's goals come from Ali Benarbia and Shaun Goater and the point is gained after the home side have twice trailed.

"We certainly did enough to win this game," says Kevin Keegan on the club's website. "We simply didn't kill off the opposition the way we have done in the past."

WHAT THE PAPERS SAY

THE MAIL ON SUNDAY

'Kevin Keegan's unpredictable Manchester City had to come from behind twice to save a point against bottom club Stockport. Shaun Goater hit the second equaliser after 83 minutes to finally calm nerves at a packed Maine Road. City made an explosive start when Darren Huckerby, who claimed four goals in the 6-0 Worthington Cup demolition of Birmingham City, hit the target again with a superb effort from the narrowest of angles after only 13 minutes. But celebrations were cut short when referee David Pugh acted on a signal from one of his assistants who ruled that the ball had gone out of play before Huckerby's finish.'

THE SUNDAY MIRROR

'Kevin Keegan lost his cool as his City contenders lost their way against their no-hope neighbours from Stockport. City's anguished boss allowed himself to be caught up in an unseemly second-half touchline squabble with County player Jason Van Blerk. Finally, ref David Pugh was forced to read the riot act to the warring duo. But Keegan explained: "I tried to throw the ball back and the player knocked it out of my hand. The fourth official saw it but the ref didn't. But it wasn't the only thing he missed!"'

THE SUNDAY PEOPLE

'Kevin Keegan showed the first signs of managerial stress in a flare-up with Jason van Blerk as Manchester City sulked to a shock draw. The cynics always reckoned Keegan would throw a tantrum one day at Maine Road, but they didn't expect him to throw the ball at an opponent as well! Keegan had just had angry words with the former City player when he went to hand him the ball for a throw-in.'

THE SUNDAY TIMES
'Manchester City's rollercoaster season continued against their lesser-known rivals, who had the audacity to show the more rigid discipline and organisation. With a little more luck they could even have taken all the points. City had to come from behind twice in a fixture that should be a rubber-stamped victory if a return to the Premiership is a priority, or even a possibility.'

15 October
KEEGAN LIKES CITY'S CHARACTER
Kevin Keegan says he likes the character his side showed in battling back for a 2-2 draw against Stockport on Saturday. The boss says he believed that his side would get nothing from the game at one point and expects to see the same character displayed again Sheffield United visit Maine Road the next day.

City's fourth round Worthington Cup opponents are Blackburn Rovers and the game will take place at Ewood Park on November 28.

16 October
CITY 0 SHEFFIELD UNITED 0
SNORE DRAW FOR CITY
It's dire stuff at Maine Road as City play out a scoreless draw with Sheffield United. Radio presenters and City fans Mark Radcliffe and Marc 'Lard' Riley call it the worst game they've ever seen at Maine Road.

"It was frustrating," says Kevin Keegan on the City website. "We three games without defeat is another way of looking at it but if we're honest we've taken two points from nine." Kevin Horlock is sent off for two bookable offences but the boss refuses to get drawn into a slanging match with a referee who many thought had a poor game.

WHAT THE PAPERS SAY
THE DAILY MIRROR
'The word is out in the First Division that you can stop Kevin Keegan's cavaliers by messing them around and muscling them about. And Neil

Warnock's Blades are perfectly suited for that type of action. City got nowhere – and for good measure had Kevin Horlock sent off for his second bookable offence in the 76th minute. United's tactics were helped by referee Steve Bennett, on a night off from Premiership duties and intent on making fussy decisions.'

THE DAILY TELEGRAPH
'Manchester City's first scoreless draw in 56 League encounters was everything but a goal affair at Maine Road last night. City, who have been involved in 63 goals from their 13 previous encounters this season, were numerically superior on an unwanted account with six yellow cards and one red.'

THE DAILY MAIL
'Manchester City were held to a goalless draw for the first time in 56 games at Maine Road in a bad-tempered clash which produced one red card and seven bookings. Midfielder Kevin Horlock was sent off in the second half for his second bookable offence as City's promotion challenge continued to splutter. There was hardly a goal attempt worthy of the name during a first half that became increasingly contentious and at times appeared on the brink of getting out of control.'

THE INDEPENDENT
'A blue moon hung over Maine Road last night as Manchester City produced that rarest of results for any side managed by Kevin Keegan – a goalless draw. "We are either very, very good or very bad," the City manager had said of his side's season thus far. Yesterday evening they were simply mediocre, facing a Sheffield United side that possessed no ambitions higher than a draw, even when Kevin Horlock's sending off for diving (one of seven yellow cards) gave them a one-man advantage. Indeed, during that 24 minutes, Shaun Goater, who earlier had been denied by the post, twice came close to scoring and might have won a penalty had Shaun Murphy's tug on his shirt been spotted.'

17 October
BORE DRAW
Keegan admits the draw with Sheffield United was a poor advert for football.

"I wouldn't rush out for the video," he says, with commendable honesty.

Paul Ritchie scores on his comeback for the reserves but they still lose to bottom-placed Sheffield Wednesday.

18 October
OUT OF THE PLAY-OFF ZONE

City drop to seventh in the league as Coventry draw at Rotherham.

19 October
WILCOX LINK DENIED AGAIN

City again refute suggestions that they have made a £1.5 million offer for Leeds midfielder Jason Wilcox.

Sheffield United manager Neil Warnock accuses Danny Tiatto of threatening Rob Kozluk's career after the player undergoes cruciate ligament surgery. "How he was not sent off I'll never know," says Warnock.

Shaun Wright-Phillips is a doubt for Saturday's game at Preston after being knocked out against Sheffield United and suffering concussion. "I tried to kid him on that he'd scored a hat-trick but he knew he hadn't done that," says Keegan.

LAKEY'S VIEW

"Jason Wilcox would have added consistency and a bit more experience at a high level and I did rate him; he's got a good left peg. To be honest I don't know if he'd be a good buy now. He's maybe not good enough for us now but at this particular time it was an interesting idea."

21 October
PRESTON NORTH END 2 CITY 1
BLUES LOSE OUT TO MACKEN WONDER STRIKE

A 40-yard wonder-strike from Jon Macken sees City leave Deepdale empty-handed, despite Darren Huckerby's opening goal. "Even as the manager of the opposition," said Kevin Keegan at the club's website, "You look at the goal and think, 'Goodness, that was something very special.'"

Eyal Berkovic is sent off for dissent and Kevin Keegan promises to have words with the player, who still hasn't completed 90 minutes for the club. City now lie ninth in Division One with 20 points.

22 October
PLAYER DOUBTS
Steve Howey and Darren Huckerby both have injuries and are doubtful for
the visit of Grimsby to Maine Road on Tuesday.

23 October
HAALAND SETBACK
Alfie Haaland's knee swells up again and he will be out for at least another
month. He is again sent to see a specialist. Kevin Keegan says it's "a bit of
a blow". Danny Tiatto is named in the Australia squad for two World Cup
qualifiers in November.

24 October
CITY 4 GRIMSBY 0
IT'S BACK TO WINNING WAYS FOR RAMPANT BLUES
City rattle in four against Grimsby with Shaun Goater opening the scoring
after a mere two minutes. Steve Howey adds a second before in-form
Darren Huckerby grabs two.

"We're back to something like we need to be," say Kevin Keegan online.
"We're not perfect but this was something like we need to produce week in,
week out if we're going to get out of this Division."

WHAT THE PAPERS SAY
THE SUN
'Kevin Keegan's tough-guy approach worked wonders as Darren
Huckerby led a Maine Road blitz. After Sunday's defeat at Preston, boss
Keegan had warned he would bring in new blood if his fading stars
didn't start winning. And what a response he got, Huckerby leading an
onslaught which had the points sealed midway through the first half.
Huckerby bagged a double to take his tally to seven in four games and
end a dismal run of four games without a win for the Division One title
favourites.'

THE DAILY MAIL
'Manchester City collected their first win in five league outings in a one-
sided encounter with Grimsby. City made the perfect start as Shaun Goater
notched his 13th league goal of the campaign. After just two minutes

Goater was on hand to beat Danny Coyne from close range after a fine left-wing cross from Danny Tiatto.'

THE DAILY TELEGRAPH
'Manchester City ended their recent barren spell in typically flamboyant fashion, sweeping aside a frail Grimsby team with consummate ease. They had taken only two points from their previous four league matches but showed no lack of confidence as they stormed to a three-goal lead inside 24 minutes.'

25 October
SCIMECA LINK
City are linked with Nottingham Forest defender Ricardo Scimeca. *The Sun* reckons it will cost £3 million to take the defender to Maine Road. Forest rather huffily deny the rumour.

Darren Huckerby is in a rich vein of form, while City move to within four points of the leadership of Division One, despite lying in seventh place.

Police say they will be taking no action over the alleged Paulo Wanchope ball boy incident at Norwich.

The reserves go down one nil away at Sunderland.

26 October
DANISH KEEPER SIGNS
City complete the signing of 18 year-old, six-foot-five goalkeeper Kevin Stuhr Ellegaard for a fee of £750,000. Kevin Keegan says he's one for the future.

Skipper Stuart Pearce admits it will be an emotional day for him on Saturday when he returns to Nottingham Forest, the scene of so many personal triumphs, for the first time as a player. Pearce says he will be very surprised if he gets any stick from the fans. It promises to be a tough game. Forest are undefeated at home and have conceded just four goals in seven home games.

28 October
NOTTINGHAM FOREST 1 CITY 1
HONOURS EVEN AT THE CITY GROUND
City manage a one-all draw with Nottingham Forest, courtesy of one of the

most bizarre and comical goals Shaun Goater will ever score. A minute after conceding, Goater capitalises on an horrendous mix-up in the Forest defence to tap the ball into an open goal.

"We are certainly not doing enough to get out of this league automatically at the moment but we can improve," says Kevin Keegan on the City website.

29 October
NO SURRENDER TO ROYLE
Chairman David Bernstein tells City shareholders at the club's AGM that there will be no backing down in the club's dispute with former manager Joe Royle. "We believe there is no substance whatsoever in the legal suit against us," he says. "We believe the situation is quite clear. It all depends on whether we were in the Premier League or not after the end of last season. It is quite obvious to me we were not. There is a moral issue here as well as a legal issue and I believe people should be able to take the down side without complaining." The Chairman also bullishly defends his own remuneration package as well as that of COO Chris Bird.

Eyal Berkovic returns to City with Israel's hopes of World Cup qualification dashed after a 1-1 draw with Austria at the weekend. Gerard Wiekens, his deputy in the draw at Nottingham Forest, is ruled out of Wednesday's trip to Barnsley with an ankle injury.

City's home game with Norwich in January is put back a day to accommodate the TV cameras. The away game at Watford in the same month will also be put back to a Sunday.

Kevin Keegan says he will most likely stick with the flat back four he employed at Forest.

30 October
JARNI BARNEY COULD OPEN THE WAY TO A MOVE
Kevin Keegan is still hopeful of bringing Croatian midfielder Robert Jarni to Maine Road. He would cost in the region of £250,000, though there are still some sticky financial issues to be resolved between Jarni and his Spanish club Las Palmas. The manager also says that Paulo Wanchope's injury has had a negative effect on fellow striker Shaun Goater, whose goal ratio has slipped considerably since his partner was injured. Keegan then warns that the side's passing must improve against Barnsley to allow playmaker Ali Benarbia, currently operating on the right side of midfield, into the game more.

31 October
BARNSLEY 0 CITY 3
ALL THREE POINTS TAKEN IN EXCELLENT AWAY PERFORMANCE
An excellent performance from The Blues, with Eyal Berkovic and Ali Benarbia both in the midfield, results in a resounding away victory. Goater, Pearce and Huckerby put City three up before the interval.

"There was some wonderful football here tonight," said a delighted Kevin Keegan on the club's website. "I thought it was the start of Manchester City. It was superb."

WHAT THE PAPERS SAY
THE DAILY MAIL
'Goal-hungry Manchester City heeded Kevin Keegan's message to come to terms with First Division football as they tore bewildered Barnsley to shreds inside an incredible 30-minute spell at Oakwell. Shaun Goater's 17th strike of the season, a bizarre Stuart Pearce goal and a third from Darren Huckerby left managerless Barnsley down and out by half-time. It was just the response City boss Keegan had hoped for after questioning his players' ability to storm their way straight back into the Premiership.'

THE SUN
'Darren Huckerby gave poor Barnsley the first-half runaround as City had all three points under lock and key by the interval.

The ex-Leeds hitman made the 14th-minute opener for Shaun Goater and scored the third himself on the stroke of half-time.'

THE DAILY TELEGRAPH
'There was no respite for managerless Barnsley last night at Oakwell, where Manchester City secured a comfortable victory, all of their goals coming in a splendid performance during a one-sided first half. Barnsley have now won only one of nine League games and they remain firmly rooted second from bottom of the table, with relegation already an ominous threat. Kevin Keegan, the City manager, whetted the appetite by pairing for the first time the creative midfield talents of Ali Benarbia and Eyal Berkovic and the outcome was a first half that left the visitors firmly in control.'

LAKEY'S VIEW

"It's places like Barnsley and Grimsby where you have to roll your sleeves up and battle. And while everyone was talking about the sweet football that City were playing, they were still capable of going to places like this and doing the business. Even with Benarbia and Berkovic in the side the steel was still there but allied with guile and skill. I also think that you can see the forward thinking there. I suspect Kevin Keegan will have looked at games and presupposed a scenario against a better side and thought about how his side would cope. Maybe he played certain players together at certain times to test things for later down the line. I think he was imagining meeting teams like Sunderland, who close down and work very, very hard, but at a higher level. I think games like this were preparation for what was to come. I think he used them as a testing ground."

NOVEMBER 2001

1 November
KEEGAN SATISFIED

Kevin Keegan claims to be satisfied with the tinkering he has done on his team, which has resulted in a three-match unbeaten run. He singles out the central defensive partnership of Steve Howey and Lucien Mettomo for special praise, as well as the striking duo of Darren Huckerby and Shaun Goater.

2nd November
GETTING WITH THE PACK

Keegan emphasises the need for City to get in with the pack of promotion contenders with the home game against Gillingham at the weekend. "We desperately need to get back in to what I call 'The Pack'. At the moment we're on the fringe of things."

Robert Jarni was present at City's winning performance against Barnsley and hopes to sign for the club next week.

3 November
CITY 4 GILLINGHAM 1
BLUES INFLICT HEAVY DEFEAT ON GILLS

A Shaun Goater hat-trick and one from Darren Huckerby ensure a comprehensive home victory. Goater takes his goal tally for the season to

20 and thanks his new striking partner for his support. "If your front men are creating chances, scoring goals and missing chances then that tells you that you are doing a lot of things right," says Kevin Keegan on the City website. Cue head-scratching over the 'missing chances' part of that statement. We know what you mean, Kev.

4 November
IS THIS THE START?

Kevin Keegan says he is happy with the team's performance against Gillingham, but that it must be the start of a more consistent showing from City. "Now we've had three wins and a draw in the last four games we mustn't think we have done anything yet," he explains.

5 November
EDGHILL BACK

Defender Richard Edghill is back in training after his knee injury while Alfie Haaland is also close to being able to play competitively. Eyal Berkovic says his country's failure to qualify for the World Cup Finals gave him the most disappointing week of his footballing career.

6 November
DICKOV INJURED

Paul Dickov picks up an injury to his ribs in training and will be out for two weeks. The Scottish striker has yet to start a game for Kevin Keegan.

7 November
ANOTHER TRIALIST ARRIVES

Kevin Keegan takes a look at Christian Negouai from Belgian club Charleroi on the advice of former Newcastle player Philippe Albert. "I can't even pronounce his surname," says a candid boss of the 23-year-old.

City's reserves beat Aston Villa 2-0 with goals from Leon Mike and Chris Shuker.

LAKEY'S VIEW

"It's just experience that makes Kevin take a good look at players in this way before committing. Certain players have ability and you know all about them but you have to look at a potential signing holistically. It's a different club, a different town and a different feel and you have to see if players can adjust to that, take it all in their stride and still be able to put in the top performances. There's also the personal side to look at, of course. What are they looking for and what can the club offer?"

8 November
JARNI DEAL SHAKY
The proposed move for Robert Jarni looks like it may fall through. The player has been in Manchester for talks but problems with current club Las Palmas seem to be the stumbling block. "He has got some problems with his club but they are his problems and we will not get involved," says Keegan.

9 November
WEATHERALL FOR CITY?
Bradford central defender David Weatherall could be on the move to City. The 30-year-old failed a medical when a move to Southampton was on the cards last week but it now looks like City could nip in for the player. With Lucien Mettomo due to be away for four weeks for the African Nations Cup in January, Keegan believes he needs more cover in the middle of his defence.

Another good Keeganism emerges. He says of Shaun Goater, "His greatest asset is that he is there to miss them as well."

Meanwhile Ali Benarbia is in Paris to marry long-time girlfriend Wafaa.

PFA members vote to strike in a dispute over the amount of cash the players receive as part of the television deals that the leagues have signed; 99% of the voters have opted to strike. "The result indicates the strength and solidarity of the players and confirms our belief that maintaining a demand for five percent of television income is both fair and equitable," says PFA Chief Executive Gordon Taylor.

10 November
WEATHERALL DEAL COLLAPSES
"Manchester City will not be pursuing their interest in David Weatherall as the player has failed his medical," explains Chris Bird. "City may renew their interest in the player in the future."

12 November
CITY DROP DOWN THE TABLE

City, who have players away on international duty, slip to seventh in the division after the weekend's games. Neither Danny Tiatto nor Richard Dunne appear for their respective countries.

Keegan admits that now might be the time to start letting some of the club's younger players go out on loan to give them more experience. Up to this point Keegan has always insisted that all the senior squad players were needed at Maine Road. This news comes on the back of the information that midfielder Christian Negouai looks set to sign for the Blues.

LAKEY'S VIEW

"The side definitely hadn't clicked by this point. The players weren't at ease with the system and it was difficult to know how everything was going to fit. The players weren't comfortable yet and that makes a huge difference. I'll never forget when I was playing at full back with David White ahead of me and we just . . . fitted. When I got the ball my first touch wasn't to control it. It was just to knock it into space for Whitey and he'd already be on his way. It was like telepathy. But it takes a while to get like that. But out of working it, getting to understand a system, came an inventive side that had many different ways of skinning a cat. I've watched the team play in certain games and thought as a pro that I wouldn't have been able to handle it. The fact that Kevin Keegan has been branded tactically naïve is rubbish, but it gives him this point to prove. And the ingredients are all there, it's all been developed."

13 November
NEGOUAI SIGNS

City complete the signing of 23-year-old midfielder Christian Negouai from Belgian side Charleroi for £1.5 million and Keegan immediately calls it the most exciting acquisition he has made since taking over at Maine Road. What? Even more exciting than Ali Benarbia? The player goes straight into the squad for the away game at Portsmouth on Saturday. At six-foot-four, Negouai balances out a midfield where Benarbia, Eyal Berkovic and Danny Tiatto are all small. "The fans were singing, 'we've got the smallest midfield in the world' when we were at Barnsley," laughs Keegan.

The reserves beat Bradford City 4-0, the goals coming from a Leon Mike hat-trick and Alioune Touré.

LAKEY'S VIEW

"I think Kevin would be the first to say that Christian Negouai has not worked out how he hoped. And that statement about him being his most exciting signing at a time when he'd already brought in Berkovic and Benarbia shows how much he rated the lad. Perhaps the player found that level of expectancy daunting and maybe that comment inadvertently added a bit more pressure. I'll never forget Alan Ball saying that Buster Phillips would be the first £10 million footballer and it absolutely killed him. Certain players can rise to it, certain players can't. But I'd never discount the lad's ability. If Kevin Keegan and his backroom team can see the ability in that lad, then there must be something there that has yet to come through. Otherwise why would Kevin Keegan be putting his neck on the block without meaning it? And I have to say I thought Christian's punch of the ball for his goal against Rotherham was quite subtle!"

14 November
DONACHIE QUITS FOR SHEFFIELD WEDNESDAY

City coach Willie Donachie resigns in order to join Terry Yorath at Sheffield Wednesday. "This has been a very difficult decision to make as I have had a lot of very good times at City," says Donachie. "However, the new challenge at Wednesday is one that I feel I should accept."

"The news has come as a great shock to me," says Kevin Keegan. "Willie has been very important in my first few months at the club, I thank him for his support. He will be missed by all at the club, but we wish him the all the very best in his new role."

Midfielder Dickson Etuhu still hasn't signed the contract offered to him by the club but it appears that the arrival of Christian Negouai on a four and a half year deal may speed up the 19-year-old Londoner's decision. The Martinique-born new boy explains. "Sunderland, West Ham and Middlesbrough were all interested in me but I really wanted to come and play for Kevin Keegan."

15 November
NAMES IN THE COACHING FRAME

Derek Fazackerley and Paul Bracewell are the names to emerge as favourites to take up the coach's role at City after the departure of Willie Donachie. Kevin Keegan explains: "I have always worked with defensive-minded people because I am a forward. I know what it takes to score goals and be inventive as that is my area of expertise. So the next coach will more than likely be someone who is different to me."

Two young City players, Lee Croft and Dorryl Profitt, are called up by England for the Under-17s match against Poland on 22nd November.

Keeper Kevin Stuur Ellegaard reveals that he is named after his manager, another slightly odd example of 'The Keegan Factor' in full effect.

Richard Dunne may be called on after international duty for the forthcoming trip to Portsmouth, despite believing he is suspended. The player only has four bookings, not five, which would have led to a ban.

16 November
NO COMMENT
Keegan refuses to comment on rumours that he was offered the role of Director Of Football with weekend opponents Portsmouth before joining City.

17 November
PORTSMOUTH 2 CITY 1
OLD BOY BRADBURY HELPS SINKS BLUES
Former City record signing Lee Bradbury scores as Portsmouth beat City 2-1. The Blues only goal comes from Darren Huckerby.

"I don't think we deserved to lose," says Kevin Keegan on the City website. "We created at least six very good chances away from home and have left with a 2-1 defeat." Keegan is at least enthusiastic about Christian Negouai's debut.

WHAT THE PAPERS SAY
THE SUNDAY TIMES
'They've long loved to berate Kevin Keegan in this part of the world, the basis of that traditional derision being his allegiance to Southampton rather than his acumen as an England manager. So imagine the delight around Fratton Park when Portsmouth rallied from a goal behind to overcome Manchester City. It could be argued that Keegan deserved all he got. Anybody who sends a team out to play in luminous lime-green socks doesn't deserve to travel home with three points. But he insisted he was hard done by when first Lee Bradbury and then Peter Crouch scored with far-post headers to end City's unbeaten run of four games.'

THE MAIL ON SUNDAY

'Portsmouth produced a second-half turnaround to claim all three points before an ecstatic sell-out crowd at Fratton Park.

For 45 minutes it looked as though Kevin Keegan's City would bury the home side as they camped in Pompey's half for long periods. But a combination of City's missed chances and fighting spirit ensured victory for Portsmouth, who have now lost just once in their last seven League games.'

19 November
"I'LL MAKE IT" – GOAT

Despite limping off with a groin injury in the defeat at Portsmouth, Shaun Goater insists he'll be fit for the visit of his former club Rotherham to Maine Road on Saturday. Kevin Keegan is blunt in his assessment of youngster Leon Mike's performance against Portsmouth, saying that the striker failed to convert two chances and strikers need to score to stay in the side. Danny Tiatto may return to City early from the Australian World Cup squad after an apparent mix-up over an international ban. Tiatto believed he had served a three-match ban for a sending off, but one of the games counted was a friendly, which FIFA does not recognise in the serving of suspensions.

20 November
FAZACKERLY NAMED AS NEW COACH

Derek Fazackerly is announced as the new coach of Manchester City. "When Willie left I was very fortunate in that I could pick up the phone to Derek," says Kevin Keegan. "I have worked with him before, I know him and he knows me. He is an excellent coach and I am delighted he is on board." Keegan and Fazackerly have worked together both with Newcastle and England. "He is strong where I am not so strong so I can get on working with the team in areas in which I believe I have expertise," says Keegan. "The relationship works well. It has been proven in the past and hopefully it can be proven again."

21 November
DANNY BACK HOME

Danny Tiatto rejoins the City squad after the ban mix-up sees him leave the Australia squad early. This also means that Tiatto could have played for

City at Portsmouth. Kevin Keegan says it is not his responsibility to check on the eligibility of his players for internationals.

22 November
FIRST IMPRESSIONS FOR FAZ

New coach Derek Fazackerly admits that City have a reputation for leaking goals and one of his first priorities will be to stop that happening. Fazackerly admits, however, that he believes the Blues have the greatest ratio of class players in the First Division. He also claims that City are one of the top six or eight clubs in the country and admits that he phoned Kevin Keegan about the coach's job when he saw that Willie Donachie had resigned on Teletext.

Kevin Keegan says he is "pretty sure" that the coach will tighten City up at the back.

Keegan rules Shaun Goater out of Saturday's home game against Rotherham, though the striker himself still believes there's an outside chance that he might be fit.

23 November
STRIKER RECALLED

Keegan recalls striker Chris Killen from a loan period at Port Vale when Alioune Touré is ruled out of the Rotherham game after picking up a knock in the reserve side's 1-1 draw with Manchester United. Leon Mike is favourite to start.

The club dismisses rumours of a £1.5 million move for Hapoel Tel Aviv's Slovenian striker Milan Osterc, while Norwich are reported to be interested in Paul Dickov.

Stephen Jordan earns City a point in the reserve team clash with Manchester United.

24 November
CITY 2 ROTHERHAM 1
CITY NOTCH UP CONTROVERSIAL WIN

There is anger from the visitors after they are beaten 2-1. City's first goal by new signing Christian Negouai was clearly a case of handball, though there is no doubting Ali Benarbia's 88th minute winner.

"A lot of people thought we didn't have the character to bounce back if we went a goal behind at Maine Road," says Kevin Keegan on the club's website. "But we showed today that we have the character to come back into the game." And the basketball skills.

WHAT THE PAPERS SAY
SUNDAY MIRROR
'It wasn't a hand of God goal that boosted red-faced City, but it was certainly the hand of a Christian. Kevin Keegan's Premiership contenders were a goal down and struggling to make any impression against a side more concerned with relegation when Christian Negouai took a leaf out of Maradona's book of black arts. Even the six-foot-four midfielder from Martinique wasn't going to reach Stuart Pearce's high right-wing cross until he flung up an arm above goalie Mike Pollitt to deflect the ball home.'

THE SUNDAY PEOPLE
'Ali Benarbia landed a late knockout for City almost on the final bell. It wrapped up a desperate day for Rotherham, who were still on the ropes and claiming City's first goal should have been disallowed – for a punch! Maine Road new boy Christian Negouai, having a shocker on his home debut, gave his side a helping hand by clearly punching a Stuart Pearce cross into the net before keeper Mike Pollitt could catch it. Pure Maradona stuff!'

THE SUNDAY TELEGRAPH
'Ali Benarbia's deflected long-range shot three minutes from time gave Manchester City an undeserved victory. It was the second stroke of good fortune for City – three minutes before the interval they had equalised through a 'Hand of God' goal from Christian Negouai – and appalling justice for a Rotherham side who deserved a point. City were without three main strikers – Shaun Goater, Paulo Wanchope and Paul Dickov. Leon Mike, on his full debut, partnered Darren Huckerby up front. Eyal Berkovic was suspended, but Danny Tiatto returned after his aborted World Cup trip to Australia.'

26 November
RESILIENCE A KEY FACTOR
Keegan praises the resilience shown by his side in the weekend win against

Rotherham and again states that City will be in the shake-up come the end of the season.

Danny Tiatto and Steve Howey were both injured in the game and may not be fit to face next league opponents Grimsby.

27 November
RITCHIE BACK IN THE SQUAD

Paul Ritchie, whose season has been dogged by injury, is included in the squad for the Worthington Cup game at Blackburn on Wednesday. Shaun Goater is still ruled out, but Kevin Keegan says he will definitely start with both Ali Benarbia and Eyal Berkovic in midfield.

Keegan also denies reports that he agreed to give a trial to 23-year-old Anthony Wheall on the strength of the City fan phoning him up and asking for one! "I read the report myself and it is one of those which you look at and think, 'Where on earth did that come from?'" he says

28 November
BLACKBURN 2 CITY 0
BLUES BOW OUT WITH CREDIT

A bad night for City as they go out of the Worthington Cup, lose Stuart Pearce for up to four weeks due to injury and see new signing Christian Negouai dismissed for two bookable offences.

Kevin Keegan lays into referee Uriah Rennie at the post match press conference. "Don't write about the match, write about the referee Uriah Rennie. That's what he wants. It was shocking refereeing, you have to have common sense. He didn't have enough common sense for the Premiership, that's why he is down in the other Divisions," says Keegan. "I am not saying anything that I have not already said to him. Here was a tie in which seventeen thousand people came to see a good game of football but he showed no common sense. I thought he was poor. I don't care what it costs me if the FA want to take it further. I will give them a tape of the game for them to have a look at."

The only consolation is that Paul Ritchie comes through his first senior appearance in 10 months unscathed.

Kevin Keegan also strongly criticises proposals being drawn up for a two tier Premiership, saying football should not be dictated by finance alone. "I don't see anything wrong with Stockport, Crewe and Rotherham, for instance, playing against Manchester City," he says. "Their players have earned the right to play in this league."

30 November
CAPTAIN GOAT
Shaun Goater will captain the side at Grimsby on his return from injury.

Keeper Carlo Nash, who played in the defeat at Blackburn, keeps his place ahead of Nicky Weaver and Danny Tiatto is also fit to return.

Manager Kevin Keegan believes the coming month will be crucial in the battle for promotion.

DECEMBER 2001
1 December
YOUTH TEAM VICTORY
The youth team records a 3-0 win over Burnley in the fourth round of the FA Youth Cup.

1 December
GRIMSBY 0 CITY 2
THREE POINTS IN THE BAG FOR THE BLUES
A crucial away win at the start of a crucial month as goals from Darren Huckerby (a penalty) and Shaun Goater on 90 minutes seal the victory.

"I thought it was a controlled performance from us today," comments Kevin Keegan at *www.mcfc.co.uk*. "I don't think we were sensational, but some of our football was excellent."

WHAT THE PAPERS SAY
THE SUNDAY PEOPLE
'It doesn't get much better than this for City's fanatical travelling army. With news of Manchester United's defeat by Chelsea safely in the bag before a ball was kicked, they watched in delight as late goals from Darren Huckerby and Shaun Goater gave the Sky Blues all three points. That made it 33 strikes this season from City's double act. And with that kind of fire power, Kevin Keegan's men will take some stopping when the prizes are handed out next May. No wonder the former England boss was in chirpy mood afterwards, insisting: "There's no doubt we deserved to win. We had a lot of possession and created some great chances throughout the game."'

THE SUNDAY MIRROR

'Grimsby may be feeling down but they're not out – and that's the view of City manager Kevin Keegan! The former England boss watched his side finally overcome the struggling Mariners with a Darren Huckerby penalty and then a Shaun Goater strike in injury time. But Keegan said afterwards: "Grimsby are good enough to stay up and certainly Lennie Lawrence gets them fired up. Their big problem is that they have a small squad and that could cost them. But they certainly have a manager who knows how to fight his way out and they have players with lots of character." Lawrence himself called the defeat "harsh" adding: "It's as well as we've played for some time, but we needed a goalscorer who could anticipate and be brave."'

THE SUNDAY TIMES

'Manchester City manager Kevin Keegan was most affronted following yesterday's first double of the season at any hint that his team were not worthy of victory at Blundell Park. "We were built to go forward today," he said. "I was pleased with everyone, particularly (Kevin) Horlock and (Eyal) Berkovic. Perhaps Ali Benarbia gave the ball away a bit more than usual. We deserved to win with a lot of possession. We missed three good efforts in the first half — two of them down to Shaun Goater." Lennie Lawrence, of course, the manager of Grimsby, begged to differ: "It was a game which turned on two points. The first was the penalty. I don't know whether it was or not, but when you're in front of 2,000 screaming fans your player is going to get it if he's brought down. Before that we hit the post when we really should have taken the lead."'

3 December
MAINE ROAD BIG SCREEN

City erect a screen at Maine Road to allow fans to see the following day's match at Millwall live. Fans have been banned from travelling to the fixture.

4 December
MILLWALL 2 CITY 3
OUTSTANDING CITY PLUNDER POINTS IN HOSTILE DEN

A great performance at The New Den sees City clinch all three points in an atmosphere that many describe as both hostile and openly racist.

Shaun Wright-Phillips scores the winner after a hotly-disputed penalty that draws Millwall level at 2-2 sees Kevin Keegan sent from the dugout by the fourth official.

"I just can't stop smiling," says Wright-Phillips.

The players applaud the empty stand where the City fans would have been after Darren Huckerby scores. City's other goal comes from Shaun Goater.

"We found we have a lot of character tonight," adds Keegan. "I have questioned that in the past but it was not questioned here tonight." City now have a record of just one defeat in eight games.

The following article was written by a Manchester City-supporting journalist and a slightly edited version was published in *The Observer* newspaper on Sunday 9 December, eliciting a huge response from fans both in agreement and disagreement. This is the original piece . . .

MILLWALL: NO-ONE LIKES THEM AND IT'S NO BLOODY WONDER

It was on the short train journey to South Bermondsey that the bravado started to wear thin.

"I'm not sure about this, maybe we should have stayed in the pub to watch Juve," said Juan.

"No, it'll be fine," I said "None of their boys will be out tonight; no-one to fight."

Arriving at the Den and putting on our best London accents for the Dibble – er, Old Bill – we took our seats about five minutes before the kick off. We breathed a sigh of relief as we looked around and saw a collection of relatively normal people; until the teams ran out.

"Ooo, ooo, ooo, ooo, ooo," screamed the white twenty-something bloke next to me whilst jumping up and down imitating a monkey.

"Ooo ooo ooo ooo ooo," screamed all his mates around us.

"Ooo ooo ooo ooo ooo," chanted approximately half the crowd.

Their target? Shaun Goater, who had the misfortune to be closest to the touchline.

"F**k off you Northern Monkey, ooo, ooo, ooo, ooo, ooo."

"F**k off you stunted coon, ooo, ooo, ooo, ooo, ooo," they screamed at Shaun Wright-Phillips.

"F**k off Paki," was the welcome for Ali Benarbia the first time he touched the ball.

"F**k off you fat Jew" was the inevitable insult hurled regularly at Eyal Berkovic. "No-one likes us; WE DON'T CARE. WE ARE MILLWALL, SU-PER MILL-WALL . . ." And on and on it went.

City, not unreasonably, were a bit apprehensive in the opening minutes. However, once they settled down they made Millwall look like the former third division journeymen they are.

"The coon's in the box. THE F**KING COON'S IN THE BOX! Ooo, ooo, ooo, ooo oh f**k he's scored." Shaun Goater silenced the racists for a few minutes by ramming their invective down their collective throats with a beautifully-taken goal from a sublime cross from Shaun Wright-Phillips.

Before the game Goater had said, "I am sure we have the experience to handle the situation and come away with the points. That match [at Millwall] three years ago was the most frightening I have been involved in during my footballing career." So how much he must have enjoyed that one.

The game and the racism continued throughout the first half and just as it looked like we were going to have a quiet celebratory half time cup of tea, Millwall equalised when Nash failed to hold onto a shot from Livermore and Sadlier netted the rebound.

"F**K OFF KEEGAN . . . F**K OFF KEEGAN . . . NO-ONE LIKES US, WE DON'T CARE . . . WE ARE MILL-WALL . . ."

By now we'd had enough and we asked if we could move into the Family Stand for the second half.

"It's just as bad in there," warned the Steward. And she was right.

"Ooo, ooo, ooo, ooo, ooo," screamed the six-year-old girl in front of us.

"Stop it. You can't do that," her father said.

"Why not?" she asked, "Everybody else is doing it. Ooo, ooo, ooo, ooo, ooo." And on and on it depressingly went on.

City were attacking the goal in front of the deserted 'away end' and by now we were so much on top it was hard to keep quiet as we tried to enjoy the fact that we were slaughtering them under such difficult circumstances. Then Huckerby scored. There was absolute silence all around the ground. It was both eerie and terrifying. The players celebrated by standing on the dead ball line and applauding the empty stand. A tribute to the fans who weren't allowed in to watch this impressive performance.

Ten minutes to go and the racial abuse had levelled out to a desultory booing of all our players. Then suddenly Millwall were back in the game,

112

scoring a penalty after Tiatto handled the ball whilst trying to take it out of the area. 2-2. Seven minutes to go and although we wanted to win we were beginning to think that a draw might be the safest option. Then a chorus of monkey noises alerted us to the fact that Shaun Wright-Phillips was in sight of goal.

"That'll be the draw safe then," I thought, when BANG! It hit the back of the net with such force you could hear it above the torrent of racial abuse from all around us.

The three of us suppressed our delight when suddenly we heard "YESSSS . . . c'mon City," from an executive box directly behind us. Unfortunately, so too did everyone around us and within seconds the box was under siege from the dads and mums and sons and daughters who make up the numbers in Millwall's 'Family Enclosure'.

Thankfully the long-suffering stewards got there first and stopped forty or so sub-humans from getting into the box for a free corporate evening out, with bonus fighting.

Finally, after what seemed like eight hours, the whistle went for the end of the game and we were able to escape.

After the inevitable train delay for 30 minutes we got back to the car and as one we screamed "YESSSSSS. WE WON." The relief all round was tangible. At last we could speak without fear.

LAKEY'S VIEW

"This was one of *the* key games of the season for us and I think Kevin Keegan's also said as much. It became a notorious match because of the fact that all City fans were banned from the game, so there was that huge empty stand at one end of the ground. And, of course, all the talk of racial abuse that went on in the papers afterwards. You might think that all that would have had a negative effect on City but in actual fact I think it had a negative effect on Millwall because the atmosphere was very hostile towards us and I think it put a lot of pressure on them to get out there, get after us and really deliver for their supporters. And when they couldn't do it . . . We competed brilliantly in this game, but there was class there in abundance. The movement for the first goal was unbelievable. Eyal Berkovic finds Shaun Wright-Phillips with a perfect pass and he drills it into the area really hard where Shaun Goater meets it full on. It really was one of the best team goals of the season for the speed of the move and the precision of the execution. What also sticks in my mind is the fact that we conceded a really dubious penalty that made the score 2-2. Now many a City side would have crumbled in the past having worked so hard to get into a great position and having had it snatched away like that. Plus we were under the cosh as Millwall went looking for the winner. But Shaun Wright-Phillips broke away and scored a beauty, his first of the season. The way he attacked the ball was awesome and I was so pleased for him, given all the stick that he'd taken all night. What a way to answer those morons. No wonder when you hear his dad talk about him he's bursting with pride."

5 December
EDGHILL RETURNS
Richard Edghill plays a full game for the reserves in a 0-0 draw with Middlesbrough as he makes his comeback from injury.

6 December
BOSS IN BOTHER
Kevin Keegan escapes punishment for his outburst at referee Uriah Rennie after the Blackburn defeat.

"We have studied the referee's report and Kevin Keegan has not gone beyond the bounds of our rules," says an FA spokesman.

It's worse news regarding the Millwall incident. "I will not be reporting Kevin Keegan for any physical offence because I did not see any. But I will be reporting him for using insulting language," says referee Clive Wilkes.

Richard Edghill is added to the senior squad for the away game at Crystal Palace. Steve Howey has still not recovered from an injury picked up against Rotherham. Paulo Wanchope returns from international duties with Costa Rica.

City's youth team draw Gillingham in the fifth round of the FA Youth Cup.

7 December
KEGGY THE BRICKIE
Kevin Keegan decides to reveal how he keeps himself busy when he's out of the game. "I love building brick walls," he explains. "My wife calls me Hadrian, as I have this habit of building walls when I have time on my hands. So you can call me Hadrian from now on!"

8 December

CRYSTAL PALACE 2 CITY 1
FRANCIS GETS HIS REVENGE

Former Birmingham manager Trevor Francis avenges two crushing defeats of his former side earlier in the season with this home victory. Shaun Goater finds the target for City but it's not enough for the Blues to avoid dropping all three points.

"We deserved something out of this game," says an upbeat Keegan online. "We played very well and found ourselves two down away from home. We have come back to score and can count ourselves unlucky not to have got a second."

WHAT THE PAPERS SAY
THE MAIL ON SUNDAY

'Trevor Francis ended his Manchester City hoodoo with a memorable first victory in charge of Crystal Palace. Francis had lost against the Maine Road club in his previous five matches as a manager. But Palace, coming off a run of four successive defeats, produced a defiant rearguard action to prevent Kevin Keegan's side moving into second place. It was a sweet victory for Francis over his former England colleague and against one of the clubs he played for. But it was also a mighty close call as Palace hung on desperately throughout the second half against a side playing vastly superior football.'

THE SUNDAY TELEGRAPH

'Trevor Francis had seen enough of Manchester City already this season after two heavy defeats while with Birmingham, so yesterday's delight at his first victory as the new Crystal Palace manager came with double helpings. First-half goals from Dougie Freedman and Jovan Kirovski sealed three precious points to end a run of four successive defeats and put Francis in bullish mood as he prepares for Tuesday's game at St Andrew's.'

LAKEY'S VIEW

"What can I say about Selhurst Park? It has always been a real bogey ground for us and I daresay it probably always will be. Absolutely no surprises that we lost there and I'm only glad that we won't be visiting the place in the Premiership."

10 December
HOME TIE

City are drawn at home against Swindon in the third round of the FA Cup. Kevin Keegan seems less sure about the quality of his side after defeat at Crystal Palace. "I knew we would get up when I was at Newcastle," he says. "I am not sure here, there is a doubt."

11 December
CITY 1 WOLVES 0
CRUCIAL HOME WIN SEES CITY PIP PROMOTION RIVALS

A first-half Kevin Horlock strike seals the win for City but Wolves boss Dave Jones is fuming after Jolyon Lescott is sent off for a tackle on Ali Benarbia. "I believe I am a reasonable person but I believe the referee got that all wrong and I will tell him so," says Jones. Kevin Keegan sees things differently on City's website. "I thought it was a bad tackle, there is no doubt about that. The player went in and did not get the ball. Whether it is a sending off or not is down to the referee. It was never a classic but three valuable points for us," he says of the game.

LAKEY'S VIEW

"Another one of those crucial games that we managed to turn our way and which made a real difference at the end of the season. Noteworthy for another crucial Kevin Horlock winner. How many times did he produce the single goal that bagged us the three points in important games? An invaluable player throughout the season for my money."

12 December
BERKOVIC OUT AGAIN?

Eyal Berkovic looks likely to miss the Christmas period with a hamstring injury picked up in the victory over Wolves. Kevin Keegan expresses his concerns about some of his players looking jaded. He gives the squad a couple of days off.

13 December
BERKOVIC IN AGAIN?

It looks as if the injury to Eyal Berkovic is less serious than was first thought. He may even be fit for the weekend game with Bradford.

Stuart Pearce still insists he will retire at the end of the season. "As far as I can see if the club gets up then I would think, looking it as coldly as I can, that we need a better player than myself," he says.

The reserves lose 1-0 to Newcastle with a side including Nicky Weaver, Alfie Haaland, Paul Dickov and Paulo Wanchope.

14 December
WEAVER DISCIPLINED
Kevin Keegan explains that keeper Nicky Weaver was dropped from the squad for the visit of Wolves after going out drinking until the early hours of Sunday morning following the previous weekend's defeat at Crystal Palace. "I think I had every right to leave Nicky out," says the manager.

Richard Dunne admits he is disappointed that City didn't show their true quality against Wolves but is keen to point out that the three points is the most important thing.

16 December
CITY 3 BRADFORD CITY 1
SLICK CITY EASE UP TO SECOND
Goals from Mettomo, Horlock and Wright-Phillips deservedly secure the points for City, despite a Richard Dunne own goal giving Bradford an early lead.

"I still think we can play better," says Kevin Keegan on the City website. "I'm not saying it was a great display but it was a step up from the Wolves game." Keegan also explains the secret of his side's success succinctly. "We don't tell Ali Benarbia how to play football, he tells us," he says. He then singles Kevin Horlock out for special praise for the way he has performed in the midfield holding role and praises the side's character.

City move into second place.

17 December
CITY TIGHT-LIPPED ON WHITLEY
City refuse to comment on stories that Jeff Whitley has been banned from the club for two weeks over concerns around training.

18 December
THE MASTERPLAN
Kevin Horlock reveals City's secret formula for winning promotion. "Our strategy is to pick up as many points as possible," he says. Cunning, eh?

The reserves beat Oldham 4-2 in the Manchester Senior Cup, with goals from Leon Mike, Chris Shuker and two from Chris Killen.

20 December
HOWEY IN TROUBLE?
More disciplinary troubles are rumoured. This time it's Steve Howey who is supposed to have been fined after being seen drinking in a restaurant by his manager.

Despite this it looks like the player will replace the suspended Richard Dunne at Crewe on Saturday, while

Alfie Haaland may also be ready for a full return to first team action after appearing for a few minutes against Bradford.

21 December
TOURÉ OUT FOR THE SEASON
Alioune Touré is ruled out for the rest of the season after the club discovers he has deep vein thrombosis.

22 December
CREWE GAME CALLED OFF
The scheduled game against Crewe is called off due to a frozen pitch. Kevin Keegan says he is not happy that the game was only postponed forty minutes before kick off, meaning that most supporters had already travelled to the game.

"The managers did not influence my decision," explains the referee. "I'm the man in charge and it was me who made that decision. I had hoped the sun would come round and soften the pitch up. The safety of the players is paramount in my mind. I had a look at lunchtime and the pitch was hard then but I wanted to give it every chance."

24 December
CHANGES FOR THE BAGGIES
Richard Dunne and Darren Huckerby are both out of the game with West

Brom because of suspension. But Paulo Wanchope looks set for his first start since 25th September.

26th December
CITY 0 WEST BROM 0
HONOURS EVEN FOR PROMOTION CONTENDERS

Battling West Brom take a point away from Maine Road in a goalless draw. Richard Edghill is sent off for diving in the penalty area but insists that he went down legitimately.

Even Baggies manager Gary Megson thinks the decision was wrong. "I cringed when the official brought out the red card because I felt it just wasn't justified," says the former City player. "No comment," says Kevin Keegan. "We played some of the best football since I came here," concludes the boss. "But we just couldn't score."

27 December
GRANVILLE GOING

City accept a £500,000 bid from Crystal Palace for defender Danny Granville. He is in London having talks while the City squad prepare for their crucial home game against league leaders Burnley.

30 December
CITY 5 BURNLEY 1
CITY ROUT HIGH-FLYING BURNLEY

An amazing City performance gives the fans a slightly belated Christmas present as a Paulo Wanchope hat-trick and strikes from Eyal Berkovic and Darren Huckerby blow league-leaders Burnley away.

"I thought some of the football, some of the goals were breathtaking," says Kevin Keegan online. "But I thought some of our football at times was also disappointing."

WHAT THE PAPERS SAY
THE SUNDAY TIMES

'Manchester City may not have met manager Kevin Keegan's goal of topping the First Division by the turn of the year but having overwhelmed Burnley thanks to a hat-trick from Paulo Wanchope, and closed the gap on the leaders to just a point, it is surely only a matter of time before they claim pole position. Despite the scoreline, a highly entertaining game was far from totally one-sided but City have the firepower to get themselves out of most tight spots in this division and made Burnley pay a heavy price for their failings in front of goal.'

THE MAIL ON SUNDAY

'Paulo Wanchope fired a first-half hat-trick as Manchester City turned up the heat on leaders Burnley with a 5-1 win in the First Division promotion race. City – and Wanchope in particular – gave Stan Ternent's side a lesson in finishing as they reduced the Clarets' lead at the top of the table to a single point. Kevin Keegan's men ultimately cruised to victory in front of a packed Maine Road but had to ride their luck on several occasions in the opening 25 minutes and were indebted to keeper Carlo Nash on several occasions, notably when he saved Glen Little's 12th-minute penalty with the score 1-0.'

THE SUNDAY TELEGRAPH

'There could be no greater contrast between Kevin Keegan – high profile, high on adrenaline, heart on the sleeve – and the invariably stony-faced Stan Ternent. Manchester City's manager has done nothing to suggest since taking up his post last May that he has progressed from being a master motivator but a vulnerably naive tactician. His teams are just as likely to take a drubbing as they are to rub the opposition's noses in it. Fortunately, with the backing of City's fanatical 34,000 following at home games and the plethora of workmanlike outfits in Division One, they are more likely to do the latter.'

LAKEY'S VIEW

"What a game. It should have been nine! We absolutely murdered Burnley, who were very average. And there was a hat-trick from Paulo Wanchope, which was great to see. Of course. consistent Paulo Wanchope is an oxymoron. It's not that I'm not a fan but there are definitely days when you want more from him in terms of holding the ball up. In certain games when things aren't going your way you're looking for the ball to stick at the feet of the strikers but he can be like a set of railings! Obviously not in this game, though!"

31 December
ALEX WILLIAMS MBE
Former City keeper Alex Williams is awarded an MBE for his work on City's 'Football In The Community' scheme.

Reserve defender Rhys Day is to join Blackpool on loan until the end of the season.

JANUARY 2002
1 January
SHEFFIELD UNITED 1 CITY 3
NEW YEAR JOY FOR BLUES
Goals from Goater, Berkovic and Wright-Phillips bring City a Happy New Year as the short trip over the Pennines to Sheffield United yields all three points. Former City favourite Michael Brown scores United's consolation goal but City are top of the table for the first time since August. Kevin Keegan is very satisfied.

"It was a very good performance particularly in the second half," he tells the City website. "It was one of those games in which it was up to us to take the initiative. I thought it was a really good team performance, but Shaun Wright-Phillips was outstanding today."

2 January
LOAN DEFENDER?
With Lucien Mettomo leaving City to join up with Cameroon for the African Nations Cup in Mali and Gerard Wiekens out for four weeks with hamstring trouble, Kevin Keegan says he may well look to bring a Premiership defender in on loan. Better news is that Stuart Pearce returns after four weeks out injured.

3 January
NO BID FOR BROMBY
City say they have no intention of bidding £2.5 million for Sheffield Wednesday defender Leigh Bromby despite reports in the papers.

Shaun Goater admits he thought he would be dropped for the game against Sheffield United despite having over 20 goals to his name already this season.

5 January

CITY 2 SWINDON 0

Goals from Wanchope and Horlock secure a straightforward third round FA Cup win over Swindon.

"It was professional rather than exciting, " Kevin Keegan says at *www.mcfc.co.uk*. City are drawn away to Ipswich in the fourth round of the competition.

WHAT THE PAPERS SAY
THE MAIL ON SUNDAY

'Kevin Horlock will always have a place in his heart for Swindon Town – though you would never have guessed it yesterday. They were the club who gave him his chance as a teenager when he was freed after two years as a West Ham trainee. And in five happy years with the Wiltshire club he made 163 League appearances and became a firm favourite with the fans. But he left Swindon for Manchester City five years ago for £1.5 million. And yesterday sentiment counted for nothing when the 29-year-old midfielder fired in the goal which finished his former club's FA Cup hopes. The free-scoring First Division leaders appeared to be stuck on their 74th goal of the season, a header from Paulo Wanchope after only eight minutes. The Costa Rican could hardly miss when Eyal Berkovic pounced on a poor attempted headed clearance by Matt Heywood and delivered the perfect cross.'

7 January
DICKSON DISPUTE

City admit to having a bust-up with representatives of midfielder Dickson Etuhu. The argument revolves around whether the 19 year old is entitled to a free transfer under the terms of his one-year contract, but what is certain is that the player will leave City.

Millwall appears to be his destination after his agent labelled a new offer made to him by City as "derisory".

Kevin Keegan is spitting feathers and says "This is a kid who had hardly played a game here before I came. I can't tell you how disappointed I am."

City circulate Simon Colosimo's details to other clubs after deciding that the Aussie defender will not make the grade at Maine Road. Stoke are believed to have offered the 23-year-old a trial.

Richard Edghill is doubtful for next Sunday's game at home to Norwich with a hamstring injury.

LAKEY'S VIEW

"I was amazed that a player like Dickson Etuhu, good as he is, could even be contemplating leaving City. He'd made some progress and reached the first team, albeit not as a regular, and had seen what was available to him, what he'd achieved and what Kevin Keegan had put into him on a personal level; how much he respected him and how much he rated him. And in spite of all that he threw it back in Keegan's face. The offer City made to Dickson to extend his one-year contract was dismissed by his agent as 'derisory' but he'd only just made it to the first team so how could that be the case? You could say he has potential but if Kevin Keegan could pull Ali Benarbia out of the hat then surely he had to know his place in the scheme of things. The point is that if he had done well in that year then he would obviously have got his rewards. I suppose you could say fair play to the lad because he's obviously got a set of gonads on him. And now he's gone to Preston, a First Division side that won't get promoted. And even if he has managed to get more money, how much more is he actually getting? I can't imagine it would be a lot more than the offer that City made. Above all it would worry me that Dickson's main concern would be getting more money right now, instead of thinking about the chance of playing in the Premiership, advancing his skills and maybe earning himself a five-year deal through his performances."

8 January
EDGY BACK, EDGY OUT

Richard Edghill's hamstring injury clears up but he will still miss the Norwich game due to a one match ban that has yet to be served following his sending off against West Brom.

Many former City players pay tribute to former groundsman Stan Gibson whose funeral takes place in Platt Lane.

Kevin Keegan reveals that he is exercising a get-out clause in Simon Colosimo's contract which states that if the player does not make 10 first team appearances by January 9th then he can be released. It also looks as if the player will not be picked up by Stoke.

9 January
ONE YEAR CONTRACTS FOR KIDS
Terry Dunfield, Chris Shuker, Tyrone Mears, Joey Barton and Stephen Jordan are all offered one-year contracts at City but no progress has been made on deals for senior players Paul Dickov and Richard Edghill. Keegan does say that he now believes Shaun Wright-Phillips and Richard Dunne will both be successful Premiership players.

Leon Mike scores the only goal of the game as the reserves beat Blackburn.

10 January
EYAL BE STAYING
Eyal Berkovic reiterates his intention to remain with City for the rest of his European career.

Kevin Keegan says he's pleased with City's run of 10 wins in the last 15 league games but that it's what the side produces from now on that really matters. Richard Dunne admits that City were not good enough for the Premiership last year. Tremendous insight.

11 January
WIEKENS BACK
Gerard Wiekens is fit and returns to the squad for the game against Norwich.

13 January
CITY 3 NORWICH CITY 1
BLUES EXACT REVENGE FOR EARLY SEASON DEFEAT
It's another three points for City with two goals from Eyal Berkovic and a Paulo Wanchope strike seeing off Norwich. Berkovic's second is a brilliant individual effort but the headlines are grabbed by Danny Tiatto, who gets involved in some argy-bargy with the Norwich bench after being sent off.

"I would go as far as saying that it was one of the best, if not *the* best, performances I have had since I became a manager," says a delighted Kevin Keegan online. On the Tiatto incident he comments, "It was harsh, but Danny did raise his hands. What Danny did afterwards I cannot condone."

WHAT THE PAPERS SAY
THE DAILY TELEGRAPH
'Manchester City resolutely overcame the early dismissal of fiery midfielder Danny Tiatto to secure a resounding victory over promotion rivals Norwich in a fiercely-contested encounter which they dominated to prise open a three-point gap at the top of the First Division.'

THE SUN
'Danny Tiatto had to be wrestled down the tunnel by Kevin Keegan after being sent off yesterday. Manchester City's fiery Aussie was red-carded for elbowing Steen Nedergaard after only 11 minutes of his side's 3-1 Maine Road win over Norwich. City boss Keegan said: "He just lost it. That is the second time he has been sent off this season and he has had eight yellow cards. I'm going to have to sit down and have a chat with him."'

THE DAILY MAIL
'Manchester City manager Kevin Keegan tonight urged midfielder Danny Tiatto to change his ways. The Australian midfielder was sent off after 11 minutes at Maine Road following a touchline clash with Danish full-back Steen Nedergaard. Tiatto now faces a three-match suspension after being dismissed by referee Roy Pearson, who was alerted to the incident by fourth official Michael Ryan. City went on to win 3-1 despite being down to 10 men, to increase their lead at the top of the First Division to three points. Speaking about the incident, Keegan said: "I think the referee just about got it right. I don't think the player should take up boxing as he wouldn't last many rounds."'

14 January
DANNY GOING NOWHERE
Kevin Keegan says he will talk with Danny Tiatto about his behaviour following his sending-off against Norwich but there is no question of him leaving the club.

The postponed away game at Crewe is rescheduled for March 12th.

15 January
THE GENERALS AND THE HORSES
Kevin Keegan singles out Kevin Horlock for praise after the Norwich game,

with a remarkable comment. "I said to Kevin Horlock that he had a great game against Norwich but no one will talk about him. As I said to Kevin, we can't all be generals. Someone has to stand on the pavement and wave as the generals go by on their horses and if there is no one there the generals wouldn't go by on their horses!" Many fans are left speechless at his erudition.

FC Copenhagen left back Niclas Jensen is at Maine Road with a view to moving to City. The two clubs have already agreed a fee for the 27-year-old.

City's FA Cup clash with Ipswich will take place on Sunday 27 January at 7.00pm. Very handy for any travelling fans.

16 January
HAALAND AND HOWEY OUT FOR THE SEASON
Steve Howey is in plaster after injuring his foot against Norwich and Alfie Haaland's knee is still not right. Both players will most likely miss the rest of the season. Niclas Jensen signs for a fee that could reach £700,000. "I'm really pleased," he says. "City are a completely different level of professional club, with huge ambition. Of course they can't promise promotion, but everything looks like the club is geared up for it," he adds.

17 January
TIATTO WILL APOLOGISE
Danny Tiatto is to write a letter of apology to Norwich manager Nigel Worthington after he kicked over water bottles in the opposition dugout following his sending off at the weekend.

"What happened made it difficult for us to defend Danny," says Kevin Keegan.

Meanwhile, Keegan reveals that City have written to the Football League expressing concern at the number of games that City have had to reschedule for the TV cameras. Nine games have already been moved.

18 January
HALF YEAR FIGURES SHOW TURNOVER IS DOWN
The club's half year figures show a 17% fall in turnover to £12.4 million with an operating loss of £2 million. But Chairman David Bernstein re-emphasises the club's commitment to a swift return to the Premiership. "We

need Premiership football for the new stadium so we are going to go flat out to get promotion and to improve the quality of the squad, even though there is a risk involved in doing that," he says.

19 January
PEARCE HINTS THAT HE MIGHT STAY
City's skipper suggests that he would be interested in a non-playing role at Maine Road when his one year deal comes to an end at the end of the season.

20 January
WATFORD 1 CITY 2
CITY BEAT THE RAIN TO OUTWIT HORNETS
A Paulo Wanchope strike and a bizarre own goal from Helguson, where he skilfully guides the ball past his own keeper, hand City all three points in the rain at Vicarage Road.

"We played really well in the first half and we should have built on that but we didn't," says Kevin Keegan on the City website. "We created numerous chances, but we failed to step it up in the second half. Sometimes you need a slice of luck and tonight we got it."

WHAT THE PAPERS SAY
THE TIMES
'Manchester City have outscored every other team in the four divisions this season so they should not really need any help from the opposition but they got it all the same at Vicarage Road last night as the softest of own goals decided this match. Heidar Helguson, the Iceland forward who had come on as a substitute early in the match, had helped to create the goal that had given Watford the lead against the run of play but he left Alec Chamberlain, the Watford goalkeeper, stranded with a misdirected back-pass ten minutes from time, increasing City's goals total to 68 in 29 league matches and their lead at the top of the Nationwide League first division to three points.'

THE DAILY TELEGRAPH
'Watford manager Gianluca Vialli had bemoaned in the build-up to this game that it was near impossible to find Division One players who had quality and spirit. Yet those two characteristics were much in evidence last

night in a pulsating match which was eventually decided in City's favour by an appalling own goal from Heidar Helguson. City began the game with top spot already theirs and a run of form – eight wins in their last 10 League games – that suggests they will take some dislodging.'

THE DAILY MAIL
'Manchester City enjoyed the stroke of good fortune which seems to attach itself to promotion-chasing sides when they were gifted a 2-1 win by Watford at Vicarage Road. Kevin Keegan's side had mustered only one second-half goal attempt but found themselves in the lead after 79 minutes when Icelander Heidar Helguson, attempting to turn the ball back to Alec Chamberlain, instead poked it wide of his goalkeeper and into the corner of his own net. Helguson, a striker having to play in midfield in Gianluca Vialli's injury-hit side, was in strange territory – but Watford appeared to be in no danger when he cut out Ali Benarbia's pass. City should have wrapped the points up in the first 20 minutes, the only stage in the game when they showed their pedigree. Chamberlain did well to stop shots from Danny Tiatto and Kevin Horlock.'

21 January
KEEGAN STILL NOT SATISFIED
Despite 12 wins in the last 16 league games Kevin Keegan believes that City can still improve. The club move three points clear at the top of the table after the win at Watford, but Keegan says: "I think this side can get better."

City have also scored an astonishing 106 goals in 29 matches.

22 January
JENSEN ON KEEGAN
New boy Niclas Jensen reveals that he signed for City mainly due to the Keegan factor. "Kevin was a big part of the appeal. After first meeting him, I had to pinch myself because I couldn't believe I was sitting in the car with him," he says.

Keegan says that Darren Huckerby will start next Sunday's FA Cup tie at Ipswich as Paulo Wanchope is away on Gold Cup international duty with Costa Rica.

City will set up an East Anglian training camp for three days to get the team prepared for the game.

LAKEY'S VIEW

"I must confess I was unsure about Niclas Jensen. I thought we'd had similar players in the past in the same position who looked as steady as he did but who were just that, steady. After five or six games, though, he was bringing the ball out better, being more positive, using the ball well and getting back well. He also had that awareness. He seemed to have a bit more class on the ball and was able to make time on the ball, whereas your Ritchies, for me, don't quite have that same ability. It took Niclas quite a few games to find his feet, which is why there were question marks, but he just got better and better and better. And I think what's helped him has been the World Cup, giving him the kind of experience that you just don't get that often. Yes, he made a costly mistake against England but he will learn from it. Some players have had a nightmare on the major stage and have gone into freefall but I certainly don't think Niclas will be one of them."

23 January
ETUHU MOVES TO PRESTON

The long-running saga of Dickson Etuhu ends with the player being transferred to Preston North End for a fee which could rise to £1million. "I wouldn't exactly say we sold him. I think Dickson just about sold himself in the end," says Kevin Keegan, while insisting there are no hard feelings between himself and the player.

Alfie Haaland is to visit a specialist in the States for yet more treatment on his knee but reveals that he still harbours hopes of being fit for the end of the season even though his manager has ruled him out.

24 January
CITY WANT TO SIGN CHINESE DEFENDER

Former Crystal Palace defender Sun Jihai will come to have a look at City in the next week with a view to signing for the club if he is impressed by the set-up. Kevin Keegan says the player is good enough to play for City in the Premiership.

Keegan also says that City should not be scared of Premiership opposition when they meet Ipswich in the FA Cup. Jeff Whitley returns after his broken ankle for the reserves against Leeds in a game which is lost 5-3.

26 January
HOWEY COULD RETURN AFTER ALL

Steve Howey's injury against Norwich now appears nowhere near as bad as previously thought and boss Kevin Keegan says he could be back within two weeks.

28 January
IPSWICH 1 CITY 4
BRILLIANT BLUES ANNIHILATE IPSWICH

An incredible performance from City sees the First Division outfit humiliate their Premiership opponents with a first class display that is witnessed live on the BBC. Two goals from Shaun Goater, an amazing Eyal Berkovic volley from the edge of the penalty area and a last-minute clincher from Darren Huckerby see City through to the FA Cup fifth round. "The fans are starting to believe in us and they are starting to get behind us even more than they usually do," says Kevin Keegan.

WHAT THE PAPERS SAY
THE DAILY MIRROR

'Kevin Keegan was left licking his lips last night after his Manchester City side beat Ipswich 4-1 to set up an emotional FA Cup return to his old club Newcastle. And the former England boss, who took the Toon Army from the Second Division to the brink of the Premiership title before quitting in 1997, revealed he had a premonition on Saturday night that he would draw Newcastle in the fifth round. Now he comes up against another ex-England boss, Bobby Robson. And Keegan said: "I'll love it. I'm not sure if it's a good draw or not, to be honest. I love Newcastle and I am getting to love Manchester City as well."'

THE DAILY MAIL

'Kevin Keegan won the perfect FA Cup fifth-round prize after Manchester City's 4-1 thrashing of Ipswich yesterday – a dream return to Newcastle, where he was idolised both as player and manager. They could sell out St James' Park three times over for the return of their favourite son, who is still fondly remembered for taking Newcastle 12 points clear at the top of the Premiership at the height of the club's resurgence in the mid-Nineties.'

THE SUN

'Kevin Keegan will take his Manchester City side on an emotional return to Newcastle in the FA Cup fifth round. But Keegan, who quit the Geordies in January 1997 after five years in charge, declared: "I don't know if it's the right time to go back to Newcastle, either football-wise or emotionally."'

THE DAILY TELEGRAPH

'The Manchester flag will be carried onwards in the FA Cup not by United but by their less fashionable neighbours City, who reduced further the number of Premiership clubs in last night's fifth-round draw. Since only four places separate City from Ipswich in football's pyramid, this was not a giantkilling in the pure sense as much as another bloodying of a Premiership nose. Kevin Keegan had suggested pre-match that this was City's chance to show they were Premiership material, despite being relegated last season – coincidentally confirmation coming in their penultimate League fixture at Portman Road. It would also, he hoped, underline that, contrary to popular perceptions, there was not a huge gulf between the top of the First Division and the lower reaches of the Premiership.'

29 January
BOSS EXCITED BY RETURN TO NEWCASTLE

City's fifth round FA Cup draw away to Newcastle sets the papers talking about an emotional return for the club's former manager Kevin Keegan. "Win, lose or draw I will enjoy the day and if we lose I will say to Bobby Robson that I hope he wins the Cup," says Keegan.

A potential move for forgotten French defender Laurent Charvet to Marseilles falls through.

Alfie Haaland returns from the States where specialists have been looking at his troublesome knee.

City could go eight points clear of third-placed Millwall if they beat the Lions at Maine Road on Wednesday night. The only selection issue is whether Nicky Weaver will retain the goalkeeping spot he won back from Carlo Nash for the cup tie at Ipswich.

31 January

CITY 2 MILLWALL 0

CITY DO THE DOUBLE OVER MILLWALL

Two late goals from Shaun Goater see 10-man City home after Ali Benarbia is sent off in the seventh minute for a raised elbow.

"It was unbelievable," says a delighted Kevin Keegan online. "I am very proud of the players, they worked very hard for each other in a team which has a lot of spirit."

City are now seven points clear of third-placed West Brom with a game in hand. Meanwhile City's reserves reach the final of the Manchester Senior Cup after beating Manchester United on penalties.

WHAT THE PAPERS SAY

THE DAILY MIRROR

'Shaun Goater sent City six points clear at the top and spared Stuart Pearce's blushes as ten-man City scrambled past battling Millwall. Goater struck his 27th goal of the season 12 minutes from time, just when it looked as though Kevin Keegan's men were going to rue Pearce's missed first-half penalty. The ace marksman settled matters with a trademark poacher's goal when he followed up after Shaun Wright-Phillips' shot had come back of the post.'

THE DAILY MAIL

'Shaun Goater grabbed the two late goals that sent Manchester City's 10 men soaring six points clear of the First Division pack on another remarkable night for Kevin Keegan's promotion challenge at Maine Road. Although it was a truly magnificent achievement against their in-form rivals, City's win seemed somehow to be written in the script even after playmaker Ali Benarbia was sent off with just seven minutes gone. No wonder Millwall manager Mark McGhee called them "awesome".'

THE DAILY TELEGRAPH

'Two late goals from Shaun Goater that took his total for the season to an impressive 28 ended a Maine Road night of frustration for Manchester City, who splendidly overcame their seventh dismissal, plus a Stuart Pearce missed penalty, to move six points clear at the head of the division. Ali Benarbia, the Algerian playmaker, received his second red card of the season after only seven minutes. This left City to battle for victory with 10 men for the second successive home game, Danny Tiatto having been sent off in the 3-1 win over Norwich earlier this month.'

FEBRUARY 2002
1 February
BOSS NAMED MANAGER OF THE MONTH

Kevin Keegan is named Nationwide League manager of the month for January after six straight wins and 16 goals scored by his side. The away game at Stockport County is moved to make way for City's FA Cup tie at Newcastle. The game will now take place on Tuesday 19th March.

City put on 20 free coaches for fans for the trip to Newcastle. "We are aware how inconvenienced our fans have been by the frequent changes in match dates and times as a result of the demands of television," says Chairman David Bernstein. "In spite of the difficulties our supporters have continued to be a credit to our club, both in their home and travelling support. The free travel offer to St James' Park is recognition by the Club of that steadfast support and will help our fans in their journey to what I'm sure will be a scintillating cup tie."

Kevin Keegan expresses sympathy for Ali Benarbia, who will miss the glamour game at Newcastle after being sent off for raising an elbow against Millwall. The manager does not, however, condone the player's actions.

3 February
WIMBLEDON 2 CITY 1
CITY GO DOWN AT THE DONS

Stuart Pearce becomes City's eighth player to be red-carded this season. He is dismissed a minute from time after a shocking City performance sees the Blues go down by two goals to one, Ali Benarbia the scorer.

"I just don't think any of the players were at it," says a disappointed Kevin Keegan at *www.mcfc.co.uk*. "We got what we deserved and if we keep playing like that for the rest of the season we will stay in the First Division."

On this same day Paulo Wanchope is on the losing side in the Gold Cup final in the States as Costa Rica lose to the host nation 2-0.

133

THE DAILY MAIL

'Manchester City's promotion charge suffered a hiccup at Selhurst Park as two goals from Wimbledon's Neil Shipperley inflicted a 2-1 defeat on the Nationwide Division One leaders. Wimbledon, currently besieged with internal politics over their proposed move to Milton Keynes, turned on the style to complete a 6-1 aggregate double over City. Visiting boss Kevin Keegan will however be kicking himself after watching his side waste an opportunity to move six points clear at the top of the table. Keegan's cavalier football failed to materialise as a below-par playing surface combined with some resolute Dons defending to frustrate free-scoring City. City dominated the opening 45 minutes, enjoying a lion's share of possession, but after an early miss by the prolific Shaun Goater the visitors struggled to reproduce the form that had seen them overwhelm Premiership Ipswich 4-1 in the FA Cup last week.'

THE DAILY TELEGRAPH

'During 14 seasons in the top flight Wimbledon had a knack of humbling the biggest teams in the land; old habits die hard, and though they are now in the Nationwide League they still like to upset the best. Manchester City are the best the First Division have to offer. Though they arrived at Selhurst Park intent on exorcising a humiliating 4-0 defeat in the autumn, the only stain on their home record; they departed with tails firmly between legs. Wimbledon thus became the first team to complete the double over City this season; they will probably be the only team, as well. It was a day for doubles. Neil Shipperley scored both Wimbledon goals – he had scored two of the four in September – and both came from Neil Ardley free-kicks. Coincidentally, City's last defeat in any competition came on this ground, nearly two months ago, against Crystal Palace.'

LAKEY'S VIEW

"There's always a part of the season where a club will have a blip. I think every side in the course of a campaign will have one game where four or five of the top players just aren't firing and I think this was City's. Selhurst Park isn't the nicest place to go but it's a good experience because you should really be able to go to places like that and show your mettle. In games like this, quality alone isn't enough. All that skill has to have a constant undercurrent of effort and commitment. As a player Kevin Keegan had all those qualities and he rightly expects all of his teams to have it too."

5 February
HOWEY BACK
Steve Howey is back in training after the foot injury sustained against Norwich in January. Eyal Berkovic, Richard Dunne, Kevin Horlock and Niclas Jensen are all expected to be missing on international duty for the FA Cup game at Newcastle.

Danny Tiatto returns to action after his three game suspension in a reserve match against Everton, which the team loses 3-1.

6 February
PLAYERS ON TRIAL
City are taking a look at Bjorn Helge Riise, brother of the Liverpool defender John Arne, as well as two brothers from Halifax Town, Chris and Matt Clarke. Sun Jihai misses an internal flight in China and will arrive later in the week.

7 February
KEVIN WANTS STUART TO STAY
Kevin Keegan announces that he would like Stuart Pearce to stay at City after his contract expires at the end of the season.

LAKEY'S VIEW
"All good clubs have characters who can not only transmit their enthusiasm to everyone else about the place but who are out and out winners, both on and off the pitch. Stuart Pearce is a guy who's reliable, who you know you can trust and who won't accept second best. So the idea of wanting him to stick around even though his playing days would be over made perfect sense to me."

8 February
"WE NEED TO BOUNCE BACK"
Kevin Keegan is keen to banish the memory of a very poor display at Wimbledon with a rousing performance against Preston on Sunday. "We need to bounce back. Wimbledon was not good enough by our standards," he says.

10 February
CITY 3 PRESTON 2

Shaun Wright-Phillips, Steve Howey and Paulo Wanchope score the goals that earn City another vital three points but Eyal Berkovic limps off with a hamstring injury.

"This was a very good game of football," says Kevin Keegan on the City website. "This was a credit to the Division. I felt we deserved to win the match. When there was a battle to be won, we won it."

11 February
WRIGHT-PHILLIPS FOR ENGLAND?

Kevin Keegan says he can't understand how Shaun Wright-Phillips hasn't made the England Under-21 squad alongside keeper Nicky Weaver. "There must be some really good players in this country if Shaun is not in the squad," he says.

City's reserves draw 2-2 away at Liverpool with two goals from Chris Shuker.

13 February
HORLOCK INJURY SCARE

Kevin Horlock is doubtful for the FA Cup game away at Newcastle after pulling a stomach muscle in training with Northern Ireland for the midweek game against Poland in Cyprus.

14 February
FIT FOR NEWCASTLE

City leave for Scotland to prepare for their Cup match against Newcastle and Kevin Keegan and admits he is saddened that Ali Benarbia and Stuart Pearce will miss out due to suspension. Richard Dunne and Niclas Jensen both return unscathed from international duty.

15 February
KEEGAN TALKS OF CUP UPSET

Kevin Keegan expresses his belief that City could go all the way to the final if they can beat Newcastle in this weekend's FA Cup fifth round tie. "If we can beat Newcastle, having beaten Ipswich, then I think we are a team which can go all the way." He also tries to dismiss talk of his time on

Tyneside. "The only real book which I am interested in writing now is about Manchester City. Whilst I will talk to people about the past, that is exactly what it is, the past."

Leon Mike leaves City for Aberdeen.

16 February
WOLVES DRAW LEVEL
Wolves beat Bradford City 3-1 to draw level on points with City at the top of the First Division.

17 February
NEWCASTLE UNITED 1 CITY 0
BATTLING CITY SO UNLUCKY
An inspired City performance wins over all the neutrals as they bravely go down one-nil at Newcastle. Richard Dunne is sent off for a professional foul in the 28th minute – *another* red card – but 10 man City give the home side a real run for their money. Boss Kevin Keegan is given a hero's welcome on his return to Newcastle.

"I am disappointed to lose," say Keegan. "We created four very good chances and three of those were when we had ten men on the field. I hope Newcastle go on and win it now."

WHAT THE PAPERS SAY
THE DAILY MIRROR
'Kevin Keegan may still be a hero on Tyneside but he came perilously close to ruining his popularity at St James' Park last night. His Manchester City team very nearly shocked the Geordie nation with the bravest of displays when down to 10 men. The First Division leaders came within a whisker of conjuring a draw, or even a win, when defeat should have been a certainty. Even Newcastle manager Bobby Robson admitted his side were lucky to scrape through to a quarter-final tie against FA Cup favourites Arsenal.'

THE DAILY MAIL
'Kevin Keegan's FA Cup hopes were shattered by his old club last night but he could still wish Newcastle boss Bobby Robson well for the tough quarter-final draw at home to favourites Arsenal. Keegan's ten-man Manchester City were unlucky to lose 1-0 at St James' Park as Robson marked his 69th

birthday with a victory that earned the tie of the round on Super Sunday. All four quarter-finals will be played on March 10 – Mother's Day – and Keegan hopes Newcastle can go all the way.'

THE SUN
'Kevin Keegan's Toon Army homecoming ended in heartbreaking defeat at St James' Park last night. Nolberto Solano's 59th-minute winner ruined former Newcastle chief Keegan's dream of an FA Cup fifth-round upset. And afterwards Keegan insisted he hoped Bobby Robson's side would go on to lift the trophy after they were drawn at home to Arsenal in the quarter-finals.'

THE DAILY TELEGRAPH
'Ten years to the month since he first brought such excitement as a manager to St James' Park, Kevin Keegan yesterday returned and once again set the pulses racing. This time, though, Keegan had the nerves jangling among those Newcastle United supporters who still cherish his name. Despite losing Richard Dunne to a professional foul and then a goal to Nolberto Solano, Keegan's City scared the black-and-white life out of Newcastle. Shaun Wright-Phillips was marvellous, Eyal Berkovic and Kevin Horlock not far behind with outstanding displays as City played with spirit and skill before bowing out of the FA Cup.

LAKEY'S VIEW
"This was one game where I watched the performance and thought it really did show that we were able to compete in the top flight. We really didn't look like conceding in the game and unfortunately it was an individual error from Nicky Weaver that cost us the game. But that performance in front of the TV cameras made people sit up and think that we were not a bad side, even though we didn't have anything like the stars in the team that we have now."

18 February
KEEGAN SALUTES FANS
Kevin Keegan acknowledges the fantastic support of the 6,000 fans who travelled to Tyneside to witness a desperately unlucky City go out of the FA Cup. "The one thing that was not in doubt in St. James' Park is that we had the country's two best sets of supporters in one stadium," he says.

19 February
PEARCE BACK FOR WALSALL
Stuart Pearce is back in contention for the visit to Walsall after being handed just a single match ban for his sending off against Wimbledon.

Title contenders Wolves play midweek and Kevin Keegan says he fully expects them to pick up three points away at Crewe.

Lucien Mettomo is back at Maine Road following Cameroon's victory at the African Nations Cup in Mali. He features in a 3-2 reserves win over Sunderland.

20 February
DEAL FOR RIISE FALTERS
Negotiations with Norwegian club Aalesund break down and a move for Bjorn Helge Riise will not happen.

Keegan also reveals that a potential trial for Nigerian Justice Christopher is also on ice after the player's club, Royal Antwerp, decide against releasing him.

Chris Killen signs a one-year deal with City, though Kevin Keegan says he could see the striker making a name for himself as a central defender, a back-handed compliment if ever one was made.

22 February
DICKOV DEPARTS
City's talismanic striker Paul Dickov, who scored the dramatic equaliser against Gillingham in the Division Two Playoff Final, is to leave the club after five years to join Premiership strugglers Leicester City. The player will move for a nominal fee as he will be out of contract at the end of the season. Dickov made 180 appearances and scored 41 goals but only wore the shirt eight times under Kevin Keegan.

It appears that Paulo Wanchope will miss the visit to Walsall because of a knee injury.

23 February
SPECIAL HONOUR FOR DICKY
Kevin Keegan says that Paul Dickov will be introduced to the crowd before City's next home game against Sheffield Wednesday as a thank you for his years of service to City.

"He has been a credit to the club," says Keegan.

23 February
WALSALL 0 CITY 0
CITY TOUGH IT OUT TO TAKE A POINT
City take a well-deserved point in a goalless draw at the Bescot Stadium.

"I thought it was a very good game of football but a disappointing result for us," says Kevin Keegan online.

WHAT THE PAPERS SAY
THE DAILY MIRROR
'Relegation-threatened Walsall did themselves and neighbours Wolves a big favour by holding second-placed Manchester City. And Saddlers boss Colin Lee, whose side face leaders Wolves on Tuesday, joked: "I'm sure my old club will return the compliment when we meet next." City have only failed to score in a handful of league games this season but Walsall did a good job in preventing them from adding to their 74-goal haul. Nobody more so than defensive rock Tony Barras and keeper James Walker, who denied City with a breathtaking save in the dying minutes from Kevin Horlock. Lee added: "If we play like that, we'll give Wolves a game."

THE SUNDAY PEOPLE
'Kevin Keegan hates coming second – but even he's starting to fancy Wolves for the First Division title. City's tense draw with relegation dogfighters Walsall leaves them five points adrift from the top. And Keegan admits: "We are nowhere near the Premiership. It's starting to look good for Wolves, so now we've just got to make sure of second place. Their fixtures are falling into place, while we've got nine games in 27 days with five out of six away in one spell. We've got two games in hand, but they are only any good if you win them. This might turn out to be a big point at the end of the season. It's a hard place to come to, and while we wanted to win, a point will have to do."'

THE MAIL ON SUNDAY
'Kevin Keegan was left in a strop over complimentary tickets after his high-flyers drew a blank at homely Walsall. **The former England manager – used to the grand stage – made it clear he was angry that none of his players had**

been granted freebies for friends and family, for a fixture played in front of a crowd of less than 8,000 at a cramped Bescot. "I can't understand it," he said after his long-time leaders slipped five points behind Wolves at the top of the table. "Last week we played at Newcastle. At least you get complimentary tickets there." But Keegan's comments earned a rebuke from Walsall's chief executive Roy Whalley. He said: "That's always been our policy. Other clubs know that in advance and should respect it. We don't ask for complimentaries from other teams."

26 February
MORE DISCIPLINARY TROUBLE

The Daily Mirror reports that stars Nicky Weaver, Richard Dunne and Jeff Whitley have all been fined the maximum two weeks' wages after a drinking incident involving an altercation with bouncers at a club in Liverpool. It is rumoured that Dunne and Weaver only kept their places in the side that draw with Walsall after senior pros pleaded with manager Kevin Keegan on their behalf. Keegan says: "If one of them steps out of line again they are finished and they know that. I have told them that." Paulo Wanchope is again out injured for the midweek home game against Sheffield Wednesday. West Brom miss a chance to oust City from second spot in the First Division table, losing 1-0 away to Preston. The scorer of the only goal of the game? Dickson Etuhu.

27 February
CITY 4 SHEFFIELD WEDNESDAY 0
CITY ROUT WEDNESDAY – FOR THE SECOND TIME

An easy win for City as goals from Horlock, Huckerby, Berkovic and Goater seal the points. The game is particularly special for Paul Dickov, who has an emotional farewell as he leads the teams out for the game. He is presented with a replica of the shirt he wore in the Division Two Playoff Final signed by all of the current squad.

"It was unbelievable," says 'Dicky'. "I was shaking like a leaf. I've never seen anything like that or been so nervous before. I only found out ten minutes before the game that I was going to take the sides out and I couldn't believe the reception that I got. People say that City fans are the best in the country but to me they are the best in the world and I hope they get rewarded with promotion."

Chairman David Bernstein also pays tribute to the striker, saying, "Paul has been a top class professional. He is a credit to the game, a credit to himself and we wish him well with his new career at Leicester. He has done very well for us and will always be remembered with great affection for that tremendous strike against Gillingham, which I feel was probably the turning point for this club."

"It was a good result," says Kevin Keegan of the game at *www.mcfc.co.uk*. "It was 4-0 at home without too many players hitting top form."

Meanwhile the deal to bring Chinese international defender Sun Jihai is completed. The player should be at Maine Road within the next few days.

28 February
PLAYERS MISSING

Richard Dunne will start a three-match ban for his dismissal in the FA Cup defeat at Newcastle and Shaun Wright-Phillips will most likely also be missing for the home game against Coventry after gashing his leg against Sheffield Wednesday. Ali Benarbia will return after suspension.

MARCH 2002
1 March
JUSTICE FOR CITY

Royal Antwerp's Nigerian midfielder Justice Christopher impresses boss Kevin Keegan during a week's training with City. The manager muses that he might be a suitable replacement for Dickson Etuhu. The reserves beat Sheffield Wednesday 2-1 with goals from Chris Killen and Chris Shuker.

Paulo Wanchope's troublesome knee rules him out of the Sunday home match against Coventry.

New signing Sun Jihai goes straight into the squad.

3 March
CITY 4 COVENTRY CITY 2
BLUES EXACT REVENGE FOR EARLIER DEFEAT

Goals from Darren Huckerby and Danny Tiatto set up a City victory but it's Shaun Wright-Phillips who again impresses with two goals, the second an audacious chip. This despite playing with five stitches in his knee due to a gash which he picked up in the midweek win against Sheffield Wednesday.

"Shaun Wright-Phillips will play for England," says Kevin Keegan at the club's website. "It might be a year or two but he will play for England because he has got everything."

Eyal Berkovic injures his ankle and is doubtful for the midweek game against Birmingham.

4 March
MACKEN MOVE SWIFTLY SEALED

Kevin Keegan admits to having watched Preston striker Jon Macken in action against West Bromwich and Birmingham. Later in the day it emerges that the two clubs have agreed a fee of £4 million for the 24-year-old former Manchester United man and the player signs after passing a medical and agreeing personal terms. The fee could rise to £5 million and means Macken is the club's biggest-ever signing. He will travel with his new team mates to the match against Birmingham City.

LAKEY'S VIEW

"I think Jon Macken's an inventive player with good movement and I think his low centre of gravity bodes well for his future, even at the very highest level. You can see he's got good feet, sharpness in his turning and good awareness. And while life is more difficult for him now given the calibre of some of the players who have arrived after him, I think he's got to show faith in the club because they've shown faith in him. One or two clubs were talked about being interested in a possible move for him when he was at Preston but there wasn't a club the size of City being touted. Jon will be thinking he's got a real chance to develop his skills at City and I have confidence in his abilities."

5 March
KEEGAN ON MACKEN

Kevin Keegan talks of his excitement at the signing of Jon Macken. "His biggest strength, apart from scoring goals, is his ability to hold the ball up and see things very quickly," he explains. "The test for him, and all the players, is if he can reproduce that in the Premiership and I think he can."

6 March

BIRMINGHAM CITY 1 CITY 2

CITY COMPLETE DOUBLE OVER BIRMINGHAM

Kevin Horlock notches City's 100th goal of the season as Birmingham are again despatched. Niclas Jensen scores his first for the club.

"It's no mean feat to score a hundred goals in a season," says Kevin Keegan on the club website. "We've missed a lot of chances along the way but I suppose you shouldn't get greedy." He also stresses that new signing Jon Macken, who watched the win from the bench, will not be guaranteed a place in the City starting line-up.

Birmingham keeper Ian Bennet says of City. "You know the style of play — stopping it is the problem. I can't remember a busier night, that's for sure." Wolves draw 2-2 with Nottingham Forest, so a win at Bradford on Friday night will see City return to the top of the division.

City announce that they will be freezing season ticket prices for supporters from the last season at Maine Road to the first at the new City Of Manchester stadium. "We feel that a price freeze is some acknowledgement of how much we appreciate our fans," says Chairman David Bernstein. "They have been incredibly loyal through difficult times and hopefully they will be able to enjoy top class football in facilities that will be second to none."

7 March

EYAL BACK FOR BRADFORD?

Kevin Keegan says it looks likely Eyal Berkovic will shake off the ankle injury he picked up against Coventry and return to the City midfield at Bradford on Friday night. He also says he expects to bring in another keeper as cover now that Nicky Weaver's season is over due to injury but refutes claims that they are to pay £2.5 million for Fulham keeper Maik Taylor.

City's players pledge £2,500 to local club Bury, who are in financial trouble. The reserves beat Oldham in a penalty shoot-out in the Manchester Senior Cup.

10 March

WOLVES BACK ON TOP

Wolves go back to the top of the First Division after a 2-2 draw with

Birmingham City. But Manchester City are now just one point behind with two games in hand. "They have to win them," says Wolves boss Dave Jones.

8 March
BRADFORD CITY 0 CITY 2
CITY SHOW CHARACTER TO PICKUP THREE MORE AWAY POINTS

New signing Jon Macken comes off the bench for the last 10 minutes of City's win at Bradford and first hits the bar, then scores. "I don't know what took him so long," says Kevin Keegan.

Darren Huckerby notches City's other strike.

"We could have been talking about a four- or five-nil win on the chances we created," says Kevin Keegan on the club's website. "If we're going to go on to the Premiership the quality of the sides are going to be better and we will not have it all our own way, so we are going to have to have plenty of character."

11 March
BERKOVIC AND HOWEY MAY NOT MAKE CREWE GAME

Eyal Berkovic and Steve Howey may be fit for the Tuesday visit to Crewe, but boss Kevin Keegan may not risk them even if they are, given that there are a number of important games still to be played.

12 March
CREWE ALEXANDRA 1 CITY 3
CITY GO TOP AFTER EXHILARATING WIN

City go two points clear of Wolves after a good win at Gresty Road.

Darren Huckerby scores again, Ali Benarbia pitches in with a wonder goal and Shaun Goater finally notches his 30th of the season.

"Two more wins and a draw should do it," says Kevin Keegan on the City website. "I think we have played better, but the result was excellent."

"What can I say about our supporters that hasn't been said before? Says Goater. "It was almost a spiritual feeling."

Meanwhile, Cameroon keeper Boukar Alioum is due to arrive at City from Turkish side Samsunspor for a trial.

13 March

RESERVES TAKE A POINT

The reserves draw 1-1 away at Middlesbrough with a goal from French striker Alioune Touré. Kevin Keegan confirms that City will not be signing Boukar Alioum.

14 March

EYAL STILL OUT

Eyal Berkovic will miss his fourth consecutive game for City when Crystal Palace visit Maine Road on Saturday. He is still troubled by the ankle injury picked up in the last home game against Coventry.

15 March

PLAYERS TO LEAVE

Kevin Keegan confirms that Richard Edghill, Andy Morrison and Terry Cooke will leave the club at the end of the season but hints that the door might still be open for Bjorn Helge Riise, a trialist in February, to hook up with the club, possibly in October. He could be one for the future, says the boss.

He also confirms that keeper Simon Royce has been signed on loan from Leicester as cover until the end of the season. He will be on the bench for the Crystal Palace game.

LAKEY'S VIEW

"Something else I like about Kevin Keegan is that he's not one of those guys who will keep players hanging on wondering whether they have a future at the club or not. He realises players have all got their own careers to get on with and their own lives to lead and they still have a chance of playing football somewhere else. That's where the honesty comes out. He'll say "I think you're a good player, you're a good lad and I'm sorry to see you go but I don't think you're quite up to it for us." He was very fair with these three players. He paid up Terry Cooke, he sorted Edgy out and he was decisive but decent in the way he did things."

16 March
CITY 1 CRYSTAL PALACE 0
HORLOCK AGAIN GRABS THE POINTS
A defeat for Wolves at Grimsby leaves City clear at the top of the First Division after an uninspiring but important win against Crystal Palace. Kevin Horlock again scores a vital goal.

"I don't think anyone has been better than him over the last three months," says Kevin Keegan. "It was an excellent three points."

A strained ligament could rule Danny Tiatto out of the game with Stockport County on Tuesday. The player starts a two match ban against Nottingham Forest at the end of the month.

18 March
BOSS TO BUY BIG
Steve Howey claims that manager Kevin Keegan will definitely buy big before the start of the next season. "I will be surprised if the manager doesn't buy any more players," he says.

19 March
STOCKPORT COUNTY 2 CITY 1
BLUES FAIL TO BREAK THE STOCKPORT HOODOO
City slump to defeat at Edgeley Park with one of their worst performances of the season after Shaun Goater is red-carded – yet another City dismissal – for handball.

Jon Macken opens the scoring but two Stockport goals in the last five minutes of the game see all three points thrown away.

"I will not make excuses for what happened," says Kevin Keegan on the City website. "Playing with ten men for more than an hour was difficult enough but we've done it before. I don't know what Shaun Goater was thinking of. I've told him that I don't like what happened."

Shaun Wright-Phillips comes off with a dead leg at half-time and is doubtful for the weekend trip to Rotherham.

20 March
SKIPPER HAD DOUBLE VISION
Skipper Stuart Pearce admits he had double vision for the latter stages of

the game at Stockport, which may explain the team's poor performance. The reserves go down 2-0 at Newcastle.

21 March
WHITLEY ON THE MOVE
Midfielder Jeff Whitley looks set to join Notts County on loan until the end of the season.

22 March
WRIGHT-PHILLIPS SET TO RETURN
Shaun Wright-Phillips looks set to make the starting line-up for City against Rotherham on Saturday after shaking off the injury he sustained at Stockport.

Shaun Goater may drop to the bench to accommodate a strike force of Darren Huckerby and Jon Macken.

Goater will only receive a one match ban for his sending off for a handball offence at Stockport.

23 March
ROTHERHAM 1 CITY 1
BLUES DOG IT OUT TO GRASP A POINT
Eyal Berkovic limps out of the Rotherham game after yet again suffering an injury. He may well miss the Easter period.

Kevin Keegan is pleased with the draw, thanks to Ali Benarbia's goal. "The lads showed a lot of character against Rotherham and a little bit more desire to hang in there than they did against Stockport," he says online. "It is a point gained." A Wolves draw also softens the blow.

LAKEY'S VIEW
"An important result for me. Not a win and not even a particularly great display, but a battling performance that really showed the heart that's within the team. For all the flair that we showed throughout the season, all the big game players and magical moments, we were still able to go away to Rotherham and grind out a point. In many ways that was just as important to show that we had that mentality when it was required. It hadn't been there early on in the season, so to see the progress that had been made was fantastic."

24 March

ENGLAND CALL UP FOR WRIGHT-PHILLIPS

Shaun Wright-Phillips earns a well-deserved call-up to the England Under-21 squad for their friendly against Italy.

25 March

RESERVES HIT LIVERPOOL FOR SIX

City's reserves turn in an outstanding performance as they crush Liverpool six nil. Four goals from Chris Killen and strikes from Joey Barton and Terry Dunfield make up the score.

26 March

NO COMMENT ON STAM MOVE

City refuse to comment on press speculation linking Lazio defender Jaap Stam with a move to Maine Road but it's rumoured that an enquiry was indeed made. Shaun Wright-Phillips makes his debut for the England Under-21 side against Italy.

27 March

ITV DIGITAL GOES INTO ADMINISTRATION

Troubled broadcaster ITV Digital is placed into administration but all of City's final four league games will still be shown as originally planned.

28 March

WANCHOPE RULED OUT FOR THE SEASON

City's injury-prone striker Paulo Wanchope is ruled out for the rest of the season and will fly to the States to visit a specialist in an attempt to sort out his troublesome knee. The former Derby and West Ham man will head for Colorado on Sunday. "He only started seventeen games for us but has done really well in them," says Kevin Keegan "He has thirteen goals, which is an incredible total for that number of games."

29 March

COOKE'S CONTRACT PAID UP

City pay up winger Terry Cooke's contract and he leaves the club immediately. He signs for Grimsby until the end of the season. Kevin Keegan insists that he will be securing Shaun Wright-Phillips' future with

City as soon as possible. He also asks for no slip-ups in the home fixture against Nottingham Forest.

30 March
CITY 3 NOTTINGHAM FOREST 0
A Darren Huckerby hat-trick is the highlight of an emphatic City win that sets up a showdown with Wolves at Molineux.

"I signed him when he was a kid and I was at Newcastle," says Kevin Keegan on the City website. "The improvements since I last saw him are unbelievable. He is a much better player now. The three points today were vitally important to us."

APRIL 2002
1 April
WOLVES 0 CITY 2
BLUES IN CONTROL AS PROMOTION RIVALS ARE BEATEN
Leading scorer Shaun Goater is left on the bench for the crucial away game at promotion rivals Wolves but manager Kevin Keegan's decision is proved right as City make April Fools of the home side and stroll to a comfortable 2-0 victory, both goals coming from Shaun Wright-Phillips.

"I don't think there was any doubt for anyone who was here today that we thoroughly deserved to win it," says Kevin Keegan on the City website. "We have come here and done a real professional job." City need just one point from their three remaining fixtures to be assured of promotion back to The Premiership but Keegan says he is looking to win all three games.

LAKEY'S VIEW
"The game where I thought we'd clinched promotion in all but name and a match which was a total testament to Kevin Keegan. The build-up to the fixture was really intense and the Wolves manager Dave Jones was really on full throttle. He was making statements about this and that, trying the old Jedi mind games by saying that on paper City were the best side and that all things being equal then they should win the game – all designed to keep the pressure off his own players and put it onto the City lads. But Kevin Keegan was totally relaxed about the whole affair. If you think about his famous TV outburst when he lost it with Alex Ferguson all those years ago, then you realise how far he's come as a manager. He didn't rise to any of the

Dave Jones bait. He said nothing but kept calm and relaxed. And didn't it show on the pitch? The way we addressed that game, we were never going to get beaten. Wolves came out on fire and really had a go for the first 10 or 15 minutes. But the team was superb; so patient, so relaxed. Our calmness, the quality of the passing we produced and our inventiveness just made Wolves panic and we simply grew in confidence as the game went on. Shaun Wright-Phillips' first goal took a huge deflection and was lucky but Steve Howey had a perfectly good goal disallowed for who knows what reason? And then Shaun's second goal was quality itself. It was a superb performance and one that I'll always remember for that relaxed feel the team showed in a pressure situation. Nobody looked uptight or stressed, just supremely confident. And as it turned out they had every right to be so."

3 April
CITY GET COQ EXTENSION
City announce an extension to their deal with sportswear manufacturers Le Coq Sportif and promise a new away shirt that will reflect the club's history for the final season at Maine Road. The reserves draw 1-1 away at Aston Villa with Chris Killen on target.

Kevin Keegan says he hopes Wolves clinch an automatic promotion slot. City face Millwall on Friday and City could be promoted before kicking a ball against Barnsley on Saturday if the Midlands side lose.

4 April
BIG NAMES LINKED TO CITY
City are linked with big money moves for Bayern Munich's Stefan Effenberg and AC Milan's Edgar Davids.

LAKEY'S VIEW
"A lot of big names were being bandied about as supposedly moving to City and we were all wondering about whether it would be exactly as it always had been in the past. City have always been linked to huge lists of players before the start of a season and we became a bit of a laughing stock over it. When I read names like Effenberg and Davids I was going 'Please, don't do this.' I wanted us to be keeping all the names under our hat until the players were actually on board. We've had so many let-downs in the

past when all these world class names have been mentioned and at the start of the season we've found that we haven't had any real 'wows' to show off. But I have to hold my hands up and say that yet again, Kevin Keegan managed to deliver."

5 April
CITY ARE BACK – WITHOUT KICKING A BALL
Wolves lose at Millwall and City are promoted back to the Premiership.

Chairman David Bernstein urges fans not to invade the pitch at Maine Road.

"The authorities have told us they are watching us carefully," he says. He also takes time out to praise Kevin Keegan's magnificent achievement in returning City to the top flight. "Kevin has made a fantastic difference on and off the field," he says. "He is always pushing the edges and always trying to test what is possible. He keeps us under pressure all the time here."

LAKEY'S VIEW
"It really was fantastic to be up without kicking a ball, but what was most poignant for me was what David Bernstein said about Kevin always wanting to push the envelope, always wanting to test the players. The fact that he is never satisfied stands us in good stead for this Premiership season."

6 April
CITY 5 BARNSLEY 1
CITY CELEBRATE PROMOTION AND THE CHAMPIONSHIP WITH ANOTHER ROMP
City turn on the promotion style with a superb performance that simply blows Barnsley away and clinches the First Division Championship into the bargain. Darren Huckerby notches another hat trick, while Jon Macken weighs in with two. But Kevin Keegan pays tribute to Ali Benarbia, "the greatest player I have ever worked with, bar none. I thought we did a really good, professional job today," he adds talking on the club website. "We have won the title the way we would have wanted to do it. We did it in front of our home fans, who were unbelievable once again today, and I think the bond between the fans and the team is getting stronger and stronger and we now have a lot to look forward to." Keegan has some

vitriol for the English FA, however. "I have a lot of good staff around me here," he says. "Arthur Cox in particular. That is the same Arthur Cox the FA wouldn't employ because he was over sixty. When Sven-Goran Eriksson wanted someone over sixty they let him do it. But he was a foreigner, so I suppose it's harder to knock. It is the most annoying thing the FA did. And it still rankles because I wasn't allowed to take the people I wanted and that was wrong. Arthur's knowledge of football is way better than mine. He managed me twenty years ago, now he sits in the background. I had Derek Fazackerley with me when I was at England and people were saying we would not achieve success. Now we have done it here and we have the chance to do it in the Premiership and maybe make a few more people eat their words.

"My return to management was always worthwhile, even if we had just made it to the play-offs I would still be saying it was worthwhile. This is a great club and it is a great club to manage."

8 April

"WE HAVE TO SPEND BIG" – KEEGAN

Kevin Keegan again states that promotion is just the first chapter of the book he intends to write with Manchester City. His ambitions are much greater than a mere mid-table position in the Premiership and to achieve that aim then the club will have to invest in new talent. "We are going to have to attract big players," he says.

9 April

RESERVES DRAW IN DERBY

The reserves earn a 1-1 draw with Manchester United, the goal coming from Ciaran Kilheeney.

10 April

COX NAMED ASSISTANT MANAGER

City's Chief Scout, Arthur Cox, steps up to become Assistant Manager to Kevin Keegan. "Arthur Cox has now been appointed Assistant Manager. That has been agreed by the Board while he will still act as chief scout. Everyone knows what I think of Arthur and what he brings to this club," explains Keegan.

"Arthur has been a tremendous influence this season and a key part in

Kevin Keegan's team," says Chairman David Bernstein. "He has been instrumental in bringing in some of our new signings and his knowledge of football and his experience is immeasurable."

Kevin Horlock is called up by Northern Ireland for next week's friendly against Spain. Horlock has missed the last two internationals, the latter withdrawal due to a neck injury. Physio Rob Harris claims the problem should clear up of its own accord over the summer and that Horlock won't need an operation.

11 April
WANCHOPE WINGS BACK
Paulo Wanchope returns from the States with the encouraging news that he won't need another operation on his troublesome knee. He hopes to be fit to play for Costa Rica in this summer's World Cup tournament.

Meanwhile, talks are continuing as Kevin Keegan tries to find a way to retain Stuart Pearce's services at Maine Road for next season. The player has already announced his retirement from playing at the end of this season. "We would all like him to stay in some capacity but that capacity has to fulfil Stuart Pearce and that is the basis of our discussions," says Keegan.

Keegan also warns the fans not to pay too much attention to the rumours of big name players coming to City, as Kevin Phillips, Stefan Effenberg, Edgar Davids, Robbie Keane and Ian Walker are all linked with a move to Maine Road.

12 April
BERKOVIC RULED OUT AGAIN
Eyal Berkovic will not be fit to face Gillingham and has now played just 20 minutes of football in the last nine City games.

Keegan also takes time out to dismiss rumours that defender Richard Dunne could be on his way out of Maine Road. "Players will leave here but Richard Dunne won't be one of them," he says.

13 April
GILLINGHAM 1 CITY 3
YET ANOTHER WIN FOR THE BLUES – PLUS SCHMEICHEL JOINS CITY!
City chalk up another win to prove that there is no letting up from the

players, despite the First Division Championship being in the bag. Darren Huckerby is left on the bench as Shaun Goater is paired with Jon Macken upfront and goals from both strikers, plus an opener from Kevin Horlock, seal the win.

However, even City's victory is overshadowed by Kevin Keegan's announcement after the game of the signing of former Manchester United keeper Peter Schmeichel. "I am delighted to say that I have signed Peter Schmeichel on a one-year contract," he explains. "He is a tremendous presence and he took only twenty minutes to decide that he wanted to play for us next season. When he walks into your club and your dressing room you know he has a winning mentality and you can't have enough of that around the club. He is a very special goalkeeper."

Keegan has stated that he wants all City's transfer business completed before the start of the World Cup.

14 April
NASH TO FIGHT FOR HIS PLACE
Keeper Carlo Nash vows to fight for his place as City's number one after the arrival of the Great Dane from Aston Villa, but admits: "I really don't know what to think, though he is one of my heroes in the game."

15 April
CITY TRIO MAKE TEAM OF THE YEAR
Shaun Goater, Ali Benarbia and Eyal Berkovic are named in the PFA Division One Team Of The Year, as chosen by their fellow pros. "When your fellow professionals vote for you it makes me very proud," says Goater.

The full team is: Russell Hoult (West Brom)
Graham Alexander (Preston North End)
Neil Clement(West Brom)
Darren Moore(West Brom)
Jolyon Lescott (Wolves)
Eyal Berkovic (Manchester City)
Mark Kennedy (Wolves)
Ali Benarbia (Manchester City)
Robert Prosinecki (Portsmouth)
Shaun Goater (Manchester City)
Dougie Freedman (Crystal Palace)

Meanwhile, Shaun Wright-Phillips is included in the England Under-21 squad for their friendly with Portugal on Tuesday night in Stoke.

Niclas Jensen says Peter Schmeichel will prove a major influence on Manchester City's first season back in the Premiership. "He is still a world-class keeper. It will be great to see him in a City shirt next season," says Jensen.

"We are definitely seeing 'The Keegan Factor' at work," says Chairman David Bernstein. "Agents from all over the world are contacting us about players."

Kevin Keegan says that Darren Huckerby will be restored to the starting line-up for the last game of the season, Sunday's home clash with Portsmouth. Shaun Goater also urges City fans to get behind new keeper Peter Schmeichel, even if he is a former Manchester United star.

16 April
SCHMEICHEL ON HIS CITY MOVE
Peter Schmeichel admits on Danish TV that Kevin Keegan was a huge factor in his opting to move to Maine Road. "It is important to have a manager who is inspirational," he says. "Kevin Keegan is a fantastic person and a great motivator. You can see that from what he has done and where he has been." He also confirms that it only took 20 minutes for a deal to be struck.

The reserves beat Bradford 1-0 away, with a first goal for Under-19 star Gary Browne. Shaun Wright-Phillips doesn't make the England Under-21 side that is beaten 1-0 by Portugal in a Friendly.

LAKEY'S VIEW
"Peter Schmeichel signed for City because of Keegan, clearly. There have been managers at City in the past, even successful managers like Peter Reid and Howard Kendall, who haven't been able to attract the names to Maine Road that Keegan has. But it's not only a question of the reputation he has and because you know you'll get a manager who's attack-minded, who will get the best out of you and who will strive constantly to make you a more consistent player. It's also the fact that you've got someone who plays such exciting football. It must be a pleasure to go into training every day, whereas in the past at City it would always be working on the back four to try and stop to rot and beat teams on the break without really having the quality players to do it in the first instance."

17 April

DUNNE OUT

Richard Dunne pulls out of the Republic Of Ireland squad for the match against the USA with a hamstring injury and will miss City's final home game against Portsmouth.

City need three goals to equal their record number of league goals scored – 108, a total achieved in the 1926/27 season.

The club announces its new shirt sponsor for next season, financial services company First Advice.

Rumours circulate that Stuart Pearce is wanted by Coventry to be their new manager.

18 April

ALI IS VOTED PLAYER OF THE YEAR – AND ASKS TO EXTEND CONTRACT

Ali Benarbia is voted the supporters' Player Of The Year, much to the delight of Kevin Keegan. Kevin Horlock comes second, with Shaun Goater in third place. "There's no doubt that Ali was the right choice," says Keegan. "He is the best player I have ever worked with."

Keegan also reveals that Benarbia has asked for another year to be added to his City contract because he wants to finish his career with the club. Keegan says he was trying to get the player more money but the former Paris St Germain player was happy to ask for an extension alone.

Shaun Wright-Phillips wins his second successive Young Player of The Year award, while midfielder Glen Whelan is voted Most Promising Player.

LAKEY'S VIEW

"Nobody could argue with the choice of Ali and what's even more exciting is that you can't help but wonder what else is up Kevin Keegan's sleeve if he can pull Ali Benarbia out of the hat. We've never had a player who's come from nowhere and been a genius. Uwe Rosler was a great buy and scored goals. Kinkladze had fantastic abilities but he was always a bit-part player for me. Ali can dominate entire games for City. It's been an absolute delight to watch the guy. And if our scouting system can bring in players like him who are they going to find next?"

157

19 April

PEARCE FOR FREE

Stuart Pearce says that if he had been told he would have won the First Division Title with City he would have joined the club for nothing.

Richard Dunne may be fit for the season's final game after all but Eyal Berkovic will miss out again due to his troublesome ankle injury.

21 April

CITY 3 V PORTSMOUTH 1

CITY BOW OUT IN STYLE. PEARCE TAKES HIS FINAL BOW – AND FLUFFS HIS LINES

City skipper Stuart Pearce bows out of professional football with a penalty miss in extra time that stops him achieving a career total of 100 goals.

"Obviously we are pleased to win again," he says. "But what a comical end to the game! It was typical of me. I got a good move to West Ham and broke my leg twice. I took a penalty in the semi-final of the World Cup and missed it. Against Portsmouth Dave Beasant says he ain't going to move and told me 'Just put it in the corner' and I miss the goal. That just about sums me up. But it has been a pleasure and an honour to represent the clubs I have. I am very proud."

City's goals come from Steve Howey, Shaun Goater and Jon Macken.

22 April

KEEPER COACH WELCOMES SCHMEICHEL

City goalkeeping coach Peter Bonetti believes Peter Schmeichel is a great signing for the club but doubts there will be much he can teach him at age 38.

"His vocal presence on the pitch is like an extra player and every side needs the kind of leadership he will be able to supply," he says.

City's reserves fail to defend the Manchester Senior Cup against Oldham, losing 3-2 with goals from Stephen Paisley and Terry Dunfield.

23 April

CITY FOR HAMBURG

Kevin Keegan reveals that it is likely City will visit one of his former clubs, Hamburg, for a pre-season friendly.

24 April
BOXER GETS MEDAL
Boxer Ricky Hatton, a lifelong City fan, reveals that he was given a First Division Championship medal – the one presented to City boss Kevin Keegan – by the manager after the final home game against Portsmouth.

25 April
EFFENBERG NOT FOR CITY
City confirm that Steffan Effenberg will not be joining the club, despite reports circulating that he had agreed a two-year deal.

Kevin Keegan visits Stuart Pearce's stud farm in Gloucestershire to discuss his future with the club. "I have an offer for him," he says.

26 April
HORLOCK SEEKS CONTRACT EXTENSION
Kevin Horlock admits that he will be looking for an extension to the year he has left on his current contract. "I want to stay at Manchester City," he says.

29 April
CITY ANNOUNCE PRE-SEASON FIXTURES
City will play two games in Ireland at the end of July and will then play four local games against Preston, Bury, Rochdale and Tranmere, with a trip to Germany for a special fixture in Hamburg against Hamburger SV sandwiched in-between.

City announce their intention to sign 20-year-old Dutch defender Tyrone Loran from Volendaam after having had him on trial at the club for a couple of days.

Shaun Wright-Phillips is called up to the England squad for the Under 20 tournament in Toulon, France in May.

30 April
WHITLEY WON'T MAKE CITY GRADE
Kevin Keegan admits that he can see no first team future for Jeff Whitley at Manchester City. "Jeff will be available," says Keegan. "I can't say he won't get a shirt here again but it would be in the reserves as I can't see him playing for the first team again."

City Academy player Lee Croft stars for England Under-17s in the Second Round of the European Championships.

LAKEY'S VIEW
"Kevin Keegan was doing his usual here being very straight with Jeff Whitley and saying that he can't see him getting a first team game at City. But you also have to think what else he meant by the statement. Is it the fact that Jeff had had disciplinary problems and that Kevin was sending a message out to the rest of the squad? Players will be thinking 'I could lose my place in an instant here and the last thing I'm going to do is jeopardise that by messing about.'"

MAY 2002
1 May
"HORLOCK WILL BE OFFERED EXTENSION" – KEEGAN
Kevin Keegan reveals that he will be prepared to offer midfielder Kevin Horlock a year's extension to his current contract, which still has 12 months to run, after his sensational performances for the Blues' Championship-winning side.

City are being linked with a £4 million deal for out-of-favour Liverpool midfielder Nick Barmby.

City Academy striker Dorryl Profitt is called up to the England Under-17 side for the final group match against Denmark in the European tournament.

2 May
SCHMEICHEL STARTS AS FIRST CHOICE
Kevin Keegan reveals that new signing Peter Schmeichel will start as first choice keeper for City next season but says there will be no other automatic starting places for any player. He also says there are no worries in his mind over the player's Manchester United connections.

LAKEY'S VIEW
"I thought it was very interesting that Keegan made the statement so early that Peter was going to be his number one choice in goal. That said two things to me. First, that he was looking for someone to take command at the back, someone who will totally dominate the penalty box, which we were lacking a little bit in the First Division. Peter's experience, his

knowledge, his awareness and his guile add that little bit more overall sharpness at the back. Let's face it, he's seen it, nicked it and spent it over the last decade. He's such a commanding figure that if he was an outfield player he'd be as influential as Eric Cantona. Secondly, it came over to me almost immediately that Kevin Keegan was going to make him captain. And I think the only reason that he went with Ali Benarbia at the start of the season was a slight worry about whether Peter was going to be fit week in, week out. No decision is ever set in stone, though, and that's another thing I like about Kevin. He's not afraid to admit it when he's made a mistake and try something different."

3 May
ONE YEAR DEALS FOR KIDS
Kevin Keegan hands one year contracts to youngsters Chris Shuker, Chris Killen and Tyrone Mears and warns that they will have to start breaking through in the next year. "We want to see if they can make a living at Manchester City as we have invested a lot of time and money in them," he says.

LAKEY'S VIEW
"When I was a City player and guys like myself, David White and Steve Redmond were coming through, there was talk of four- and five-year deals for us. But I like what's been done in offering these guys one-year deals. What does this say to these players? It says 'Yes, we want you. Yes, we've invested a lot of money in you. But it's now time to start showing what you can do or you'll be on your way.' It's difficult for top clubs with big squads full of quality players because you can be a victim of your own success with youngsters coming through who have a lot of potential to succeed but who may not get a first team game with you in the next two to three years. So shorter deals are surely sensible. It's also a knock-on effect of the ITV Digital fiasco. Clubs simply can't afford to give out massive deals any more, especially to players who haven't shown they can do it at the top level. In a year's time, if these lads have made the first team and done it week in week in, week out, then sure, give them the big deal. But the game is in a precarious state at the moment and if clubs aren't successful in the Premiership and get relegated, then they may never make it back, which would put undue pressure on them if they had all

kinds of players on long-term deals. Not that I think City will go down this season, of course!"

4 May
THERE'S NO PRESSURE TO SELL
Kevin Keegan says that he is not actively looking to sell any players at the club but that should there be any interest in his squad members then the players themselves will be the first to know about it.

7 May
DUNNE CALLED UP
Richard Dunne is confirmed in the Republic Of Ireland squad for the World Cup and Niclas Jensen is selected for the Danish squad. Paulo Wanchope feels confident that he will be fit to represent Costa Rica at the tournament, saying his knee is feeling fine.

Kevin Keegan admits that no representatives from Manchester City will attend the tournament as he has already identified all the players he would like to bring to the club.

8 May
WRIGHT-PHILLIPS PULLS OUT OF UNDER-20 TOURNAMENT
Shaun Wright-Phillips decides to spend the summer resting rather than compete in the Under-20 Tournament in Toulon on the advice of the City physios.

City abandon their plans for a pre-season trip to Ireland.

Lucien Mettomo is named in the Cameroon World Cup squad.

9 May
DISTIN FOR CITY?
City are rumoured to be in hot pursuit of Newcastle's French defender Sylvain Distin. The 24-year-old made 34 league appearances for Bobby Robson's side, but is currently on loan on Tyneside from Paris St. Germain. Blackburn and Newcastle are both keen on his signature.

Kevin Keegan also says the door has not been closed on another Frenchman, Laurent Charvet, who has hardly featured for City over the last season. Keegan says the player has two years left on his contract and must come back and force his way into the reckoning next season.

11 May

NO LONG-TERM LOANS

Kevin Keegan says there will be no long-term loans of City's younger players, despite requests having already been received. Keegan argues that long-term loans would effectively be curtailing the City careers of players who only have one year deals to start with. He says he would consider loan moves of three months or less.

13 May

"WE SHOULD BE TOP SEVEN," SAYS WANCHOPE

City striker Paulo Wanchope believes the Blues should be aiming for a top seven finish on their return to the top flight. "For the first year teams like Spurs and West Ham, for instance, should be the benchmark for us," he says. "In the long term we have to think of being near to Arsenal, Manchester United and Liverpool." Meanwhile, Stuart Pearce claims his boss is not tactically naïve, as some have claimed in the past.

14 May

TRANSFER ACTIVITY

City are linked with a move for Independiente's 20-year-old Argentinean striker Vicente Matias Vuoso and Lyon's Cameroon midfielder Marc-Vivien Foé. Foé was previously at West Ham and left for £6 million.

Meanwhile, the club have agreed a £1 million buy-out to bring Volendaam defender Tyrone Loran to Maine Road.

Kevin Keegan identifies the improvements being made at the club's Carrington training centre as pivotal to the club's future development.

15 May

ANOTHER DANE ARRIVES

City announce the signing of 20-year-old defender Mikkel Bischoff from AB Copenhagen for £750,000, taking the number of Danish players in the squad to three. Bischoff joins Peter Schmeichel and Niclas Jensen. The club insist he's one for the future.

Stuart Pearce signs a one-year contract in what is effectively a coaching role. "Manchester City is a club going places and I am delighted we have sorted something out," he says.

LAKEY'S VIEW

"City's youth system has always been good but the idea of bringing certain players in from other clubs at a level where the idea is that they'll be developed into first team players is very refreshing. That's the situation with Mikkel Bischoff and while I've not seen him play I've heard a lot of very good things about him. It's the Benarbia approach at a lower level, if you like. These guys aren't known to the English football community but you certainly trust Kevin's judgement on these players. He might well make mistakes following this approach but it doesn't look like he's made too many so far."

20 May

DISTIN JOINS UP

Sylvain Distin's £4 million move from French club Paris St. Germain is completed, with the player agreeing a four-year deal. City admit they tried to bring the player to Maine Road during the previous season, but that Distin was looking for a Premiership side at that time. Sun Jihai is named in the Chinese squad for the World Cup Finals and Lucien Mettomo makes the Cameroon 23.

LAKEY'S VIEW

"I took the signing of Sylvain Distin as a good sign that City were showing real ambition not only to stay in the Premiership but to achieve something in it. You could not have envisaged Joe Royle investing heavily in really top quality players like Distin but Kevin Keegan was under no illusions that even a side which had taken the First Division by storm would not be strong enough for the Premiership. It might seem harsh on the players already at the club, the ones who'd done the business the previous season, but the arrival of players like Distin means that there's real competition now. Now as a player you can look around at players like Sylvain and say 'Fantastic. All these great players around me can make me a better player and I can learn a hell of a lot from them.' It can also make you think 'My God, I've got some stiff competition around me now and I have to raise my game to match them.' That's healthy at any club. As players we have all looked around at other players and said to ourselves, 'I can pull up as many trees as I like, but that guy will always get in ahead of me because he's a better player and if he's doing it week in week out, then I can't argue with that.' We all know there are guys who've been at the club in the recent past who are good players and good servants, who wear their hearts on their sleeves and would die for City. Good players and cracking guys, but let's be honest, not Premiership quality. Guys like Paul Dickov. There are a lot of good lads who've played out of their skins to get City to the position we're in now, but they won't be able to mix it with your Marc-Vivien Foés or your Sylvain Distins. They'll know that and they'll thank their lucky stars they'll have had the chance to get the club up to the Premiership and to have been involved in the highs of that First Division campaign. All good players hope to achieve as much as they possibly can in their careers and all players want to grace the Premiership if it's at all possible but you also have to know what your level is."

21 May
CITY ADMIT TO INTEREST IN ANELKA
After Liverpool announce that they won't be signing Paris St Germain striker Nicolas Anelka to a permanent deal City admit to an interest in taking the player. Fulham and Newcastle are also rumoured to be watching the situation closely. Anelka scored five goals in 23 appearances for Liverpool.

22 May
VUOSO TALKS TO BEGIN?
City look set to begin negotiations with Argentine striker Vicente Matias Vuoso. Vuoso, who partnered Manchester United's Diego Forlan at Independiente, could be a City player by next week.

23 May
ANELKA NEGOTIATIONS HOT UP
"We are continuing to have positive dialogue over the potential transfer of Nicolas Anelka and it is expected we will have a much clearer picture in the next twenty four hours," says Chief Operating Officer Chris Bird. A fee of £13 million is quoted, with City defender Lucien Mettomo possibly moving to Paris as a makeweight in the deal.

The club denies any interest in unsettled Leeds midfielder Lee Bowyer. City fans mourn the death of former legend Roy Paul.

24 May

ANELKA MOVE IS ON

City announce that they have agreed a fee with Paris St. Germain for the French international striker Nicolas Anelka. The player will undergo a medical at the weekend and the club hope to tie up the deal by the start of next week. Director Of Football Dennis Tueart says: "The signing of Nicolas Anelka re-enforces the message that as a club we are moving forward. When Nicolas was with us we showed him a video of the highlights of the promotion-winning season so he could see the quality of supply which he can expect."

25 May

KEEGAN AT THE HELM FOR A YEAR

Kevin Keegan celebrates his first year in charge at Manchester City.

27 May

ANELKA CLOSE TO COMPLETING MOVE

Nicolas Anelka is close to completing his move to City from Paris St. Germain and says: "I have a good feeling about the club and manager Kevin Keegan."

It looks like City's French striker Alioune Touré will move the other way.

Talks also open with Argentine striker Vicente Matias Vuoso.

City announce they will compete in a pre-season round robin tournament in Denmark against FC Aarhus, Silkeborg and HFK Sonderjylland.

29 May

RELEGATION WON'T BE CONTEMPLATED

City Chairman David Bernstein says: "Relegation is an horrific possibility but it is one which we won't even contemplate. Kevin doesn't know the word 'relegation'."

LAKEY'S VIEW

"The Anelka move was reported at this stage as being on and then close to completion and City fans must have been wondering if this was all just nothing but paper talk. Then two days later at the end of the month David Bernstein was talking about relegation not being an option for City this season. I agree with him. We really have to cross that word out of our dictionaries for the next year because it's unthinkable that we will go down. I don't think any City fan has seriously contemplated relegation. It must be the first time in many years where we haven't even spoken of it. I've heard people saying "I'll bet a year's salary that City don't go down", whereas in the past they wouldn't have even bet a week's wages on it!"

Blue skies overhead?

WE'RE sitting on the couch in Lakey's front room. It's mid-October and the nights are starting to draw in around this neat little corner of Stockport. And while we're chewing the fat before we discuss City's performances in this Premiership season that's so heavily loaded with expectation, we get onto the subject of the footballing shakedown that's currently happening, sparked by the evaporation of TV money.

"It's frightening for players now," says Lake. "There's a real reality attack happening throughout the game and players are having to wake up and smell the coffee. The gravy train is over. A lot of guys who were thinking it was going to be a great thing to let their contract wind down, become a free agent and then pick up a nice fat pay packet somewhere else are now starting to see the other side of the coin, where they're struggling to find any kind of work. To be fair, average players have had it too good for too long. They're going to have to be a lot more realistic and I think there's going to be a big correction in the future."

So Nicolas Anelka's going to have to tighten his belt, is he?

"Yeah, he'll be struggling, I should think! Actually, if you look at City they're one of very few clubs that are bucking the trend right now. The board have set their stall out where their ambition demands that they're in the Premiership. There's a gamble involved in that. They're having to invest in their future by paying top drawer wages for top drawer players. In fact, I think we're one of the biggest spenders in the Premiership currently. But we had to do it and City are lucky in that they have such a solid fanbase – which has been proven even in the bad times. Additionally, they seem to have cut a sensible deal with the council for the new stadium. The prospect of a big stadium with full houses means it is hard to see the club falling flat on its arse.

"Of course, the big proviso is that they stay in the Premiership first and foremost, even more so since the ITV Digital fiasco. And then the ultimate goal has to be the Champions League, because that's where the real money is."

Those are lofty ambitions and there is the small matter of City's first season back in the top flight to deal with. How is the team shaping up?

"If anyone thought we would be in for an easy ride, I think they've seen that they were very much mistaken,'" says Lake. "I'm still very confident about our chances, but there's no doubt that we're going to have to work for everything we get in this division. There was always going to be a steep learning curve for the first 10 to 15 games of the season. Back in the First Division it took us that long to find our feet and the quality of the opposition was nothing like it is now. By New Year we need the players to have got up to speed and what I would like to think is that Maine Road will be something of a fortress from then on. Then, with the attacking players we have and a pretty decent depth to the squad, we should be grinding out some results away from home. There's no doubt that with players like Sylvain Distin and Peter Schmeichel in your defence you have to be looking to start collecting clean sheets away from home . . . and that's not something we were even managing to do in the First Division!"

There have been some defensive frailties exposed. "No doubt about it. You take a game like the home win against Newcastle. We were creating chances in the first half that were phenomenal. Eyal Berkovic reckons Shearer said to him at half time that we could – and maybe should – have been four or five up. But then we could have ended up giving the game away with silly mistakes. There was one in particular, from Distin of all people, that I remember. Awful. The games against Liverpool and South-ampton were extremely disappointing too. But you have to remember that it's a steep learning curve and these things are bound to happen. You have remember, too, that we have proved in certain games that we've lost that we can compete. I doubt many teams will got to Arsenal this season and give a better account of themselves. The major problem has been in conceding goals early which has meant that we've been chasing the game, which naturally leads to a less disciplined performance as you strive to get the goal back. They need to show more mental strength, but I'm very confident that we'll be fine."

Arsene Wenger says he expects City to finish in the Top 10. Is that still realistic? "A lot of it is down to the attitude that the management have instilled at the club," says Lake. "Kevin Keegan, Pewter Schmeichel and Stuart Pearce are winners who will not accept second best and that attitude has a very positive effect on the club. The class is there. We've already seen it. The first 20 minutes of the game against Newcastle was probably the best football I've ever seen from City. It is the consistency that's lacking and it is the consistency that we need to strive for. We were absolutely terrible away at Aston Villa and you know that would have been one of the games the management had earmarked as a match to get something out of. There can't be too many days like that in this division.

"Equally, we must not forget that there are a lot of new faces to integrate into the team and that always takes time. Admittedly, the guys who have been brought in are better players so they should respond quicker than the new faces did last season but it will not happen overnight."

What are Lake's views on the players Keegan has opted to start the campaign with?

"It's no surprise that the four players he brought in to form the spine of the side – Schmeichel, Distin, Foé and Anelka – have all been playing and started well, with the possible exception of Foé. Keegan was man enough to tell the lads who got us up last season that, come the start of the Premiership campaign there would be a metamorphosis in exactly the same way that there was a metamorphosis of the First Division side. The side that got us promoted could not be the one we took into the Premiership. Keegan is not naïve about the demands of this division and, even with those new, quality players, it's still been hard work. But we've already seen that when we're on song we're very, very exciting. We've gone to Leeds and Arsenal and although we've been beaten in both games we've shown a lot of nice touches and shown that we really can play. We've got so many facets to our attacking play that it must shock the hell out of some of the back fours and back fives that we're coming up against. And Keegan's always looking at different ways of using the options that he has. I think Darren Huckerby has proved a lot of people wrong already. He started the season on fire and while I still believe that sometimes he'll beat himself, there's now a different confidence in the man that bodes well. I think he deserves a real run."

Defensively?

"Well we've been caught out a few times already but I say again, it's a steep learning curve. I was surprised that Keegan started the season with Steve Howey in the back three instead of Richard Dunne but I think that's because Kevin's found he likes the way Steve works with Distin. And I think Steve's risen to the challenge well – he wants to prove he's still capable of performing at the very highest level. Maybe Dunney had one or two bad games in pre-season but I think over the course of the season he'll play his way back into the first team.

"Jihai has done OK. He's a bit wild and unpredictable at times but he uses the ball well and he sees more than you think he sees. He's got good vision and good awareness and he passes a ball well, so I think we'll be OK with him."

The rotational system looks certain to play a part, though Keegan started off the early games using a settled side with few changes. Lake agrees: "I'm sure we'll see changes but whether it'll be the way the very top sides mix and match I'm not so sure. He might keep the same side for three or four games at a time. And you have to ask yourself: 'Will a rotation system work where the players coming in might only just be good enough for the Premiership?' That's the key question for me. It is about squad depth. Anelka might be rested against the supposedly weaker teams like Southampton or West Brom if the season is going well. If we are in the bottom half of the table then I don't think Keegan will contemplate it. We're certainly not strong enough to be resting players of that calibre against Arsenal, Liverpool and Manchester United."

How will other teams view City now that they have had a chance to assess them properly? "I think of it the other way around,'" says Lake. "If I look at the other teams in the division – sides like Charlton, Birmingham, Southampton and West Brom – then I'd say those are the teams where we would have been looking to bank all the points from the home games. Then I ask myself whether other clubs will have been lumping City in the same bracket and I do not believe they will be. I also think we have the personnel in place to drag us out of a bad patch if we do happen to go into one. It won't take four or five matches to get back on message because it won't just be the manager driving people on. It will be the four or five senior pros too. Players will be only too aware that they'll need to get their arses in gear and get with the script, otherwise they'll have six people on their back.

"I don't necessarily mean ranting and raving on the pitch. It will happen more on the training ground, more behind the scenes. Schmeichel will have a go during a match, of course, but lads like Berkovic will say their piece away from the public eye. They'll all sit down and watch re-runs of matches and the senior players will drive the upping of performances."

Video howlers will be called in evidence as the squad strives for success. Lake says: "They will use video a lot to illustrate a point. A player might think he is tracking and using the ball well but video shows how, even over the course of five minutes, he has not stayed with his man, he has not used the ball, instead giving it away and failing to see the options worked on in training. They will be shown to have switched off. Video helps you make amends on the training pitch the next day. You repeat the positive moves and psychologically you are trying to erase the stuttering side to your game where you have three or four options, but don't instinctively know which one to use.

"You hope to get to the point where you've seen what's available before you've received the ball and already made the right choice. I think it's been noticeable that the team has been doing it in fits and starts early season and the hesitation has been pounced on and we've been done as a result. Visual analysis and psychology work side by side and will be a constant for City.

"It was interesting to see that there came a point last season where all the mistakes they made on the pitch could be corrected. It wasn't that mistakes were not being made. That will always happen. But they were recognised earlier by the players' own anticipation, and other players then fell into place to cover. The key to it now, having stepped up to a higher level, is for different and better players to bring the best out of others. They will do it in different ways, of course. Schmeichel is positive, vociferous, demanding and dogmatic. But Anelka looks almost shy and retiring on the pitch. Will he lead by example? Is he going to be the kind of bloke who'll take it on the chin from Berkovic when he's ranting and raving? Will they all help the younger players like Shaun Wright-Phillips? That's yet to be seen. It's still a learning curve. It may not work because of the personalities but what you hope is that Kevin Keegan can make everyone see how the team is what matters.

"And I'm positive. Even Nicolas Anelka has said he's prepared to work at the team side of things and he's so far proved that on the pitch. That's a good sign, for my money."

What else is going to be key throughout the season?

"I believe there's a lot of pressure on the medical staff at City to keep Eyal Berkovic fit and out on the pitch. He missed a hell of a lot of games last season and he's one of those few players who have the ability and the awareness to change games in an instant. We have got a fantastic medical set-up at City now but despite the depth of the squad there are players like Eyal and Peter Schmeichel who are so important that you really have to keep them on the pitch. He needs to play more games this season."

And Paulo Wanchope, another player prone to long lay-offs?

"We are told he is out until New Year although I am not fully aware of what the problem is. The talk from the World Cup was that he would be OK for the start of the season so this is definitely worrying. A fit Paulo Wanchope has the ability to start alongside Nicolas Anelka though I don't think Keegan would have gone for it even if he had been available. Their styles of play are so different that they would find it hard to operate effectively together. Paulo is too enigmatic for Nicolas, who needs structure to his game. Paulo will nutmeg two people and create something. Nicolas doesn't have a jink and a trick, but you know if he is getting service for 90 minutes he will get you goals. He's got amazing movement and amazing awareness. I don't think the two are suited although we have seen many times that players who do not appear to fit together somehow strike up a great partnership. If Paulo is fit, of course, he would make an ideal option if Nicolas was not doing the business. But I don't think he would get in the side in front of Nicolas Anelka and I don't think he would sit well alongside him."

Overall, then, a positive future. Kevin Keegan is Manchester City's Messiah?

"Absolutely. As I said, it's personal with Kevin now. He has a point to prove to the Premiership and to the rest of the footballing world. He has not had top flight success. He has not won anything and I am convinced he will not stop until he has the Premiership title in his grasp. Keegan has the drive and the momentum. He is able to bring the best out of people and the players love working with him.

"It is fantastic for all the Blues who have sat around Greater Manchester and beyond and thought we were nothing but a yo-yo side, up and down between divisions. Now you talk to all the pundits, talk to any managers and say to them: 'Be honest. What sides do you believe will be catapulted back into the First Division?' And City aren't in that line-up. City fans now have to realise that on our day we *can* beat Manchester United, we *can* beat Arsenal, we *can* beat Chelsea. We can actually do it. It's not pie in the sky. It could actually happen. It will actually happen."

VIEWS FROM THE TERRACES
MIKE PICKERING

Top DJ and M People mentor Mike Pickering first started supporting City when he was five "just about the time when Mercer and Allison joined". Despite being in Collyhurst, an area that was almost exclusively Red, his dad and maternal grandfather were both staunchly Blue. "I had no choice in the matter, really." He says. Despite living in London he is still a season ticket holder at Maine Road and hardly misses a game.

If you started watching City at the outset of the Mercer/Allison era, you must have got a slightly false impression of what it was going to be like supporting the Blues?

"Definitely, yeah. I think it took about seven years before I realised that you didn't just automatically win a trophy every year. But I soon found out that life wasn't really like that and settled into being a City fan, watching over a decline at the club ever since really. At least until recently. I remember thinking that the Glory Days were really over when Peter Swales said that City would never be able to compete with United. That was when we were consistently finishing higher in the league than them and consistently thrashing them in the derbies. I thought 'Bloody hell, we've thrown the towel in.' Then immediately after that they sold Trevor Francis and bought David Cross and I really did know we were in for a bad time. From then on we've had a succession of hapless managers and we've stumbled from one fiasco to another. Until now."

And is your new-found optimism entirely down to the arrival of Kevin Keegan?

"Not really. I think it goes back to the changes that were made in the management set-up two or three years before Kevin got there. I can remember coming back from a game one time when David Makin and John Wardle from JD Sports were on the local radio station talking about somebody needing to turn the club around and I remember thinking 'This is a seminal moment.' I'm a great believer in the fact that football clubs need to be run like businesses. Yes, of course by supporters, but by people who know what they're doing as well. The days of football clubs being run by greengrocers and bog roll salesmen are over.

"So when Wardle and Makin got involved and brought Dennis Tueart in, then made David Bernstein Chairman I thought 'Hold on a minute. Things are happening here.' Because let's not forget, David Bernstein was no slouch either. I think he was responsible for turning French Connection round, wasn't he?"

But those guys brought Joe Royle in to manage the club, didn't they?

"Yes they did but that wasn't a bad move at the time. It worked in the short term but it just became obvious that he wasn't a Premiership manager, didn't it? I think I knew it when we got up out of the First Division the season before. We were playing alehouse football. And when we got up the tactics were a joke. Royle didn't bring a creative midfielder to the club when everyone knew we were crying out for one. He couldn't attract any big names to play for City and then when he did, he decided that Paul Dickov was a better striker than George Weah. I mean, I never really liked Paul Dickov, unlike most City fans. Too much falling on his arse and moaning for my taste. But no-one in their right mind would claim he was better than George Weah. I remember one time taking the train back down to London after a match and ending up talking with David Bernstein *(this isn't unusual. I've done it myself – HJ)*. His phone rang and it was Joe. 'Oh dear,' he said when he hung up. 'It appears that George Weah is throwing tea cups around.' That was a funny couple of years, really."

So did you feel confident the minute that Keegan was appointed that things would turn around?

"I have to admit I didn't feel too sure about Kevin Keegan because I think that, like many people, my opinion of him was clouded by what had happened when he was in charge of England. But you have a look at what he achieved at Newcastle and it was nothing short of phenomenal. Talk to any Geordies and they still think he's a God there. And it's supporters that count, don't you think? But no, I wasn't sure at first and think I would have been happier if the club had brought in someone who was younger and who had more to prove, someone like David Moyes. I would have gone for Kevin Keegan over some of the other names that were being bandied around, though. Do you remember? It was all David Platt and Dave Bassett. Horrific!"

And I assume you accept that your reservations have turned out to be unfounded?

"Well yes but let's not forget that it didn't all happen overnight. We had a pretty sticky start last time around with that game against Coventry away when we lost four-three and then particularly the pasting we took at West Brom when we lost four-nil. I remember driving back to London after that game and saying to my mates that if Keegan didn't do something quick then he'd be better off buggering off. I remember being disappointed by the fact that most of the players who were in that team that day were players who'd been part of our Second Division team. I think he'd only signed Pearce and Berkovic by then. But to be fair to him he cites that game as the turning point as well. He brought Benarbia in pretty much straight after that. He'd obviously given everyone a chance and decided that there were quite a few of them who weren't up to the job."

But he always said he'd do that.

"That's right. Maybe I was being a bit harsh on him, because it's that loyalty which he shows to his players that has meant he's so well liked by them. He's certainly improved a lot of the players who were at the club before him. I mean, you could hardly recognise Wanchope as the same player under Keegan as he was under Royle. A massive improvement. Richard Dunne is much improved too. But probably the best example is Kevin Horlock who just blossomed last season. Joe Royle called him a sulker and I can remember being at some dire game when Horlock was on the bench and we were screaming at Royle to get him on but he just refused to listen to us. He was a bit like that, was Joe."

I haven't heard one player who's been disgruntled under Keegan, not even the players who have been on the fringes of the team.

"I have. I heard from someone who bumped into Alfie Haaland in Norway that he wasn't happy and thought he hadn't been given a fair chance. But I think your point is right, generally. And the other thing he's doing is blooding the youngsters. He brought Shaun Wright-Phillips on a treat and now Chris Shuker seems to be making a real push for the first team. He's a real player's manager from what you hear. I hear that he doesn't go into any of the lounges at City because he prefers to be with his players. It's kind of a 'I'm with you 100% so long as you give me your all' vibe. He just seems to have galvanised the whole place. He has that infectious enthusiasm that just seems to rub off on people and that's a happy knack to have. Plus one of the biggest assets that he has – and it's one that I for one definitely underestimated – is the quality of the players he can attract to the club. There's no way that some of the players who are now wearing our shirt would be there if it wasn't for Kevin Keegan."

And that enthusiasm is certainly infectious when you've got people talking about a Top Six finish in this first season back in the Premiership.

"Well to be fair he's said that himself. He's said he's banned the word 'consolidation' from the club, which is kind of a nice, positive vibe to have. But to be honest I think we have to have confidence without aiming too high. I think we'll finish mid-table. Maybe it's because I've been a City fan for so long but I tend to look at the teams in a division that are worse than us and I reckon this season we can count Birmingham, West Brom, Everton and Southampton in there. And we've got to be better than Tottenham, haven't we? I think we'd do well to take a long, hard look at Fulham, though. They walked the First Division the year they came up, everyone said they were going to do well because their style suited the Premiership, they spent £30 million or whatever it was on players and look at them. They were rubbish. The thing is you really do need a goalscorer in this division and we certainly hope that we have one in Anelka."

And Keegan. Has he got the bottle to stick at it no matter how things go this season?

"I think he has, actually. I don't think he'd walk away from this thing. So long as he had the backing of the board I think he'd really dig his heels in. Don't forget, things only went wrong at Newcastle when he felt he didn't have the backing of the board."

So who would you rate above Keegan as a Premiership manager, then?

"Well Ferguson and Wenger, obviously. But apart from that you're starting to struggle. I think Sam Allardyce is a good manager, though I wouldn't say he's better than Keegan. I like Glenn Roeder too, for the way he handled himself under a lot of pressure last season. David Moyes could be good, but we'll have to wait and see. Graham Taylor? I don't think so. I don't like Gordon Strachan either. And Gerard Houllier? Well, he said Danny Murphy was his Platini and then he tried to buy Lee Bowyer, so I can't rate him after that, can I? When you look at the managers who are operating we shouldn't have any worries about Kevin Keegan at all. The Premiership isn't the fantastic league everyone tries to tell you it is."

So where do you think it might end with Keegan? Can City really become a genuine European power?

"I don't see why not eventually. The expectation is certainly there at the club now. We've got a big name manager, we're going to a new stadium where we'll give the impression to anyone who comes there that we are a big club. And the really big spenders seem to have disappeared from the European scene. Not even Real Madrid have been lashing out fortunes on new players. So yeah, why not City a big European club? Not now, but in three or four years time, why not?"

Well, because this is Manchester City, where anything can – and usually does – happen.

"Yeah, but not this time, eh?"

CELEBRITY FAN – SUSAN BOOKBINDER

Five Live radio presenter Susan Bookbinder got hooked on broadcasting when she used to watch Denis Law summarising at Maine Road as a child. Her family are City daft and brother John actually played in the same City youth team as Paul Lake, after turning down an offer from United. Good lad! Susan's also President of the Milton Keynes branch of the City Supporters Club.

You're known on Five Live for your laudably biased attitude in favour of City, so you must be enjoying The Keegan Era . . .

"Oh definitely. Let's face it, we've had a bad time of it these last few years, so suddenly to be managed by such a charismatic character as Kevin Keegan, to have had the kind of performances we've seen and to see the quality of players who are now being attracted to the club, has been absolutely brilliant. Having a bit of glamour and success makes up for all the grey hair, the heart conditions, the wrinkles, the eating disorders, the misery, torture and despair that so many people in my family have suffered from supporting The Blues. My grandfather actually had a heart attack at the 1955 Cup Final when we lost to Newcastle Final, so in a way you could actually say that he died for City.

"My stepmother is a psychologist and I'm sure one of the main reasons why she married my dad was so that she could have her own private case study!"

All this suffering and you're not even from Manchester!

"That's right. I grew up in Derby, but my grandfather and father were both City season ticket holders so I had no choice in the matter. Anyway, coming from Derby and supporting City's nothing. I've just got back from a trip to Yancheng in southern China and there's a growing Manchester City Supporters' Club there. There's a young guy called David Peng and together with his dad, Giangbaio, they both follow the Blues through the website and, of course, get regular bulletins from my Dad and me. I was amazed. There were loads of advertising hoardings with Beckham's face on over there but because of Sun Jihai playing for us it was City that everyone wanted to know about. It's refreshing to see that, despite all the efforts of United's massive propaganda push in China, it's City that are becoming the Chinese *people's* team of choice!

Having a world football figure like Keegan as manager obviously helps with those kind of things too. You're a big Keegan fan, aren't you?

"Oh yes, from way before his City days, actually. When I was growing up I thought he was a real hero though I must stress I never, ever had a bubble perm as a tribute. I've always liked him and I think that Keegan managing City is a marriage made in heaven. The drama and the controversy that's always surrounded both parties is just perfect. I've always thought there was a fairy tale quality in the idea of the two of them together and I've always thought this is where Kevin Keegan belongs. It took City and Keegan 30 years to find each other but now they're together and it's wonderful."

So no doubts about him when he was announced as manager?

"None at all, unlike a lot of City fans. The day that Keegan was appointed I was driving up to Maine Road with my dad because I'd been asked to 'manage' the City ladies team in a game against United, a game which I'm pleased to say we won 2-1. On the car radio on the way up they said reports were coming through that Kevin Keegan was about to be appointed Manchester City manager but we thought it surely wouldn't be that very day. Anyway, the story builds up until it's dominating not only the sports news but all of the national news! Surely no other club, never mind a First Division side as we were at the time, could do that. That just proved to me that Keegan was right for City. To have all that glamour and cult status rolled into one package . . . *it was national headline news!* Brilliant.

"The only downer was that when Keegan was actually announced as the new boss the Manchester Evening News announced the result of the ladies' game against United the next day and said that 'The Keegan Effect' was already in operation. I thought "Cheeky Sods. How about 'The Booky Effect?'" But seriously, I was *so* excited. All the fans were outside Maine Road singing 'Super Kev' and he was there signing autographs, but I must admit I did think 'Poor old Joe'. I thought that was a good example of how fickle football fans can be, because if Joe Royle hadn't got us up out of the First Division in the first place with all that followed, then he probably would still be our manager today."

179

You weren't one of the "Keegan will be off in six months" brigade, then?

"No way. People were all saying 'I'll give him till the middle of the season and he'll walk out.' But I call that 'The Goebbels Factor'. You know, if you tell a lie often enough it becomes the truth. I think it's a pity that although Keegan's achieved phenomenal success as a club manager, whatever he does at City will always be tainted by the fact that he quit the England job. When the appointment was made I heard Rodney Marsh saying 'Keegan walked out on Newcastle, he walked out on Fulham, he walked out on England. Let's see how long it takes him to walk out on City.' I never felt that for a minute and I'll tell you why. If you look at what he achieved at Newcastle he got them to phenomenal heights despite the fact that there was always a lot of politics going on on that board. Everyone knows that. I think Keegan turned around and simply said he didn't need it anymore, which is fair enough by me, and the reception he got when we were up at Newcastle last season shows what the people up there thought of his efforts."

"He didn't walk out on Fulham either; he was released to take the England job – and I honestly think that the foundations of what England have achieved under Eriksson were laid by him. I think because he wears his heart on his sleeve he told everyone how he felt at half time in that World Cup qualifying game against Germany, the bit about not knowing how to put things right. Coming out to the press and telling them something as personal as that was an incredible thing to say and obviously it was bad from a PR point of view. Maybe if Alastair Campbell had spoken for him he would have got away with it. I think it's such a shame that he couldn't get along with the England job but I think he's proved with City beyond any doubt that he really does know what he's doing."

So when were you really convinced that everything really was going to be fine at Maine Road?

"I'd have to say the very first game of the season at home to Watford. It was billed as Keegan versus Vialli, The Big One, two of the main candidates for promotion. We had Pearce and Berkovic both making their debuts and it was a year since I'd seen us get absolutely annihilated by Charlton 4-0 in our first game back in the Premiership. I couldn't believe how well the team played. It was like coming out of a coma of misery and the performance was just so exciting. Seeing Stuart Pearce *organising* things. Seeing the team playing like they actually *knew* each other, like they were in a football team together. It was magic – and then both the debutants scored just like it was written in the fairytale script! Berkovic ripped his shirt off, everyone was singing 'mazeltov, mazeltov, mazeltov' and I thought, 'This club is going up.'"

Any moments of doubt?

"Going to West Brom and getting beaten four-nil early on was humiliating. We didn't play that badly, but it was that sinking feeling of 'Oh no, here we go again'. I mean, with City you expect it to be a rollercoaster each season, but with Keegan it was more like a rollercoaster within each game. But he quickly got players like Berkovic and Benarbia in, which made a real statement about how a Keegan team was going to play. And thinking about it, it was a great example of how to get people working together. George Bush should call off Colin Powell and get Kevin Keegan to negotiate in the Middle East!

"In the end that season was utterly bizarre. You're usually sitting there biting your nails right to the very last kick with City but there we were, sitting back and relaxing. The only thing we had to worry about was whether we were going to beat our all-time season goals record which wasn't a bad place to be."

Mind you, from what I heard on the radio you weren't exactly sitting back and relaxing when you went to the infamous Millwall away game . . .

"That's true. I went to Millwall and it was the most awful night – I really felt like I was in Nazi Germany. I went on 606 afterwards with their Chairman Theo Paphitis and we had a real spat. He said 'You shouldn't have gone along' because City fans were banned. He didn't know my boyfriend's a Millwall fan. I've been made to feel welcome in all away ends across the country but even my father was afraid to celebrate when City scored at Millwall. The anti-Semitism was worse than the abuse that the black players were getting; it was like an NF rally. You could hear a pin drop when Shaun Goater scored and my dad let out a bit of a cheer. They were turning round going 'Where are you, you Manc c***s?'. Somebody said 'If we can find Bin Laden we can find you c***s,' and I stupidly said 'But you can't find Bin Laden, can you?' It was a nightmare. My boyfriend was obviously very ashamed of what happened but the hooligans seem to have won down there.

"Still, the result was right and Darren Huckerby scoring and clapping the empty seats where the City fans would have been was awesome."

You had a much better time at Wolves . . .

"Ah, that was funny. I was on 606 talking about whether Wolves or the Baggies would go up with City and we were playing Wolves at Molineux on the following Bank Holiday Monday. I didn't have a ticket so I appealed on the air to see if anyone could help me out. Alan Green said 'You're abusing your position Booky' and I said 'I don't care, it's an important match.' I got this call from Rachael Heyhoe Flint, who's a Director at Wolves. 'I heard your plea, do come along as my guest.' So my dad and I ended up in a box, which was brilliant. I ended up doing something for 606 from Molineux and the next time I saw Adrian Childs, who's a Baggies fan, he said 'I heard you on 606 after you'd been drinking Rachel Heyhoe Flint's wine! You were saying you hoped Wolves went up.' Well, I said 'If you'd actually been listening Adrian you would have heard that I said I hoped Wolves went up so we could take another six points off them!' As a result of that interview I had several death threats, including one from a Baggies fan that said 'If that Susan Bookbinder ever comes up North we'll chop her up into little pieces and eat her.' The last time I looked West Bromwich was in the Midlands so I'm not too worried about that one!"

Another rumour was that you were, how shall I put it, 'tired and emotional', when you did that piece from Wolves.

"Not true. I was asked something along the lines of 'Are you biased whenever you report on City?' and I said "I want to nail my colours firmly to the mast and say I am definitely a City fan." But I was quoted as having said 'I want to colour my nails to the mast.' I categorically deny it and I'll get the tapes to prove it! I had had quite a lot of wine but not that much! You've got to be careful, though. I was invited by the Chairman David Bernstein to be his guest at City on the last day of the season, which was brilliant. He's a lovely man. But his wife remembered every single comment I've made on 606 over the last year, which can be a bit disconcerting!"

So you've met the Chairman. But what about the manager?

"I've only met him once when he came to Five Live to do an interview when he'd declared his interest in the England job while he was still at Fulham. I was reading the news and when I walked into the studio he was just sitting there, which made me a bit nervous. Anyway, I went out and someone told me later that Keegan said 'I've always wanted to know what she looked liked. I've always imagined this gorgeous bird surrounded by books.' I was so chuffed. Kevin Keegan wanted to know what *I* looked like!"

So it's a love thing between you two? No, only joking. Anyway, what of the future under KK?

"Not that long ago people were talking about survival in the Premiership and nothing else but I was talking to Mark Bright the other day and he said 'Booky, it's not about survival any more, is it?' The ambitions at the club are so much greater now. There are no more Man City jokes. I really quite enjoyed it in the First Division because it was great to go round winning everywhere and scoring bags of goals and The Premiership is so different but I think we'll finish in the Top 10, I really do. We've got some real quality players at the club now and I'm even happy having a former red like Peter Schmeichel at City. Surely he's always had the ambition to play in Manchester rather than Salford, anyway! I sat next to a Liverpool Director at an awards do not that long ago who said he would give Anelka until Christmas before he started asking for more money. But the way he said it, though, I thought he was really jealous. I thought to myself "We've got him and you're p***ed off." I think it's sad that a lot of the players who got us up last season won't make the side this year, but I guess that's football.

And if your optimism turns out to be misplaced?

"Well, having witnessed the way we "played" against Southampton, leaving the country seemed the best course of action. By this time, I was sick of hearing that old cliché from the press that "Keegan can't defend" but to be honest, in that game, there was no attack either. The 2-0 scoreline was flattering to us and I was disappointed that Shaun Wright-Phillips was substituted. He was the only one having a good game; still, I speculated to the City fans around me that maybe it was a unifying tactic – at least there'd be consistency – they were all useless together!

"If it all goes horribly wrong by the end of next season I'll just remember how I felt when it was all going brilliantly in the First Division and I travelled all the way to Stockport believing we were guaranteed a win. Then it was raining all the way through the game, obviously we lost, and it was difficult to tell which team was going to be relegated and which was about to become First Division champions. We were appalling. And remember, this was the City that had played so brilliantly at Newcastle and that annihilated Ipswich in the F.A. Cup. It was a good lesson to learn. Just when you start to get confident the old City comes back and bites you. Still, this time I really feel that things will be different but if not, then my advice is 'Don't get too depressed. Have another drink!'"

STEVE ANGLESEY

Steve Anglesey is Editor of the website Football365, a former editor of the official Manchester City magazine and a lifelong Blue.

You wrote an infamous article on Football365 when Keegan was announced as manager, didn't you? There was one line in particular . . .

"Oh yes, it was 'Some say that Kevin Keegan will provide entertainment . . . but so would a half-time juggler.' Obviously I feel fairly foolish about that now but it was even worse. I don't think I actually said in the piece that he'd be out by Christmas, but I certainly believed it. I thought bringing Kevin Keegan in as manager was a profoundly bad idea for two reasons. Firstly, in his last job as a club manager he'd built a half decent team at Fulham but it was far from outstanding. Secondly, the England experience. I was horrified that such a tactically naïve manager could get the England job on a wave of public opinion and nothing that happened during his time with England dissuaded me from that view. Let's be honest, only Graham Taylor has had a more disastrous reign in charge of the national side and if you look at the qualifying results from when he was in charge, Kevin Keegan is probably the worst England manager in living memory; only Don Revie has come close. Keegan said he would play a very exciting game and young people would get their chance in an England shirt and I don't know why – maybe simply blind loyalty – but that didn't turn out to be the case. It was *awful*. All those old players at the fag end of their careers and Keegan's own admission that he wasn't up to it tactically made that period a very dispiriting time."

OK, so your reasoning may have been sound, but you must be prepared to eat a bit of humble pie now, given the way things have gone at City.

"Absolutely. Now I have a bit of an understanding of 'The Keegan Effect' that the Newcastle fans always went on about. Only they really knew how special that time was for the club because to outsiders it all looked like a bit of a joke. You know, the over-fanatical fans, how it all came apart at the end of that season, with the Geordies crying on the telly every week . . . to me, that period only reinforced what I'd thought for ages and that was that Kevin Keegan was a bit of a comic figure. All I thought of when I thought of Keegan was the header in 1982, falling off the bike in Superstars, the bubble perm, 'Head Over Heels', the boot-shaped soap on a rope and those homoerotic Brut adverts with Henry Cooper. The list goes on. Remember that ridiculous helicopter that came to spirit him away from Southampton when he retired? Then when he came back to Newcastle within three weeks he'd resigned saying 'It's not like what it said in the brochure'. All of this made him a comic figure to me ... and then he became a tragi-comic figure with England."

"So I don't think it was crazy when he came to City for me to think 'Another joke manager. Oh God, it's Kevin Keegan, the man who's walked out of every management job he's had and he's the soap-on-a-rope-meister.' Here was a guy who'd already admitted that he didn't understand tactics at the highest level, so I thought it was a fairly unappetising proposition. And having seen what had happened at City in the last six or seven years you just thought 'Here's another daft episode of the longest-running soap opera in football'. I'm absolutely delighted to have talked absolute rubbish but I suspect I'm not the only one who's saying that right now."

So when did you first realise you had been wrong?

"Well to be fair the first few results of last season did nothing to dissuade me from that point of view. Plenty of mad wins, but plenty of defeats too. It seemed like it was five-three or three-five every other week. There were no draws at all for ages. And given the fact that we won the league at a canter in the end it's easy to forget that it took until Christmas to really turn it round. But it was around that time that you suddenly saw the team develop this real belief and things simply took off."

So what turned it round?

"I think the signing of Benarbia. To think that he was at Sunderland and they weren't sure about him! That signing summed everything up for me. It sort of freed everybody up, spiritually as well as physically, and changed the whole feeling about the place at City. There's a real arrogance about the way Ali plays, the way he teases defenders. He's one of those great players who's always thinking a couple of moves ahead, a real artist, and the fans love him for that. I'd been worried about the way the press conferences would go during that topsy turvy period, when if we'd won Keegan would say 'We're definitely going up' and then when we'd lost he'd go 'We're definitely, definitely not going up with these players'. I certainly wondered if it would all go off the rails then but then in came Benarbia and it was just obvious from the very first game he played in that he was special. It was just the way he directed things from the get go, bringing other players into the game, pointing and cajoling, helping his team mates. He was very gracious with his talents and it made everyone feel 'Yes, we've got a world beater here'.

He made people love the team, didn't he?

"I think I'm beginning to realise that Keegan makes people love the teams he puts out and that's a really great thing. We all remember when Peter Reid was in charge at City and the team was fifth or sixth in the league when he was sacked. But nobody enjoyed what was going on, nobody loved that team. And people do love this team. So you have to hope that the next person who comes in understands that this way of doing things is re-established as part of the City tradition. When we've had our good teams they've always been attacking sides. The first thing most people try and do in a failing team is shore up the defence, but Keegan's outlook has been very refreshing. When you look at the chances that we created and let's face it, Shaun Goater missed, we could have scored 150 goals last season, no word of a lie."

Do you worry that people have got carried away by how good we are, then?

"I think a lot of people have, but bizarrely not Keegan. He's actually quite ruthless and his actions have shown that he knows the team that took us up really isn't good enough to compete. I know this sounds sound very 'showbiz matey' but I remember when he first came to City I did some interviews with Mark Lawrenson, Barry Venison and Lawrie McMenamy's son, Chris, who were all with him at Newcastle. They all said to a man that Keegan would get them up with pretty much the same team he inherited but that we had to watch because he'd start shipping plenty of them out. And that's pretty much what happened. He showed he was prepared to do it with a fans' favourite like Paul Dickov and I think that, sad as it is, he'll be doing it with guys like Shaun Goater too. It's only really the creativity in the midfield that he added last season but he's already done some radical re-shaping for The Premiership."

So what do you think of his signings for the Premiership?

"Well I don't know anything at all about the young kids he's brought in but I like the fact that he always seems to be on the lookout for talent that he can develop cheaply. I think Peter Schmeichel didn't have a great season at Aston Villa but there could be other reasons for that. He's been a fantastic goalkeeper in his time and he's still better than either of the two guys we already have by a distance. The Anelka thing could go either way, but what's the worst thing that could happen? If it doesn't work out, then they'll sell him for £10 million and lose three on the deal. It's got to be worth taking a chance on him. He's 23 and he's going to get a load of chances. He must be rubbing his hands at the thought of it, the balls that will be threaded through for him by Benarbia and Berkovic."

So you won't be making any rash predictions of failure for Keegan?

"No, I've learnt my lesson there. Of course there's a tantalising suspicion that it may still all go wrong, just in the same way as when Joe Royle was the manager we thought 'This is it, we're well organised' and then it went horribly wrong within the first two to three months of being in the Premiership. We've obviously had a poor start to the season, so we're not out of the woods yet. I still worry about Keegan's history of fragility and his habit of walking away from things. It might not have been his fault, even, but things can push you over the edge. Let's not forget that City fans are notoriously fickle. We've had to put up with a lot over the years, but we've also been fairly impatient in the face of severe provocation and the success of Manchester United. I'm worrying about relegation a lot. Going down would be a disaster, much worse than the last few because of the way we've taken out loans against future earnings and because of what's currently going on in the Nationwide League. There are a few current City players I'd like to see take a 15 per cent pay cut – there are some I'd like to see take a 100 per cent pay cut – but the thought of being forced into taking those decisions like Derby and Leicester have been is dreadful."

"I don't think it's going to happen because we have a core of four or five players of real quality – Schmeichel, Wright-Phillips, Distin, Foe, Anelka – which puts us in a different bracket to West Brom, Bolton, Sunderland and maybe Birmingham. We do need to find some consistency from somewhere and we need to eliminate the basic errors that we've been punished for. We also need a couple of players to find their form – Bernarbia and Jensen are, I think much better than they look. We need another striker to play off Anelka and we need another ball-winning midfielder. Keegan recognises that and so we will be alright provided we can bring the personnel in. But I'm already losing sleep about City a good two months ahead of the usual schedule.

"Still, I don't want to sound too negative. The obvious fact is that it's a much healthier club than it was when he first joined. The playing squad is so much better and the attitude of the team is right. Plus they're committed to the attacking ideal and it's so enjoyable to watch. I can't remember the last time it was this enjoyable to watch Manchester City and that's magnificent, wonderful."

187

So where will City finish in the table?

"I would hope they'll be able to finish in the top 12 but I don't think they'll get into Europe like a lot of City fans are saying. My greatest wish would really be that they have a decent Cup run because we haven't had one for years. I'm convinced that the other teams who've gone up will struggle because it was the poorest First Division for many, many years last season. West Brom won't be able to score and they will concede, while Birmingham have no depth or quality. I would hope we'll be at least as comfortable as Fulham were last season but with a team that's as committed to attacking as City obviously will be, there's always a danger. And we don't know the character of the team, how they'll react in adversity. The key issues are whether they're good enough defensively and whether Keegan will be able to keep a sizeable squad of players all happy."

JOHN STAPLETON

The TV broadcaster John Stapleton has presented many national programmes including Nationwide and The Time The Place. He is currently one of the mainstays of GMTV. He has a long family association with City. His grandfather attended the very first game at Maine Road against Sheffield United in 1923 and John went to his first City match in 1953, aged seven. "I can still remember sitting on the wall by the tunnel," he says. He claims that City is still his biggest passion in life and despite living in London attends most home matches. "I use air miles, though I'm running out," he laughs. "It's my one indulgence. I'm not a member of a golf club. I don't own a yacht. I spend my time watching Manchester City."

Did you think City had made a wise move bringing in Kevin Keegan at the time of his appointment?

"To be honest with you I didn't give too much thought to Kevin at first, because I was surprised and – I have to say – slightly disappointed when Joe Royle was dismissed, because Joe has been a professional friend of mine for a number of years. I've known him since he was at City as a player. I remember interviewing both Joe and Rodney Marsh years ago and I loved him at once; I thought he was smashing guy. I thought he deserved another chance and the board had said they would stand by him immediately after relegation, so I was surprised and disappointed when he went. I was very sorry for him because he's a really, really nice guy. I thought he'd done his best by City and it was an unfortunate end, to put it mildly. I think Joe would be the first to admit that one or two of his buys hadn't come off but he wouldn't be the first manager that had happened to, would he? Old softy me would have given him another chance. But football is a tough old game and Joe knows that and I have no axe to grind with Kevin Keegan at all. But it was in that slightly subdued spirit that I welcomed Kevin Keegan in.

"Of course people looking at the situation now would say the board were right to do what they did, because Kevin Keegan got City back up, which we're all delighted about. So Kevin Keegan has proved himself a great manager and in many ways what's equally important is that City played some of the most attractive football I have seen in my life last season. And I'm not kidding about that."

So how did Keegan achieve such instant success?

"Well it wasn't exactly instant, was it? We had a pretty slow – or should I say inconsistent – start to the season. People tend to forget about things like that four-nil defeat away at West Brom but I don't. I'm still one of those City fans who will be going 'Well, we should get a point' when we're three-nil up with 10 minutes to go.

"I think things settled down properly when Benarbia and Berkovic got it together in the middle of the park."

Everyone says Benarbia was the key signing of the season.

"I'd agree with that. The purchases of Ali Benarbia and Eyal Berkovic were acts of genius. I was at Maine Road for Ali's debut against Birmingham. I was told that Keegan had lunch with him the day before the game and couldn't believe that he was available after Sunderland 'ummed' and 'ahhed' about him. Keegan said 'Come and play for Manchester City'. Benarbia went back to Paris on that Friday night and landed back in Manchester on the Saturday even later than I did – and I was only there to *watch* the game!

"Well, he walked onto the pitch and bossed the game like I've never seen anyone boss a game in my life. He ripped Birmingham to shreds and even Trevor Francis, Birmingham's boss at the time, said he was astonishing. I've never seen a more creative player than Benarbia. Kinkladze was good, obviously, but he was a very individualistic player. This guy is a real team player and the way he creates chances for other people is absolutely brilliant.

"Eyal Berkovic arrived with a reputation of being a bit of a pain in the backside, the kind of guy who could cause trouble in an empty room. But apparently he hasn't been difficult at all which I think says a lot for Keegan's man-management skills. And on the field those two guys have been a joy to watch. I sat next to an old boy one day when I was there and he said 'I've waited 25 years to see football like this'. He's right. We haven't seen play like that since the '60s. Astounding stuff . . . and goals, goals, goals."

So you obviously like the playing style that Keegan has introduced? What about his management style in general?

"Well I like the attitude he takes with the players from what I've seen. When there was any trouble in that first season he dealt with it very efficiently. Jeff Whitley had some troubles and they were dealt with. And players who had an uncanny knack of being in the wrong nightclub at the wrong time were carpeted in no uncertain terms. I'm not sure that people realise quite how bright Keegan is. I met him when I was working on the TV programme *Nationwide* many years ago. I was sent to an England training camp to do a piece on him and he talked and talked and talked and a three-minute item became a 25-minute piece. We talked about everything, from his upbringing in Scunthorpe, where a nun had taken him under her wing, right through to his religious beliefs . . . and he's a very switched on guy."

It's all gone very well for Keegan so far, of course. But how do you feel he would react if there was a very difficult period for him at City? The question mark that hangs over him is still the fact that he has a reputation for walking out when the going gets tough?

"Absolutely. In the back of my mind – and probably in the back of a lot of other people's minds – is that knowledge that Kevin Keegan does not have a great reputation for staying power. When things go wrong he goes. Now that perception may be totally wrong but there's no question that that is the public's sense of Kevin. And I guess I also wonder sometimes whether he really fits the glove, as it were. I still think there's a bit of Kevin Keegan that feels his natural home is St James' Park, which is understandable. I know a lot of City fans were a bit put out when he made that comment about loving Newcastle and beginning to love Manchester City. But that was a very honest comment. Let's put it this way. I suppose if I moved to Brighton and went to watch them I could grow to love them but it's not a natural thing to do, is it? I ain't complaining about his loyalty, certainly not. And from what I hear from people at Maine Road he is 150% committed to the cause. He really is work, work, work. He doesn't go out very much. His wife comes down from the North East to see him and they go out for dinner but that's about it. He is a real hands-on, 100% grafter. I've seen him on match days right up till half-past-two glad-handing people; kids, corporate folk and all the rest of it. Kevin does it all and so I don't think anyone can really criticise him."

So he won't up and run?

"I certainly hope he won't panic and walk. I really don't think he will. I don't think he can afford to, actually, because he's been seen to do it once or twice, albeit unfairly. He left Fulham because of the England job, which is totally understandable, and at Newcastle I suspect there were some things going on behind the scenes that we don't know about. I sincerely hope he proves that he can survive not only a battle, but the war itself, because what City want is some stability, for everyone's sake. I think Keegan's mature enough to cope with adversity and whatever his inner feelings might be, he won't let them show as much any more. The board risked a great deal in appointing him and I don't think from their point of view they'll want to admit defeat if things get sticky either."

And do you think his signings for the Premiership suggest he'll do that?

"Yes, I think so. The most impressive thing is that the club have put their money where their mouth is and spent 20-odd million pounds buying some class acts. I don't know much about Distin but people tell me he's a very good player. If Anelka can behave himself and not be the moody, enigmatic figure he's been in the past, then he'll be fantastic for us. We have six strikers to choose from now. It does show the type of commitment you're looking for and also a commitment to playing the right type of football. Everyone says Marc-Vivien Foe's a good solid player and will be a good buy for us. I have no problem with Peter Schmeichel coming in and City fans should swallow any negative thoughts they might have. Hey, we've had United players before, haven't we? Overall I think Keegan's made some very good signings since he's been at the club and as I said before, I'm amazed where the money's come from. It's disappointing that some of the younger lads won't get a chance to break through now but that's a problem with every big club these days. I like Lucien Mettomo too. The jury's out on Christian Negouai and while Jon Macken's a good player I think five million's a lot of money for someone who's relatively unproven. The Argentinean, Vuoso, I know nothing about."

So do you think there really is this 'Keegan Factor' that everyone is so fond of talking about?

"Yes, I do think there's a real Keegan Factor. There aren't many clubs that can boast a manager who's managed England, who's been really successful at club management and who's also been known as a world class player. Not many clubs in the world, never mind The Premiership. Kevin Keegan's been there and had several T-shirts both as a player and as a manager. And that in itself is worth a lot to Manchester City."

DAVE WALLACE

Dave Wallace is Editor of King Of The Kippax, City's best-known fanzine. While he's now a familiar fans' voice on City, you'll still always be able to spot Dave on match days selling the latest edition of 'K.O.T.K.' from underneath his regulation flat cap.

When City wheeled out Keegan to announce him as the new manager how did you feel about him?

"I thought he'd had enough of football after the whole England fiasco so it was surprise to see him back in management again. Was I happy about the appointment? Well, bizarre as it sounds, I didn't really know enough about his abilities at the time. He had that big thing hanging over him after quitting the England job because he looked a broken man after that Germany game. There were doubts over his attitude at Fulham. And that spat with Ferguson on the telly had cast a few doubts over whether he had the bottle for managing at the highest level. But on the other hand he's always liked a challenge throughout his career. He left Liverpool at the height of his powers for Hamburg. He came back to an unfashionable club in Southampton. You know what I mean? And the one thing I didn't realise about him was just how big a personality he is. It wasn't until I saw 12-year-old fans of opposition clubs asking for his autograph at games last season that I realised the pull he has."

Did you speak to anyone at the club at the time of his appointment?

"Not really. A brief conversation with one the directors, that was all. I just did a few radio interviews where I said I hoped we got the Keegan who'd done so well at Newcastle rather than the one who'd been in charge of England. That might have sounded a bit pessimistic but to be honest we've been right to be pessimistic in the past. City have always made such a hash of their managerial appointments in the past, haven't they? I was worried that here was someone else arriving at Maine Road to ruin his career but my main concern was that he'd last more than five minutes and actually stick it out in the position."

The football didn't come straight away, though, did it?

"No. The pre-season wasn't good and then the early season form was patchy, to say the least. We got hammered away at West Brom and at home to Wimbledon and it was all looking a bit shambolic. But Keegan was true to his word. He said all along he'd give the squad a chance to show what they could do but when he realised that some of them weren't up to it he made changes. He brought Ali Benarbia in and we notched up a 3-0 away win at Barnsley and I think that was really the turning point. He put Ali, Eyal Berkovic and Shaun Wright-Phillips into the team and everyone was saying there was no way he could have three creatives in the same team, but I think he proved throughout the rest of the season that football can conquer."

He was pretty tough when he had to be, wasn't he?

"Definitely. He's got a reputation for being very matey, but if you've ever read his book you'll realise that he can be tough when he has to be. There was a story about John Beresford and him falling out at Newcastle because he kicked up a real stink when he was substituted one time. There was a bit of a barney and that was pretty much the end of Beresford's Newcastle career. I also think he learnt a lot from what happened to him with England. It certainly made him more wary of the press and he was fairly cool towards them all through last season. Not that that bothers me. I don't care whether he talks to the press or fanzines or whatever, so long as the team's performing on the pitch."

But his attitude to the fans has always been first class, hasn't it?

"Definitely. Joe Royle didn't have much time for the fans when he was in charge but Keegan's top man with them. Joe never attended Supporters' Club meetings but Kevin has. He was there at the Junior Blues Christmas panto larking about and having a great time. And the fans have responded to him. There were 2,000 who went over to Germany for the pre-season friendly against Hamburg. That shows what the fans think of Kevin Keegan."

His PR skills have never been in doubt. But the age-old accusation is that he's tactically naïve.

"I'm not sure that's fair. The year he could have won the title at Newcastle I think he was just plain unlucky. Yes, he made a bit of a mess of the England job but managing a club is completely different and Keegan's very much a man who loves the day to day cut and thrust of it. I actually think he's put a very good team around him with Derek Fazackerley, Arthur Cox and Stuart Pearce and all through last season you could see that there was a plan; tactics were changed during games and what have you. You can't argue with the amount of goals that we scored and to be honest the lion's share of the goals we conceded were during the first quarter of the season when he was getting things sorted. Don't forget he masterminded some fantastic victories away at Millwall and away at Wolves, for example. He won lots of games with just 10 men too. So how tactically naïve is that, then?"

Fair point. You talk to lots of City fans when you're selling the magazine before games. Has there been anything negative said?

"Not really. A couple of people have said they're worried about our defence, but what fan in the country isn't worried about their defence? I would say 99.9% of the fans are delighted with Kevin Keegan. Some people might say that the Premiership is a different kettle of fish but Keegan's already been there and done that. We like the signings he's made. He's not made many mistakes – maybe the signings of Negouai and Toure – but that's not too bad a record so far, is it? Of the new singings Distin looks a good player and Anelka's looking very smooth. I think having last season end so early was good for us because it gave him time to make early signings and to get them bedded in. I think the squad is looking good. He's got some great players with speed, strength and guile and he's already proved that he wants to play the kind of football that football supporters like to see. There was absolutely nothing to get excited about when Joe Royle was in charge of the team, but Keegan's been marvellous so far. And if there's amazement in my voice it's because by winning the First Division Championship he's already done better than any other City manager in the past 20 years."

But do you think he can go on from that to create something special at City?

"I see no reason why we can't go on to become one of the top clubs in the country. We were back in the '70s and I'd say we're a Top 10 club even now. We have a fanbase that is largely untapped and we're moving to a fantastic new stadium, even if I think it's too small for our needs. But yes, things are looking good. And from a personal point of view I think Keegan's got a real point to prove. He wants to show that everyone was wrong when they said he wasn't up to it when Newcastle blew that massive lead in the title race. He wants to show that everyone was wrong when they said he was a quitter after the England job. He's desperate for success and to win trophies. He's older and more mature and I think he'd be happy to finish his career at Maine Road, though not in the way that most of our recent managers have! I think he's a very honest guy with a good team around him and a good team in the boardroom too, which is obviously very important. Of course this is Manchester City, so anything can happen, but this time it feels right."

And if Keegan really can bring major success back to the club?

"It'll be knighthood status, won't it? I mean, City fans wanted to knight Joe Royle when we beat Gillingham in a Division Two Playoff Final, didn't they? If we get a major trophy they'll certainly give Keegan the freedom of Manchester. And while I don't think it will happen in the next couple of years I really do think it will happen eventually. Right now it will be nice to think that we can get a bit of competitiveness back into the city and to think that we can give United a real game again. That will be nice."

KEVIN CUMMINS

Rock photographer Kevin Cummins has been fanatically supporting City since 1961 and is currently working on 'We're Not Really Here', the official photographic book which will document the club's last year at Maine Road.

How did you feel about the sacking of Joe Royle?

"I was delighted when he got the boot. I'd had a run-in with him professionally when he was at Everton. I was taking photos for a magazine called *Goal* and we'd arranged everything with Royle for us to do a session at a certain day and at a certain time. When I got to the training ground at the appointed time the secretary said 'Oh, Joe won't be in today' – and he knew I was coming all the way from London.

"Anyway, I had to go back again 10 days later and it was at the time of the Andre Kanchelskis transfer to Everton from Manchester United. I was standing outside the secretary's office and Royle came out and thought I was one of the tabloid photographers sniffing around looking to get a shot of Kanchelskis and that I had somehow managed to sneak my way in. So he grabbed me in a headlock, told me to get out, swore at me and tried to throw me down the stairs! The secretary came running out and said 'Joe, Joe, this guy isn't from the papers.' It was only after he realised his mistake that he started hugging me and apologising profusely but I didn't think too kindly of him after that! He never seemed like a very nice bloke so no, I wasn't disappointed when he was sacked."

Did you have strong opinions about who the next manager should be?

"Not really. I couldn't decide who I thought the best person for the job was. There were a lot of yesterday's men being touted, like George Graham and 'Harry' Bassett and people were talking about David Platt too. But I wasn't keen on any of them, especially Platt. I think he showed his true colours with the England Under-21s performances at the European Championships.

"When Keegan got the job so quickly I did think it might be another case of 'jobs for the boys', which I'd always thought was the case with the Royle appointment. Keegan was Dennis Tueart's mate, they'd been on holiday together and all the rest of it. I wasn't all that positive to start with, but I think that negativity came mainly from so many years of supporting City. I mean, who's ever really replaced Joe Mercer? I was prepared to give Keegan the benefit of the doubt and in retrospect I think he's done fantastically well. He's definitely the best manager we've had since Mercer."

What made you change your mind about Keegan, then?

"Well, when he first got to Maine Road there was no 'Kevin Keegan's blue and white army' from the fans, no chanting for him at all really. It was very much a question of 'Show us what you can do'. But I did remember going to his first press conference as England manager and being really impressed by the way he talked a good fight. He was very inspirational and I think we quickly saw at City that the players loved playing for him because they came out of the dressing room thinking they were unbeatable.

"He was very fair with everybody too. He gave all the players a chance, like he said he would right at the off and it was only after we got beaten four-nil at West Brom that he said 'The players we've got here aren't good enough and I'm going to replace a few.'"

So in which areas has he really worked his magic?

"He bought creative midfielders who could put a telling ball through and whether it was in the First Division or not you've still got to create chances and you've still got to score them. Mind you, I don't think it needed a managerial genius to work that one out. Joe Royle decided to go into the Premiership without a creative midfield and anyone could see that that was madness. But let's look at City's strikers last season. Darren Huckerby scored 20-odd goals, Shaun Goater got an absolute hatful and Paulo Wanchope was a revelation. And that's all down to Keegan. He's very self-deprecating about his skills, saying he wasn't a great footballer, that he was just a hard-working footballer, but that's obviously not true. Let's not forget he won the European Footballer Of The Year award when it really meant something, when coaches sought out the players they liked rather than simply being given a piece of paper with David Beckham's name on where you just have to tick the box. So he's got the track record. Keegan improved all of our strikers' games because they've responded to Keegan's pedigree. Everyone does, which means there's a big difference between signing for Dave Jones at Wolves and Kevin Keegan at Manchester City. Someone like Nicolas Anelka is going to want to play for Keegan because he really thinks he'll be able to improve his game. And he will. I mean, Anelka could score 50 goals in a season!"

What was the best thing about City under Keegan last season?

"Most of the people I go to football with have never seen City win anything and they all agreed that last season was the best football they had ever seen a Manchester City team play. I think Brian Horton had a bit of a go in the early to mid-nineties when he had Paul Walsh and Niall Quinn upfront, but he was forced out because he was an unknown, which I thought was ludicrous. But Keegan has made watching City enjoyable again. He's gone back to playing football the way Manchester City have traditionally played it. When we won the league in 1968 we conceded a lot of goals – 43 – but nobody complained because we scored 86. We were an exciting team to watch. The attitude was 'If they score two, then we'll score four', which suits me fine. Instead of sitting on the train out of Euston thinking 'Four hours up to Manchester for a load of misery and we'll probably lose', we're now thinking 'I don't care how long it takes to get there, we're going to see a fantastic game of football.'

"It's been exciting, positive football. But that's what Keegan's always produced as a player and as a manager. He's never failed wherever he's been. The papers like to go on about the England situation, but you talk to Newcastle fans, to Southampton fans, Fulham . . . nobody has a bad word to say about the bloke."

So what did happen to him with England?

"If you look at some of the players that he had at his disposal it's not surprising he didn't do that well. I mean, the Nevilles? It's no coincidence that fans around the country sing "If the Nevilles play for England so can I." And I don't think he had too happy a time with the F.A., judging from what he said not so long ago about wanting to bring Arthur Cox into his backroom team at the time and being told that he was too old."

What's the single most inspirational thing he's done since arriving at City?

"Signing Benarbia, no doubt about it. In England it's rare to find a player of that vision. We've still got to see over the course of a whole season what we think of the players he's brought in for the Premiership but I think Anelka will be a fantastic signing for us. You've already got idiotic fans on Blue View saying 'It's a terrible signing. He gets caught offside all the time.' But that's his game, sitting on the shoulders of defenders and doing them for pace. Imagine having either Benarbia or Berkovic, two of the best creative midfielders in the country, putting balls through for him to run onto . . . it could be carnage!"

And the worst thing?

"At one point I thought it was the signing of Peter Schmeichel. I was most disappointed by that at the time. Most City fans hate Man United more than they like City and Peter Schmeichel is so much a part of *them*, isn't he? But that's an emotional response. In the light of the purchases he's made since you can understand it. He's gone for a keeper who costs nothing for a season rather than shelling out six million on David James, which has given him more money to spend on top class strikers. And the performances Schmeichel's turned in have made me eat my words. He's been magnificent."

Things couldn't have gone better for Keegan at City last season, but he's had a very sticky start to this campaign. How do you think he will respond?

"The problem for Keegan is that a large proportion of the British press pack are desperate for him to fail for several reasons. They've never forgotten (or forgiven) him for having the temerity to take on their beloved ManYoo when he was at Newcastle. His 'I'd love it . . . if we beat them' outburst has now become a stick to beat him with at every given opportunity. His so-called failure with the English national team and his supposed lack of defensive nous are two other British tabloid notions that are regularly trotted out when the anti-Keegan brigade sharpen their pencils.

"Keegan's Newcastle team finished runners up in the Premiership in 95-96 and had the second best defensive record in that division. The following season they again finished runners- up to ManYoo, but this time their goals against tally was four less than United.

"The British press were so desperate for Keegan to take the England job because they wanted someone they considered malleable in that position. When he didn't allow them to pick his team for him, they quickly turned. It's interesting that now they claim Keegan was the peoples' choice for the job and have exonerated themselves from the whole affair.

"Keegan's natural instinct is to attack with style and flair, but not to ignore defence and midfield as he is often wrongly accused. In Nico Anelka, he's bought potentially one of the most exciting strikers in Europe – for Manchester City. This is the club who five seasons ago had Gareth Taylor and Danny Allsop as two striking options. He also brought Sylvain Distin, Ali Benarbia, Eyal Berkovic and Marc-Vivien Foe to our club. The Premiership is a tough division and the gap between it and Division One has never been wider. It takes time to adapt to the relentless pace of the game. After an opening day defeat at Elland Road, City, according to the press, were relegation material. ManYoo aren't, despite losing there too. After beating Newcastle and Everton (with ten men) at Maine Road we might just stay up. After picking up a point at West Ham we were boring, etc. etc. As far as I can see, Keegan's only problem is the British press. He should ignore them and carry on doing what he does best, producing exciting, attacking football that people will travel to see.

"The man is smart and well-respected by most people in the game. More importantly he has the respect of his players and staff at Maine Road too. He's a self-motivator on and off the field. He was a winner as a player. Trust him and he will repay that trust by becoming the best manager Manchester City has ever had."

And he'll definitely stick around, will he? He's often been accused of walking away from difficult situations . . .

"I'd like to think so. They always say Keegan bottles out, but I don't think he does. I think Keegan does what he does and when he can't go any further with something then he moves on. That's what I think he'll do at City but given the way that the club have turned things around off the pitch I would really hope that won't be for a long, long time. From being a club run by a bunch of newsagents they're now a really professional operation. Now they don't just want the club to tick along. Now they have real ambition and I think that the ambition within the club matches Keegan's. I suspect if we won the Premiership, then got knocked out in the semi-finals of the European Cup Keegan might think that he'd underachieved, because that's the nature of the bloke. But that's great for City, isn't it?"

So where will City finish at the end of the season?

"Oh I don't know. I always think they'll finish top. But who would have thought three years back when we were away at Colchester that this would be happening? It's quite telling that the longest odds you can get on City to finish in the top six is 6/1. And we're not even quoted for relegation. People think we're going to have a great season, because we've got the nucleus of a great side, the best City have had since 1976. I'm still optimistic."

WILL GREENWOOD

British Lions, England and Harlequins rugby centre Will Greenwood grew up in Blackburn but his mum wouldn't let him go to football on his own. Fortunately his older cousin James was from a family of fanatical City supporters and ended up taking the young Will. "I used to sit about 10 rows behind Big Helen with her bell. It's a wonder I'm not deaf! But I got the bug straight away and I've been fanatical about City ever since."

How did you feel when Kevin Keegan took over the reins at Maine Road?

"I had no worries, no feelings of caution at all, just total optimism. Kevin Keegan's footballing philosophy has always been 'Attack! Attack! Attack!' and that was what I wanted to see at City after the dour performances of the previous season. Of course, having a team that plays for a manager who thinks that way can have its downsides. You know, we were always going to have our shocking days as well as our great ones. Who doesn't remember getting pasted four-nil at West Brom early doors last season? But think about it. Imagine supporting someone like Aston Villa? How boring would life be? Kevin Keegan is the type of manager who will live by the sword and die by the sword. We have a saying that we use with England rugby that success is on the far side of failure and that's so true. The line between the two is so very, very fine and the only thing that's certain is that you will be a failure if you don't try that something just a little bit more special, that bit more out of the ordinary. I mean, let's face it, you want to see goals don't you? You know you watch the live game on Sky on a Monday and you get certain teams that seem to delight in scraping a 1-0 win away from home. But as a fan on the other end of that scoreline I'd rather lose 4-3 than 1-0 and give myself a bit of real excitement. And you never know how many times you might come out on top if you go in with that attitude. I'd really love to see Keegan go back to Anfield and be on the right side of a 4-3 scoreline. That would be awesome."

So is Keegan exactly the kind of motivational manager that you would love to play under as a professional sportsman?

"Totally. He has passion and he has real emotion. He doesn't just sit there quietly. When things go wrong he's up out of the dugout shouting and cajoling and having a go. When things are going well he's there clapping and backslapping. He really lives it and that's what would inspire me as a player."

But it's that kind of 'heart on the sleeve' approach that some people are sceptical of. They see it as a lack of astuteness, a lack of nous.

"They do, that's true. And I don't know what his statistics are as a manager, especially in the Premiership, but what I do know is that whenever Kevin Keegan gets hold of a team something always seems to happen. I mean, if you were to look at pure stats we should never have got rid of Peter Reid when he was in charge at Maine Road. His record was superb but look at him at Sunderland. He's had a hard time. Managers will always have ups and downs but whatever happens you always know that Kevin Keegan will have tried and Kevin Keegan will have given it a go. The worst thing to feel about the team that you support is that they gave up or that they didn't try. I don't think Kevin Keegan will ever put out an uninspiring team."

So how do you rate this current City side against all of the teams you've seen in sky or 'laser' blue over the years?

"Keegan's built a great team, no doubt about it. But I have a real emotional attachment to the side that beat Gillingham in the Division Two play-off final. I mean, I know that that team was nowhere near as good as the one that Keegan's put together. But for my money that will always be the greatest City team ever. That game beats anything that I have ever been involved in, either as a spectator or as a player!"

What? Surely you're not serious. You're an England rugby international!

"No, I mean it. That game gave me 40 of the maddest minutes of sport that I've ever experienced. My mood went from hope to disappointment to utter dejection to hope to . . . I don't know, going f***ing crazy! There was so much hanging on that game. Who knows where the club would be now if we hadn't managed to get out of that division at that moment? It really could have been the death of Manchester City. So yes, that's my greatest City team, but looking at what we've got at the club right now really makes me very excited. The thing is, I was excited by the way we were playing in the First Division, but there was always that nagging doubt about how good we really were. I mean, look at the season before when Fulham absolutely ran away with the First Division. Everyone was saying that they had the style and the quality to really make an impression in the Premiership and they did absolutely nothing last season. But then we went to Ipswich in the FA Cup, who were obviously a Premiership side at the time, and we absolutely destroyed them. It was a demolition job and a performance that was as good as just about any I'd seen in the Premiership. So it does make me confident that we'll be OK this season."

Especially with the signings Keegan has made to strengthen the squad, yes?

"Well definitely. You look at the squad and there are certainly five, six, maybe seven top class Premiership players at the club. There's Anelka, of course, who's the third most popular striker in the *Daily Telegraph* Fantasy League behind Van Nistelrooy and Henry, so that means it's not just City fans who think he's going to do well. I think Tiatto has been Premiership quality all along and has only stayed at City this long because he loves the club. And Wanchope. My mate is a West Ham fan and he says it was the best thing they ever did to get rid of him. But I like Paulo. I think he's quality. And I hope Goater gets his chance. Steve Howey's an international defender and Ali Benarbia and Eyal Berkovic would grace any Premiership midfield. So I think we have a top squad. We may well let in a few goals and a lot depends on Richard Dunne, who played really well last season after looking out of shape at the start of the season. But if he's fit that will really help."

We looked like a very fit team in the First Division. Do you think the Premiership will find us out?

"I hope not and I don't think so. But there's no doubt that there will be a lot of very fit teams in the top division. When I was on my holidays in the summer I happened to be staying at the same hotel as the Spurs lads and they were in incredible shape. There is not an ounce of fat on those boys and they're so light they can just run and run all day. But I don't think we have anything to fear on that score."

Presumably you don't get to see too many games, given your day job?

"No, more's the pity. I only made it to three last season, but at least now we're back in the Premiership it's easier because there's so much Premiership football on Sky. And I think City will be an attractive proposition so they should be on a lot."

And where do you think we'll finish?

"Well I'm supremely confident, actually. You have to be bullish, don't you? Keegan bought Nicolas Anelka when no-one else was spending money and I thought that was a great statement of intent. So I really do think that the Champions League isn't beyond us. I hope so, because it would help me shut some of the England lads up who've always given me stick these last few years. Lawrence Dallaglio is a big Chelsea man and Austin Healey is an Evertonian and it's been so boring having to listen to them going on. It would be nice to stick it to them a bit!"

EDDIE LARGE

The comedian Eddie Large, 61, has been following City ever since his family moved down from Glasgow into a terraced house opposite Maine Road when he was 10 years old. 'The Little And Large' show was the BBC's most prestigious light entertainment show throughout the 80s. Despite living near Bristol, Eddie is a regular at Maine Road.

What were your feelings when you first heard that City had appointed Kevin Keegan as manager, Eddie?

"Before I answer that I'd better declare my interest in this. I'm actually very friendly with Kevin. I've known him for about 20 years, we speak on the phone probably once a week and my wife goes in his box at Maine Road."

Really? How did you get to know him?

"There's a story behind this one. When we played Spurs in the 1981 FA Cup Final we were due to be on holiday. I remember doing a deal with my wife where I said if we got to Wembley, then we'd have to holiday in Europe so that I could fly back for the game. If we didn't make it to the final then we would go to America. Anyway, when we made the final we opted for Spain and who should be staying at the same hotel but Kevin Keegan? We got talking and got to know each other and ended up being friends. So to answer your question, I think that Kevin is a special person as well as being an excellent manager, so I was delighted when he got the job.

I was very upset when Joe Royle was sacked, because he's a top notch fella and after everything that he'd done for us I felt the decision was very harsh. But that's football, I suppose. I was actually with Joe doing some after dinner speaking on the Friday before he was sacked on the Monday and he had no idea at all that it was about to happen."

"Anyway, once it had been announced that Joe was going I actually phoned Kevin up and said 'Why don't you come and do the job?' and he made a joke. He said 'What contract should I ask for, then? Three months?' But what he didn't tell me was that at that very moment when I was speaking to him on the phone the Chairman or Dennis Tueart was actually in his house negotiating with him! So when I put the telly on later in the day and saw that City were in negotiations with Kevin I thought 'You bastard!' I was so chuffed, though, and the sadness I felt about Joe leaving did evaporate a bit."

So presumably you had no doubts that Keegan was the right man for the job?

"No doubts at all. I remember being at Maine Road for the last match of last season against Portsmouth and watching those great scenes with Dennis Tueart. I turned to Dennis, who also knows Kevin very well, and said 'You and I knew that he would do this, didn't we?' It was a nice moment. But people should never have underestimated Kevin, because he's very cute. People wanted to try and invent this story about Kevin being tactically naïve after the England job, but I think that's rubbish. We didn't look tactically naïve when we took Ipswich to the cleaners, did we? And Mick McCarthy, who was analysing that night, said that the tactics were absolutely spot on."

But Keegan did admit after the Germany World Cup qualifying game that he hadn't known how to put things right.

"That's true but what a lot of people don't realise is that the night before that game there was a programme on Sky with four journalists – Steve Currie, who's a Red by the way, Brian Woolnough – and two others. And not only did these four journalists absolutely slate Kevin, but they also gave away his tactics by telling the whole world that he was going to play Gareth Southgate in midfield. I thought that was dreadful – and then those were the same guys who jumped on him afterwards and said he was tactically naïve. Let's be honest, Sven-Goran Eriksson hasn't done much better. We only qualified for the World Cup Finals with a lucky last minute free kick and we were absolutely outclassed by a Brazil side with 10 men."

Is it just a question of Keegan being more suited to club management, where he can really get his hands dirty?

"I think so. What I do know is that he's in work before anyone else watching anyone who's rolling in at half ten drunk from the night before. He's everywhere, watching the reserves at Hyde Road, watching the youth team on a Saturday morning. He knows everything that's going on at that club. My son is at university in Manchester and he knows some girls who told him that they were out with three of the City lads and the usual stuff was going on, drinking and all that. Well, my son told me this, so the next time I spoke with Kevin I said 'I hear some of your boys have been out on the town' and he said 'You mean him, him and him' and named all three of them. Believe me, he's on the ball."

So how do you think he's turned things around so comprehensively at City?

"Well I'm sure that there are lots of reasons, but I think he's managed to start changing the attitude of the club. I've always said City fans are optimistic pessimists and Stuart Pearce said on the end of season video that he felt we were manic depressives, which is probably a better description. But Kevin has got everyone actually believing in ourselves again. I would say to him 'Oh, it would be great if we could get a draw today' and he didn't like that. He said 'What's wrong with you City fans? You've got to get rid of this attitude.' And I really do think he's gone a long way to getting rid of it. You can feel the optimism running through the club and the fans. You can feel it when you read the fanzines. People believe that this dream of greatness isn't a pipe dream, that it isn't yet another false dawn. Nothing negative ever comes out of Kevin's mouth and that has to rub off. Even when we were beaten four-nil by West Brom and then four-nil by Wimbledon early last season and I was going 'Oh, here we go again,' there was Kevin being positive as ever.

"I also think that he's prepared to make the tough decisions when he has to. Despite the fact that he really is a very nice fella, football has taught him over the years that he has to be hard. That's important, to be able to be good and bad cop in one body! But because he's always very honest and straightforward with people I think the players respect that. I've often said to his wife that I think sometimes he's too honest for own good. Football makes you a liar, inasmuch as you can't tell the world your star striker's struggling to be fit for Saturday's game. But there's no doubt that Kevin is more honest than most. Plus, I think you also have to give credit to the Chairman for the way the club is run now. It's a very professional outfit these days and I think that has really helped in terms of providing the finances to allow Kevin to do the things he's wanted to do. It looks as if he's been backed all the way, which will have given him confidence to get on with managing the football side of things the way he wants to."

You can certainly see a positive attitude in the way his City team plays.

"Definitely. He transformed a lot of the players. Darren Huckerby couldn't score for toffee the previous season and then he knocked in, what was it, 20 or 30 goals? I didn't think Berkovic was that brilliant at West Ham or Celtic but look at the performances he turned in. I think all that stems from the positive attitude he puts out. He gave Shaun Wright-Phillips a go because he could see that the boy had talent but that he also had the right attitude, that he really wanted to be a footballer. I think the same thing will happen with Chris Shuker. Kevin has that dynamism that people respond to. I've stayed at his house and I couldn't believe it, he was always on the go, always doing something."

Is there any danger that that might lead to something not getting the attention it deserves when he's trying to keep too many plates spinning at once?

"That's where his backroom staff, the likes of Arthur Cox, come in. Kevin trusts Arthur with his life and I think he's now got the team in place behind the scenes that means he's comfortable that he can handle things. That's natural. You're always going to feel more comfortable with your own people behind you. What manager in the history of football hasn't brought his own team in?"

True enough. It was interesting to see how we improved defensively once Derek Fazackerley was brought in.

"That's right, but even in the pre-season this year there was a 4-3 at Bury. Kevin told me 'that's a typical Keegan performance', which made me laugh."

But you're still confident that we'll do well in The Premiership?

"Very confident. I just think that we have to learn to trust Kevin and that's a difficult thing for a City fan to do. With the exception of Joe the list of our previous managers has been shocking. None of them achieved anything, so we've all felt let down so many times. But we really do have to just sit back, trust him and relax. I mean, his judgment has been so sound we'd be crazy not to. Look at the Benarbia signing. Who would have thought that he would have turned out to be our Player Of The Season and such an inspiration? None of us had heard of him. And I'm excited about the players he's brought in. I know for a fact that Kevin's really excited about Anelka and I was dead chuffed about the signing of Foe; he's a superb player. I'm not very happy about Schmeichel for obvious reasons, but Kevin brought him to the club fully aware of what the attitude of some fans would be. He knows all about local rivalry from Liverpool, with Everton, and from Newcastle, with Sunderland. But I think he was really looking at what Schmeichel can do for the other keepers at the club, as well as the fact that he needs a leader on the pitch now that Stuart Pearce has retired. Like I said, we have to trust his judgement. And anyway, Schmeichel's had two clubs between us and *them*, so it's not all that bad, is it? The one thing we can all be certain of is the effort that the team will put in, because Kevin won't accept anything less."

Do you think that Keegan's stated ambition to turn us into one of the top sides in England is realistic?

"Yes, I do. I'm a great believer in riding the wave when things are going your way and at certain times things just seem to fall into place. When Anelka was on loan at Liverpool last season who would have thought that he would end up joining City? Then the Commonwealth Games came along and everyone loved the stadium, then found out that was where we're going to be playing. I think we're on the up and I really do think we'll be challenging Manchester United before very long. I think their empire's crumbling over there and ours is very much growing."

So where do you think we'll finish this season?

"Well it's very hard for a City fan not to say top ... or bottom, I suppose. But let me put it this way. I would not be surprised to see us finish in the top six. And I would be surprised if we finished in the bottom three."

Talking outside Maine Road, the Gardeners' Arms or winging their way through e-mail hyperspace, City supporters have all got an opinion on KK.

"Keep the faith, that's what I say. Don't be fooled by the media constantly going on about Kevin's tactical naivety. I read Stuart Pearce saying these people were talking out of their ... hats! And if King Kev is good enough for Psycho, then he's good enough for me. It has been a disappointing start but finding your sea legs in the Premiership isn't easy. We need to back the manager, not sack the manager and I'm convinced that by the end of the season Kevin will have turned things round and established us back in the elite."

Ian Watson, Chester

"Well it's not been the start we wanted, has it? But we've already shown that we have the ability, if not the consistency. I don't think there'll be a better performance from a visiting team at Arsenal all season, so it shows that we have got what it takes. There are too many unforced errors happening, but once they're ironed out we'll be just fine."

Alan Aldred, West Bromwich

"Kevin Keegan has been superb for Manchester City. Win or lose, he wants the team to play exciting, entertaining football. Joe Royle could only take us so far and I think Keegan's the man to take us to the next level. There'll be some bad days this season, of course, and that worries me. But City fans are always worried. I think we'll finish tenth."

Stuart Martin, Northern Ireland

"I was very cynical to start with but I've been blown away to date by everything that Keegan's done. He wasn't the man I would have chosen after Joe Royle. After the England fiasco I thought it was the last thing that City needed, more inconsistency, but he's been fantastic. I think City can easily survive this season. He's brought the right players in, Schmeichel in particular. And it's long enough ago that he was playing for that lot that I can now say that with a smile on my face."

Tom Hutton, Bristol

"I have no problem with Keegan, I think he's doing a great job and is the best thing that's happened to City since Joe Mercer. We knew the sort of footballer he could attract. Joe Royle wasn't capable of bringing big names in and Mr. Keegan has done that. And it's exciting. Win or lose it doesn't matter, because we're getting real quality entertainment. I think we'll be fine in this division. We'll win some and lose some and it would have been good to hit the ground running at Leeds, but it wasn't to be. Still, I think we'll send a few shivers down a few other teams' spines. I'm sure Keegan's made one or two mistakes since he arrived, but when you look at all the plus points the odd mistake isn't all that big a deal. He bought Negouai and we haven't seen him since but we can forgive him that. I think Keegan's great – and he won't walk away."

Phil Hare, Brighton

"I've only just become a supporter. My partner has followed City for the last 35 years and he's converted me in the last 18 months because I used to be a Leeds fan. I think Kevin Keegan's brilliant. He's got us this far and things can only get better now. In fact, my partner has had a 200/1 bet that City will finish above United this season, make the Champions League and that Leeds will get relegated!"

Jeanette Evans, Wakefield

"Keegan's done well for us, which hasn't surprised me because he's got a good pedigree. All he needs to do now is keep it going. I don't think we'll finish in the Top Six. I think he's only said that to gee the players up. But Top 14 and then move forward next year is a realistic ambition. There's no danger of relegation. The players he's brought in for the Premiership are very good. But only time will really tell, especially with Anelka. He's one of those guys with a different take on life, isn't he? But overall we're doing well."

Dave Reid, Alderley Edge

"It's the best football I've watched at City in the 20 years since I became a season ticket holder. I can't fault Keegan; he's really enthusiastic. People were sceptical when he arrived. I live down in Reading and people down here say he's a bottler and walks away, but I've got no reason to think he will. I'm quietly optimistic. It was awesome to watch the team last season and I really enjoyed every game I saw. I would say we'll finish at the bottom of the Top 10."

Stan Smith, Reading

"I've got to say this Keegan Era is the best ever. I think the football City are playing is the best I've seen in the 11 years I've been watching them. If I could afford it I'd be at every game because it's such a joy to watch. I don't know what Keegan's done to change things around so much, especially after the England situation. But he was great at Newcastle, wasn't he? He seems to be able to get every player believing in themselves. And he's shrewd in the market too. No-one would have bought Eyal Berkovic and made him such an important player, but Keegan did. And everyone knows him and everyone wants to play for him. Joe Royle could never have signed Nicolas Anelka but the way Keegan wants to play, with a constant commitment to attack, excites players. I think we'll survive this season and I'd be happy with that. Keegan's talking about Top Six, but he's in Never Neverland there."

John Graham, Cumbria

"He's turned it around, hasn't he? I'm really pleased with what Keegan's done. You can sum it up in that he's just added confidence. He got an extra 25% out of players last season; guys like Horlock suddenly became that much better overnight. How does he do it? I don't know, but I'd like to find out, because I could do with a bit of that at my work! The only thing I worry about is balancing it all out, making sure that the big names who come in on the big money don't upset the apple cart. I think it will be a difficult season, but he's made great buys. Schmeichel is a superb signing, Sun Jihai is a quality player and getting better every week. But it's all down to confidence – and Keegan can deliver that."

Anthony Bent, Stockport

"I think Keegan's done amazingly. I was really pleased that he came to Maine Road in the first place and the fans are all really happy that he's here. The most important thing he's done is get top players to sign for us. Joe Royle had taken us as far as he could, but Keegan's reputation has transformed things. The team has been fantastically entertaining, though it probably still lacks a bit in defence. But I like it. It's attacking football, you're on the edge of your seat all the time and you know that goals are going to be scored either way. There's no two ways about it, this season will be much harder than last. Everyone knows the quality of the Premiership and it will take a bit of time to gel. If we finish in the top half of the table I'll be very pleased and then in the next couple of years we can start going for Europe. Three seasons ago we were playing in the Second Division, so that just shows how far we've come."

Mark Armstrong, Middleton

"When Keegan first came I was a bit worried because he had a reputation to hop it if things go wrong but he's proved to be a good choice. Last season was just so enjoyable. I come three hours up the motorway for home games and his style of play really made the journey worthwhile. I'm not remotely worried about surviving in the Premiership, because there are a lot of teams that are far worse than us. And I think our defence is a lot better than people give us credit for. Best thing Keegan's done? Signing Ali. That was wonderful and he's helped to bring other great players to the club. He's not made a bad signing, has he? Sun Jihai was a bit hot-headed when he got here, but look at him now. All in all I'm delighted."

Anne Parker, Buckingham

"I wasn't sure about Keegan at first. I think City treated Joe Royle disgracefully, giving him the usual vote of confidence three weeks before they sacked him. But having said that, how wrong can one be proved? His first season was the best season anyone's ever seen here, so you swallow your principles for the sake of 124 goals, don't you? I think he's yet to prove himself at the very highest level but there's no reason why he can't succeed. He's had the money and he's got the money going forward. The only thing that worries me is that he seems to have amassed a massive squad again and we've seen the dangers of that before. I'd like to think we'll finish anywhere outside the bottom three. The objective is to stay up and if that's achieved then it's job done. You can't go into that fantastic new stadium and play Colchester United on a wet Wednesday night. I think he's got enough resources, so if we don't stay up then I think it will be his fault. I reckon he's bought wisely. Nobody can question the signings he made last season with Berkovic, Benarbia and the like. We like the look of Anelka. He can move. Yes, I think he's bought pretty astutely. What annoys me is the fact that there are players like Litmanen moving on frees and we didn't even seem to be looking. Still, how many strikers can one team use?"

Greg Parkinson, Swinton

"It's too early to really make a judgement on Kevin Keegan. Obviously he did fantastically well in the First Division last year and he's turned the club around completely. The best thing about him is that he attracts players, which Joe Royle couldn't do. If we finish anywhere in the top 10 this season then I'll be happy; very, very happy. Sometimes I think he leaves things a bit late in games when you'd be looking at him to change things but so far I'd give him seven out of 10, but moving upwards. Anelka looks great, Distin makes the odd mistake but is very solid, Marc-Vivien Foe has the potential to become the new Paul Lake and at last we have a goalkeeper in Peter Schmeichel. And I think we like the idea that *they* hate him playing for us more than we hate the fact that he played for them!"

Dave Garner, London

"Having seen Keegan on the pre-season tour of Denmark it just really brought it home to me what a superstar the man is. The Danish fans were all over him as soon as he got off the coach and fair play to him, despite having his job to do he still had time to stop and chat to them all. He seems a pleasant man. I thought it was a totally unexpected and exciting choice when he came to City. We all said at the time that it would all end in tears, but that it would be an exciting ride, and I think that's what City fans want. I still think it'll end in tears, but not because Keegan's tactically naïve. If you're tactically naïve you don't get any points and he's managed to get some. No, I think we'll get *that* close to being fantastic but there won't be the funds available for the last few players needed. Whether he walks or is pushed or gets a better offer I don't know, but I can't see Keegan finishing his career here."

Robin Samuel, Seven Kings

"Of all the changes Keegan has achieved, his greatest is the transformation of our expectations. Two seasons ago we were contenders for the worst home record in all four leagues. Home wins were as rare as an edition of the *MEN* without a Beckham story. Now Maine Road really is a fortress. We are no longer satisfied with merely defeating the opposition. To avoid disappointment we must obliterate them. Now we demand style, a flourish, panache and flair. Winning is no longer enough. Once more the spirit of adventure reigns at Maine Road."

Joe O'Neil, Tangled Up In Blue

"Walking out of Maine Road after the first game of last season against Watford there was a buzz in the air; we had all just experienced something special. For the first time in many years I had actually enjoyed watching my beloved Man City. We had gone out and played attacking, entertaining, flowing, exciting football and after a season and a bit of it I have to confess I'm addicted. There have been a couple of blips along the way (Wimbledon at home, WBA away) but my God, Kevin Keegan transformed a very average team into something which was an absolute delight to watch in just one pre-season! To call him a genius is an understatement. The detractors who claim he only possesses good motivational skills and is tactically naive can only be described as retarded. To achieve what we did last season takes a hell of a lot more than motivational skills, as any real football fan will readily acknowledge. We are exceptionally lucky to have the legend that is KK. He is a proud, passionate man who wears his heart on his sleeve. I think he has learnt not to be too open with the back-stabbing English media whose knowledge, understanding and experience of the beautiful game could be written on the back of a stamp. As for the simpletons who claim he needs mega bucks to build a team, he has probably spent less during his reign at Maine Road than the PLC in Stretford splashed out on a single player!! No longer do we have to put up with signing also-rans and has-beens, every KK signing has got quality written all over him. He knows a good player when he sees one. After all, he won European Player of the Year twice himself. I hope The Messiah stays and puts us back where we truly belong, competing with the best in Europe. He has achieved a hell of a lot in a very short time and it's difficult to keep your feet on the ground sometimes. I have to admit I found myself taking the new standard of football for granted myself last season once or twice. But we have to remember where we have come from and where we are now and I bloody well know where I'd rather be!! Join me please, ladies and gentlemen, in raising a toast to Our Messiah, the football genius, the one and only Kevin Keegan."

Tim Bennett, Blue Heaven

"When Kevin Keegan was announced as the new City manager I was quite pleased, but like many others I worried about his staying power. The media portrayed him as having a problem dealing with difficult situations and as things often go wrong at Maine Road we were optimistic, but cautious. His commitment to attacking football was a refreshing change following the sterile, defensive play of the Royle era and within a few months he'd brought the entertainment back to Maine Road. In summary, the 2001-02 season was the most exciting I can remember, and it's all thanks to Keegan."

Ged Isaacs, Contributor to King of the Kippax Fanzine.

"Kevin Keegan's influence at Maine Road is enormous. He has transformed a relegated side into an exciting team that strode confidently into the top flight. The First Division Championship season of 2001/2002 saw Keegan's flair-filled side play beautiful attacking football and score a record-equalling 108 goals. His and Arthur Cox's ability to identify and attract top class players such as Benarbia and Berkovic, Foe and Anelka, and to nurture young talent (particularly in Shaun Wright-Phillips' case), together with Keegan's enthusiasm and excellent powers of motivation fuelled this resurgence. In short, Keegan is a total breath of fresh air that blows through Manchester City."

Phil Banerjee

"When the City board appointed Kevin Keegan as the next manager of The Blues it was a god-send. The club itself was becoming a yo-yo outfit, umpteen managers who had spent mega money and with nothing to show for it. Keegan was about to change all this. In his first season as Blues boss Keegan brought in quality players at little cost, combining youth and experience, and this proved to be a winning combination. The team played exciting football and more than matched the expectations of the City fans. Records broken, goals galore and the Championship in the bag, happy faces and happy days were back again at Maine Road as City re-claimed their rightful place, back in The Premiership. City will become a major force again in The Premier under Keegan's guidance. The Board have seen what he can do and the type of players he can attract to the club. It might take a couple of seasons for City to gain major honours. One thing that is guaranteed though, it's going to be one hell of a ride."

John H Rigby, Bluemooner

"As a City fan it's impossible to truly get excited about an upcoming season. A certain Mr Royle would have us climbing the Premiership ladder with ease, winging our bandwagon through Europe, giant killing and slaying dragons en route. Giants and dragons don't exist, of course, and our exploits were destined for the humble First Division again. No fantasy about that. However, after the initial shock of Sir Joe being relieved of his place on the chipboard throne, an instalment was made in the form of the gigantic tiny figure of Kevin Keegan. Everything about the guy was/is impressive. Thoughts on England never really clouded the

Maine Road faithful's view. The club-level theory was tested well enough, thank you very much. Time to steady the course. The route was already charted, but the implications were deemed a little more trying than first expected. How in God's name do we motivate a recently-demoted side and get them through the stormy waters that is the First Division? Then in he strides, sporting a Sky Blue old skool Adidas top, playing us down but inadvertently playing us up too. 'This team isn't good enough to get to the play-offs, never mind win the Championship,' he hollered, whilst sitting ruefully in eighth position. Whoosh – Masterstroke. Ali Bernabia. In. They're off. This City team charmed, teased, oozed confidence, disposed of opposition, ran riot, dug in, excelled, boasted class, style (except for Huckerby's hair) and flair, with swagger verging on arrogant. Most importantly, they WON. If memory serves me correctly I saw 'em get beat three times at Maine Road all season. On and on went the swashbuckling. You could see opposition teams running out on to the Maine Road pitch, heads hung, thinking 'Hope its only one or two we concede . . .' Try Three. Records smashed here, there and everywhere, the Manchester Ship pulls in winning a trophy and a degree of pride. Keegan had the pride from the start, it transpires. We took a little longer coming round. We did arrive though. Brought into a wider context, this season we – albeit cautiously – do expect. Not because we think in terms of Charlton, going down and then re-appearing at the top end of the table, come the top flight season's end. But because Keegan makes you believe. You try and stop yourself, but you just can't help it. It's like falling in love – or re-falling in love as the case may be. Ambition is a word bandied about a lot at the moment, but you can taste it. Bob The Builder last year. Nicolas Anelka this. Come on. No one is denying that this is going to hard, but the belief and positivity close season has been tremendous. How long has it been since we had a full squad assembled a month or so *before* the season starts? I shan't even mention the new stadium. You listen to David Bernstein and he's gushing. Yes, maybe Swales was a Blue, but he was also naive. Lee was just a imbecile. The club was in a desperate state of disrepair when he left. Don't forget that it was our current Chairman who had to sack his friend for the good of the club he loves. Brave, that. David Bernstein? Thanks. And so we go on. Can this ascension continue? Probably best not to expect too much – and being a Manchester City Fan (don't those three words sound good together?) we shall have to wait and see. But we've been watching – and the signs are pointing up."

Joel Perry, BB Lower Kippax

"KK brings inspiration and passion. Anyone unable to raise their game for him shouldn't be in the game, let alone play for City. Keegan and the new board appear to have rid the club of the negative cancer which has dragged us down for years. European football is a real possibility by 2005."

Harry Higham, Manchester. CTID

"It was another bad City appointment. Keegan – a quitter who lacked tactical knowledge – wouldn't be able to handle the pressures of MCFC. How wrong we were as, after an indifferent start, Kevin transformed City from sloggers into artists. Flair and excitement are now synonymous with the laser blue shirt. One player is key to the revolution. Ali Benarbia's vision, intelligent passing, flicks and back heels have unlocked defences all over the country. Our captain carries our expectations on his shoulders. We hope that his pedigree leads us to Europe, but I fear an injury or loss of form. Years of supporting City leads me to anticipate the latter."

Louise Deeks, Appleton, Cheshire

"Well, after supporting City since 1990 there ain't been many high points, but since KK has come in he has brought a brand of football I didn't think I would ever see at City. Nor did I ever expect the type of players we have now. It's too early to say how we will do in the Premiership long-term, but for once I can genuinely be excited about a season and the future."

Adam Raby

"Well, what a season it was last time around. I went to three matches; Portsmouth at Fratton Park, Wimbledon at Selhurst Park and Pompey on the last day of the season. I thought I was a bad curse after the games at Portsmouth and Wimbledon, where City lost 2-1 both times. But it was a different story at Maine Road for the last game, 3-1 to City! What a job Kev has done. I couldn't have imagined it! City Till I Die."

Richard Canham, Hampshire

"I started off as a Keegan pessimist and ended up as a Keegan disciple! This has happened in just the first year or so of his reign as MCFC's new manager. From the impressive first game against Watford to the inspirational purchase of Ali Benarbia, Keegan's first season was superb and has given me so much enjoyment and – most importantly – hope for the future of this great club. My personal highlight was the Ipswich Cup game which showed just how good a footballing side we had become! The Premiership will be tough and after all the optimism of the pre-season, the new season has started in typical City style (Jekyll and Hyde). Top class performances followed by mediocre ones. Yet there have been enough good performances already to show we can be a force under Keegan and hopefully break into the top half of the best league in the world. Maybe not this season, but definitely next season. Then again, this is Manchester City we are talking about. Oh well, relegation battles are exciting for football fans, aren't they?"

Joe Hulme, Westhoughton

"Some people raised their eyebrows when we appointed King Kev but quite simply it has proved to be a match made in heaven. No Blue under the age of thirty will have seen as exciting football as we have witnessed this last season and it will be a long time before we see 108 league goals in a season again. Keegan has become a legend in less than 12 months in the job. We used to laugh at the daft Geordies who had his face tattooed on their arse cheeks, but now tattooists in Manchester are doing a roaring trade. Hopefully, the journey has only just begun."

Nick Jackson, Withington.

"The Keegan appointment was a terrible decision. We needed a man with a proven record of handling the pressure of managing the Blues and the ability to get us into the Premier League. Joe Royle was that man. That was my view, and how wrong could I have been? With hindsight, Keegan is the perfect soul-mate for City. After just one season he has secured himself in every Blue heart. For the first time our team's abilities match our ambitions. Long live the King."

Simon Jones

"The Keegan era started as a real rollercoaster, the first few matches of the season we didn't know what would happen next. A win against Watford and a four-nil home defeat to Wimbledon had everyone a little confused. As the season wore on and we neared Christmas things settled down. I didn't have that feeling of impending doom I used to get just before kick off. The way in which we won the league has brought a new feeling of hope to the blue half of Manchester and this is thanks to Kevin Keegan. Let's hope he can carry on the success and improve on his time with Newcastle, putting Manchester City back where they belong . . . making them a force in European football."

Simon Morris, Cumbria (Manchester ex-pat)

"City fans want success, but more than anything they want their team to play exiting football. In a twelve month period Kevin Keegan has turned Manchester City into the type of team we have collectively longed for since Joe Mercer managed the club in the late '60s and early '70s. Since his arrival the so-called drinking culture has been eradicated, the deadwood has been pruned (e.g. Tony Grant), world class talent like Anelka and Foe have signed up, exciting, skilful players have been brought in very cheaply (e.g. Eyal Berkovic and Ali Benarbia) and the best has been brought out of existing players (e.g. Darren Huckerby, Shaun Wright-Philips and Paulo Wanchope). We have scored more goals in a season than any City team in history and also equalled our all time league scoring record. True, we conceded a lot of goals, but as the season proceeded, the average goals-against ratio also fell. Indeed, the second half of the season saw us concede around 19 goals in 25 games, which is nearly as good as WBA's record. You have to give Keegan 9 out of 10 for such a record. Indeed, it could only have been bettered by winning a real trophy and we did well in these too. In the League Cup we lost to Blackburn (the eventual winners) 2-0 away, conceding a very late goal after outplaying them for long periods of time with only 10 men. In the FA Cup we thumped Ipswich 4-1 and should have beaten Newcastle in the fifth round, losing 1-0 after having Richard Dunne sent off and outplaying them for much of the match. Only the inability of the referee to see Robert's foul on Niclas Jensen caused us to lose. Indeed if Ali Benarbia had played (he was suspended at the time) Newcastle would have lost. As to this season, well I'm very hopeful. Ali's passing ability will rip Premiership teams defences to shreds and Keegan's assault on the transfer market has and will improve all aspects of the team. Indeed the final amount spent (around £30 million) shows the board have the cash and the will to back Keegan. Keegan is our Messiah and he is taking us back to the promised land at great speed. If you want a prediction I believe that we will qualify for Europe this year and if we're lucky we could be the first team to win the title after promotion since Nottingham Forrest in the late '70s and Ipswich Town in the early '60s."

Blue Anorak.

"I think that since Keegan took over at City we have suddenly had our expectations raised. We now have a manager who can attract the best players in the world and carries a name. He plays the most entertaining football I've ever seen played by a City side and now he has some great players there as well. Ali Benarbia is a total genius, Eyal Berkovic his partner in crime, Nicholas Anelka is top quality along with Sylvain Distin, Jon Macken, Niclas Jensen, and Lucien Mettomo. I think his only bad signings were Simon Colosimo, Alioune Toure and Peter Schmeichel, but the first two he's realised his mistake with. I think that in the next 12 months we will be established within the top seven of the Premiership and will only keep improving with King Kev at the helm. Thank goodness we sacked Royle and persuaded a brilliant man-manager with the ability to attract top class players to come to City."

Neil Allen

"The football played last season was superb and it's all thanks to Kevin Keegan. He has brought some quality players into the side and everyone has had to earn the right for a regular first team place. We were by far the best side in the First Division and put in excellent performances against the likes of Ipswich and Newcastle to show we are ready for the Premiership. I'm really pleased that Shaun Wright-Phillips got voted Young Player of the Year; he worked so hard for us and just got better and better. But I thought everyone was outstanding!"

Helen Rodgers, Manchester

"The tremendous optimism surrounding Keegan's sparkling new squad may be tempered by that niggling feeling that we've been here before. With the vultures waiting to swoop at the first sign of problems at City, you can't help but feel we've reached a crossroads. Cynics suggest that last season was the honeymoon preceding the broken marriage. This time, I don't think so. I'm completely sold on the Keegan dream. He's restored my belief that we can achieve absolutely anything and I've stopped fearing the worst. That's what Keegan has brought to City."

Scott Turton, Droylsden, exiled in Middlesex

"What has Keegan ever done for us? I mean, apart from the vision of Berkovic, the all-round genius of Benarbia, the swansong from Pearce (and the next phase of his career), the authority of Mettomo, the blossoming of SWP, the reinvention of Horlock, the self-belief of Huckerby, the coolness of Jensen, the fanclub of Sun Jihai (pretty big), the bravado of signing Anelka, breaking all our own club records, the statement of intent of his current spending.

"Nah, give me the good old days, any day."

Andy Noise, Derby